INCHON

GREAT BATTLES

INCHON

S. P. MacKenzie

OXFORD
UNIVERSITY PRESS

Great Clarendon Street, Oxford, OX2 6DP,
United Kingdom

Oxford University Press is a department of the University of Oxford.
It furthers the University's objective of excellence in research, scholarship,
and education by publishing worldwide. Oxford is a registered trade mark of
Oxford University Press in the UK and in certain other countries

© S. P. MacKenzie 2025

The moral rights of the author have been asserted.

All rights reserved. No part of this publication may be reproduced, stored in a retrieval system, transmitted, used for text and data mining, or used for training artificial intelligence, in any form or by any means, without the prior permission in writing of Oxford University Press, or as expressly permitted by law, by licence or under terms agreed with the appropriate reprographics rights organization. Enquiries concerning reproduction outside the scope of the above should be sent to the Rights Department, Oxford University Press, at the address above.

You must not circulate this work in any other form
and you must impose this same condition on any acquirer.

Published in the United States of America by Oxford University Press
198 Madison Avenue, New York, NY 10016, United States of America

British Library Cataloguing in Publication Data
Data available

Library of Congress Control Number: 2025933841

ISBN 9780198851653

Printed and bound by
CPI Group (UK) Ltd., Croydon, CR0 4YY

Links to third party websites are provided by Oxford in good faith and
for information only. Oxford disclaims any responsibility for the materials
contained in any third party website referenced in this work.

The manufacturer's authorised representative in the EU for product safety is
Oxford University Press España S.A., Parque Empresarial San Fernando de Henares,
Avenida de Castilla, 2 – 28830 Madrid (www.oup.es/en or product.safety@oup.com).
OUP España S.A. also acts as importer into Spain of products made by the manufacturer.

FOREWORD

The phrase 'great battle' carries four immediate connotations. The first relates to time. The standard narrative, whether applied to Marathon or Waterloo, Salamis or Trafalgar, assumes that the events occurred on a single day—or at most over two or three days. Secondly, a battle has to be on a scale large enough not to be deemed a skirmish. Fighting may characterize war but fighting itself does not constitute a battle. If the forces involved are too small or the commitment to engage by one or both sides too slight, then what happens is not a great battle. At least one side, and possibly both, must want to fight. Third, a battle occurs in a defined, and in some cases a confined, space. On land it is sometimes so geographically limited that it takes its name from an otherwise little-known geographical feature, such as Bunker Hill, or an obscure village or hamlet. At sea, its name may be more capacious but as often it gains precision by adopting the name of the nearest landfall. Lastly, a 'great battle' implies that the consequences are commensurate with the commitment; in other words, that the result proves decisive.

The infrequency with which all these four conditions have been met helps explain why 'great battles' have been rare. Great battles need to be infrequent or they lose their cachet. Calling some forms of combat battles may be no more than a rhetorical device, coined for effect, or, more pragmatically, to give shape to otherwise seemingly inchoate episodes. Since the nineteenth century the word battle has been applied to events that are not concentrated in time and space. Persistent fighting in all seasons and all weathers combined with technological innovation and full social and economic mobilization to make outcomes more cumulative than singular. In the Second World War, the 'battle' of the Atlantic was decisive, both in the economic war and in enabling the D-Day landings, but it was not clearly defined in time or space. It lasted nearly four years and, although largely restricted to the North Atlantic, still embraced an expanse of sea larger than any major continent.

At sea especially, battle in a traditional sense was rarely decisive. As the British naval theorist Julian Corbett observed in 1911, man lives upon the land, and so 'it scarcely needs saying that it is almost impossible that a war can be decided by naval action alone'. The Greeks may have checked the Persians at Salamis in 480 BC but they did not topple the Persian empire. The Christian victory over the Turks at Lepanto in 1572 was similarly a great defensive success, which checked the Ottoman advance into the Mediterranean but not into continental Europe. On 21 October 1805 Nelson 'decisively' defeated the French and Spanish fleets at Trafalgar but war with France continued for another decade. In the short term too, while Nelson's victory ended the danger of a French invasion of Britain, it did not end Napoleon's freedom of manoeuvre within Europe. Just over six weeks after Trafalgar the French emperor won possibly his greatest victory, defeating the armies of Austria and Russia at Austerlitz on 2 December 1805. However, even in land warfare 'decisiveness' can be a relative, rather than an absolute, term. At Austerlitz Napoleon smashed the continental alliance which threatened him in the short term but he did not prevent its resuscitation in 1813. Nor did he win the economic and commercial war waged by Britain and underpinned by its maritime power.

In Corbett's day, the ability of warships to cope with adverse weather conditions enabled by the invention of steam power and the end of sail ought to have made naval battle more possible, but it did not necessarily do so, partly because improved navigation and advanced technology opened up more of the world's oceans and so created greater space in which an opponent could hide. Since the beginning of the twentieth century, war at sea has been increasingly fought under and over the surface, as well as on it. In the Second World War 'great battles' were fought in the Pacific simultaneously at sea and in the air with devastating effects—at Pearl Harbor in December 1941, the Coral Sea in May 1942, and Midway in the following month. Each was conducted at scale and was limited in time, if less so in space. Each was more clearly a 'great battle' in the classical definition than the whole of the battle of the Atlantic, but the war against Japan was also won by sustained economic warfare conducted by submarines and by island-hopping amphibious assaults. The Second World War did not end in a climactic battle like Waterloo in 1815. That final defeat of Napoleon, for many then and since, embodies the concept of decisiveness, not least because it introduced nearly a century of comparative European peace, but its outcome too rested as much on the exhaustion of France, and of its enemies, after two decades of conflict as it did on the results of a single day on a confined battlefield, however sanguinary the fighting.

For those who practise war in the twenty-first century the idea of a 'great battle' can seem no more than the echo of a remote past. The names on regimental colours or the events commemorated at mess dinners bear little relationship to patrolling in dusty villages or waging 'wars amongst the people'. Contemporary military doctrine downplays the idea of victory, arguing that wars end by negotiation not by the smashing of an enemy army or navy. Indeed it erodes the very division between war and peace, and with it the aspiration to fight a culminating 'great battle'.

And yet to take battle out of war is to redefine war, possibly to the point where some would argue that it ceases to be war. Carl von Clausewitz, who experienced two 'great battles' at first hand—Jena-Auerstedt in 1806 and Borodino in 1812—wrote in *On War* that major battle is 'concentrated war', and 'the centre of gravity of the entire campaign'. Clausewitz's remarks related to the theory of strategy. He recognized that in practice armies might avoid battles, but even then the efficacy of their actions relied on the latent threat of fighting. Winston Churchill saw the importance of battles in different terms, not for their place within war but for their impact on historical and national narratives. His forebear, the Duke of Marlborough, fought four major battles and named his palace after the most famous of them, Blenheim, fought in 1704. Battles, Churchill wrote in his life of Marlborough, are 'the principal milestones in secular history'. For him, 'Great battles, won or lost, change the entire course of events, create new standards of values, new moods, new atmospheres, in armies and nations, to which all must conform.'

Clausewitz's experience of war was shaped by Napoleon. Like Marlborough, the French emperor sought to bring his enemies to battle. However, each lived within a century of the other, and they fought their wars in the same continent and even on occasion on adjacent ground. Winston Churchill's own experience of war, which spanned the late nineteenth-century colonial conflicts of the British Empire as well as two world wars, became increasingly distanced from the sorts of battle he and Clausewitz described. In 1898 Churchill rode in a cavalry charge in a battle which crushed the Mahdist forces of the Sudan in a single day. Four years later the British commander at Omdurman, Lord Kitchener, brought the South African War to a conclusion after a two-year guerrilla conflict in which no climactic battle occurred. Both Churchill and Kitchener served as British Cabinet ministers in the First World War, a conflict in which battles lasted weeks, and even months, and which, despite their scale and duration, did not produce clear-cut outcomes. The 'battle' of Verdun ran for all but one month of 1916 and that of the Somme for five months. The potentially decisive naval action at Jutland spanned a more traditional twenty-four-hour timetable but was not conclusive and was not replicated during the war.

Clausewitz would have called these twentieth-century 'battles' campaigns, or even seen them as wars in their own right. The determination to seek battle and to venerate its effects may therefore be culturally determined, the product of time and place, rather than an inherent attribute of war. The ancient historian Victor Davis Hanson has argued that seeking battle is a 'western way of war' derived from classical Greece. Seemingly supportive of his argument are the writings of Sun Tzu, who flourished in the warring states period in China between two and five centuries before the birth of Christ, and who pointed out that the most effective way of waging war was to avoid the risks and dangers of actual fighting. Hanson has provoked strong criticism: those who argue that wars can be won without battles are not only to be found in Asia. Eighteenth-century European commanders, deploying armies in close-order formations in order to deliver concentrated fire, realized that the destructive consequences of battle for their own troops could be self-defeating. After the First World War, Basil Liddell Hart developed a theory of strategy which he called 'the indirect approach', and suggested that manoeuvre might substitute for hard fighting, even if its success still relied on the inherent threat of battle.

The winners of battles have been celebrated as heroes, and nations have used their triumphs to establish their founding myths. It is precisely for these reasons that their legacies have outlived their direct political consequences. Commemorated in painting, verse, and music, marked by monumental memorials, and used as the way points for the periodization of history, they have enjoyed cultural afterlives. These are evident in many capitals, in place names and statues, not least in Paris and London. The French tourist who finds himself in a London taxi travelling from Trafalgar Square to Waterloo Station should reflect on his or her own domestic peregrinations from the rue de Rivoli to the gare d'Austerlitz. Today's Mongolia venerates the memory of Genghis Khan, while Greece and Macedonia scrap over the rights to Alexander the Great.

This series of books on 'great battles' tips its hat to both Clausewitz and Churchill. Each of its volumes situates the battle which it discusses in the context of the war in which it occurred, but each then goes on to discuss its legacy, its historical interpretation and reinterpretation, its place in national memory and commemoration, and its manifestations in art and culture. These are not easy books to write. The victors were more often celebrated than the defeated; the effect of loss on the battlefield could be cultural oblivion. However, that point is not universally true: the British have done more over time to mark their defeats at Gallipoli in 1915 and Dunkirk in 1940 than their conquerors on both occasions. For the history of war to thrive and be productive it needs to embrace the view from 'the other side of the hill', to use the Duke of Wellington's words. The battle the British call Omdurman is for the Sudanese the battle of Kerreri; the Germans called Waterloo 'la Belle Alliance' and Jutland Skagerrak. Indeed, the naming of battles could itself be a sign not only of geographical precision or imprecision (Kerreri is more accurate but as a hill, rather than a town, it is harder to find on a small-scale map) but also of cultural choice. In 1914 the German general staff opted to name their defeat of the Russians in East Prussia not Allenstein (as geography suggested) but Tannenberg, in order to claim revenge for the defeat of the Teutonic Knights in 1410.

Military history, more than many other forms of history, is bound up with national stories. All too frequently it fails to be comparative, to recognize that war is a 'clash of wills' (to quote Clausewitz once more), and so omits to address both parties to the fight. Cultural difference and even more linguistic ignorance can prevent the historian considering a battle in the round; so too can the availability of sources. Levels of literacy matter here, but so does cultural survival. Often these pressures can be congruent, but they can also be divergent. Britain enjoys much higher levels of literacy than Afghanistan, but in 2002 the memory of the two countries' three wars flourished in the latter, thanks to an oral tradition, much more robustly than in the former, for whom literacy had created distance. And the historian who addresses cultural legacy is likely to face a much more challenging task the further in the past the battle occurred. The opportunity for invention and reinvention is simply greater the longer the lapse of time since the key event.

All historians of war must, nonetheless, never forget that, however rich and splendid the cultural legacy of a great battle, it was won and lost by fighting, by killing and being killed. The battle of Waterloo has left as abundant a footprint as any, but the general who harvested most of its glory reflected on it in terms which have general applicability and carry across time in their capacity to capture a universal truth. Wellington wrote to Lady Shelley in its immediate aftermath: 'I hope to God I have fought my last battle. It is a bad thing to be always fighting. While in the thick of it I am much too occupied to feel anything; but it is wretched just after. It is quite impossible to think of glory. Both mind and feelings are exhausted. I am wretched even at the moment of victory, and I always say that, next to a battle lost, the greatest misery is a battle gained.'

Readers of this series should never forget the immediate suffering caused by battle, as well as the courage required to engage in it: the physical courage of the warrior, the soldier, sailor, or airman, and the moral courage of the commander, ready to hazard all on its uncertain outcomes.

HEW STRACHAN

CONTENTS

List of Figures   xv
List of Maps   xvii
Abbreviations   xix

1 Introduction   1
2 Operation Chromite   5
3 News Media   24
4 Official Histories   38
5 Memoir Battles   52
6 Analysis Wars   68
7 Projecting History   84
8 Commemoration Sites   99
9 Conclusion   113

Notes   119
Bibliography   167
Picture Acknowledgements   191
Index   193

LIST OF FIGURES

3.1	Douglas MacArthur observes the success of Operation Chromite aboard *Mount McKinley*, flanked by Court Whitney and a pointing Ned Almond.	29
3.2	US Marines scale the seawall, Red Beach, 15 September 1950.	31
3.3	Photo taken by Pfc. Ronald L. Hancock, Inchon, 16 September 1950.	35
4.1	Roy E. Appleman.	42
4.2	Kim Il Sung.	45
4.3	Park Chung-hee.	48
5.1	Cover of the initial 1965 paperback edition of *Reminiscences* (1964).	57
5.2	Cover of *War in Peacetime* (1969).	60
5.3	Cover of *First to Fight* (1984).	63
6.1	A helmeted Oliver Smith in conversation with Ned Almond.	76
6.2	Cover of *Hell or High Water* (1968).	79
6.3	Cover of *Victory at High Tide* (1968).	82
7.1	M-G-M publicity poster for *Inchon*.	92
7.2	Kim Jong Il gives on-the-spot film-shoot guidance.	94
7.3	Press conference for *Operation Chromite*.	97
8.1	Douglas MacArthur statue in Freedom Park, Inchon.	101
8.2	Exterior of Inchon Landing Operation Memorial Hall.	103
8.3	Heroes of Wolmido statue, Victorious Fatherland Liberation War Museum, Pyongyang.	107

LIST OF MAPS

2.1 Korea: August 1950. 7
2.2 The Inchon assault: 15 September 1950. 14
2.3 The fight for Seoul: 20–28 September 1950. 18

ABBREVIATIONS

AP	Associated Press
CBS	Columbia Broadcasting System
CPV	Chinese People's Volunteers
DMZ	Demilitarized Zone
DPRK	Democratic People's Republic of Korea
GHQ	General Headquarters
INS	International News Service
IWM	Imperial War Museums
JCS	Joint Chiefs of Staff
KIMH	Korean Institute of Military History
KPA	Korean People's Army
MMA	MacArthur Memorial Archive, Norfolk, VA
NARA	National Archives and Records Administration II, College Park, MD
PFC	Private First Class
PRC	People's Republic of China
ROK	Republic of Korea
ROKA	Republic of Korea Army
ROKMC	Republic of Korea Marine Corps
UN	United Nations Organization
UP	United Press
USAF	United States Air Force
USAHEC	United States Army Heritage and Education Center, Carlisle, PA
USMC	United States Marine Corps
USMCU	United States Marine Corps University, Marine Corps History Division, Distinguished Marine Interview Transcripts, Quantico, VA
USN	United States Navy
USSR	Union of Soviet Socialist Republics

1

Introduction

The armed struggle in Korea between 1950 and 1953, known in the northern half of the peninsula as the Fatherland Liberation War (with reference to its purpose) and in the southern half as the Six-Two-Five War (from the month and day it began), was a conflict marked by dozens of battles great and small. In the decades since the armistice a variety of different military engagements, commonly involving heroic actions by fellow countrymen, have established themselves in popular consciousness within various individual states involved.[1]

However, 'Inchon'—shorthand for the American-led amphibious seizure of the port of the same name and subsequent fight to wrest control of the capital city it served from North Korean hands in September of the first year of the war—is in a class of its own. Almost everywhere it is understood as a momentous turning point in the conflict; a battle orchestrated by General Douglas MacArthur that generated the collapse of a hitherto largely successful North Korean invasion of South Korea, setting the stage for an initially triumphant counter-invasion of North Korea that would in turn produce headlong retreat due to Chinese intervention. What is more, Inchon stands out as a clash of arms that came to be celebrated as a triumph by both sides.[2]

In the Democratic People's Republic of Korea a version of events was constructed which explained failure in terms of sabotage and emphasized the spirit of self-sacrifice among both soldiers and workers under the direction of Kim Il Sung; a heroic mentality that delayed the enemy landing and advance inland long enough for long-term strategic victory to be wrested from the jaws of a short-term local defeat. On the opposing side, Inchon quickly came to be celebrated as the masterstroke of its prime mover, Douglas MacArthur; though over time, questions would arise about operational leadership and its actual strategic significance, and significant differences of opinion over the nature and meaning of Operation Chromite would eventually emerge in certain quarters of the Republic of Korea and the United States.

Just as striking as the development of either radically or subtly different interpretations of Inchon are the variety of forms in which they have been expressed. In the arena of toys and games, for instance, the last quarter-century has witnessed the unveiling of a virtual reality game and Lego-style building-block set devoted to the landing for South Korean consumers, while a version of the famous GI Joe action figure packaged to represent one of the US Marines taking part in Operation Chromite was produced for the American market to mark the fiftieth anniversary.[3] On the musical front, to take an alternate form of rendition, an Inchon March was composed in Pyongyang to celebrate the battle even as it unfolded, a symphonic band piece was produced in the United States to mark the golden jubilee, and seventeen years after that North Korea staged a full-scale revolutionary opera devoted to the battle.[4]

The sheer range of representation, coupled with the need to keep within the word limit set for this series and focus on the national forces directly engaged, has meant that not every manifestation of Inchon is covered in this book. Operational analysis of the landing and advance from Inchon to Seoul, moreover, cannot be as complete as might otherwise be the case due to any pertinent North Korean military records—indeed, archival documents of all kinds—being closed to outside scrutiny in one of the most secretive societies on earth. Nonetheless the chapter-by-chapter discussion of the half-dozen particular types of representation that follow the initial operational chronicle and outline of the wider strategic significance of the battle—contemporary press accounts, officially sanctioned histories, published war memoirs, debates among historians, cinematic dramas, as well as memorials and museums—will hopefully leave readers with a sense of the enduring importance of Inchon as a socio-cultural phenomenon as well as a militarily consequential clash of arms. The conclusion will also address the place of the Inchon landing in the history of modern amphibious operations alongside its role in securing the future of the United States Marine Corps.

Note on Transliteration

In theory, the Revised Romanization (RR) system, as officially approved in the Republic of Korea for over twenty years now, ought to be the *modus operandi* in this book. A number of issues, though, make this highly problematic in practice. For one thing, it is not the form used in North Korea over the past thirty years, a revised adaptation of the McCune-Reischauer (MR) system, the original of which is still in widespread use among Western scholars and libraries. More significantly, much of the relevant source material printed in English, whatever its provenance, displays evidence of a phonetic approach roughly similar to the original MR but usually without the trademark apostrophes or breves and displaying a somewhat freestyle approach to hyphens and/or lettering.

I have therefore adopted a policy of using in the text whichever form of spelling on the whole appears dominant in the English-language literature related to the subject matter of this book, with the exception of direct quotes, which are reproduced verbatim. Thus, for example, Kim Il Sung is used for the North Korean leader rather than Kim Il-sŏng or Kim Il-sung, while for place names Pusan is used rather than Busan and, most obviously, Inchon rather than In'chon or Incheon. Source citations are repeated in whatever system they appeared in online listings such as WorldCat used for inter-library loan purposes. Korean materials translated for the author by Dr Daniel Pieper are cited in the manner he, as an historian of Korea, prefers: namely, McCune-Reischauer.

Acknowledgements

I owe particular thanks to three scholars in making this book possible. Professor Hew Strachan, for agreeing that a volume on Inchon would be a useful addition to the OUP Great Battles series and for his subsequent thoughts; Dr Daniel Pieper for his yeoman service in identifying and translating numerous Korean-language sources on my behalf; and an anonymous external reviewer for several pertinent suggestions for improvement. Responsibility for the uses to which recommendations and translations have or have not been put rests solely with me. In addition, I am grateful for the assistance of Jim Zobel in obtaining copies of material held by the MacArthur Memorial in Norfolk, Virginia, and to the staffs of various other repositories and libraries in the United States, including the National Archives and Records Administration, College Park, Maryland; the US Army Heritage and Education Center, Carlisle Barracks, Pennsylvania; and the US Marine Corps University, Quantico, Virginia. Especially the context of the Covid-19 pandemic and its aftermath, either direct assistance or indirect help, via primary-source material posted on institutional websites, proved to be invaluable. Maps were produced by the incomparable Elbie Bentley. Lastly, as in the past, this book could not have been written without the services of the inter-library loan department of Thomas Cooper Library, University of South Carolina.

2

Operation Chromite

The amphibious assault on Inchon and consequent advance on Seoul in the second half of September 1950 cannot be understood in isolation. They were part of a wider American response to what was perceived as an increasingly critical military situation on the Korean peninsula. And their success would have major repercussions concerning both the immediate and longer-term future of a conflict that had its roots in recent events.

Context

In theory, Korea was supposed to become a fully independent unitary state in the wake of Japanese defeat at the end of the Second World War. In practice, reflecting the politics of the victorious powers that had occupied each half of the peninsula in the years immediately afterward, two competing regimes had emerged by 1948. South of the 38th parallel was the Republic of Korea (ROK), a repressive and unstable state led by Syngman Rhee given only conditional military and diplomatic support by the United States. North of the 38th parallel was the Democratic People's Republic of Korea (DPRK) headed by Kim Il Sung, a solidly communist entity which enjoyed much more robust military and economic backing from the Soviet Union. Each claimed suzerainty over the entire peninsula, and border clashes were frequent. However, the Korean People's Army (KPA) in the north was by 1950 significantly larger, better trained, and more lavishly equipped—not least through possession of a sizeable number of T-34 tanks—than its southern counterpart, the Republic of Korea Army (ROKA). Kim was confident that an offensive from the north, producing in turn uprisings in the south, would rapidly succeed; and after obtaining agreement in Moscow and Beijing, he launched his forces across the parallel on 25 June in an all-out assault.[1]

Though there would be no mass civil insurrections in the south, and the northern invasion would quickly provoke military counteraction by the United States and its allies acting on behalf of the United Nations, the KPA seemed virtually unstoppable through the summer months. Despite some heroic actions ROKA formations were repeatedly put to flight, as were the first understrength and underequipped US Army combat units of the Eighth Army deployed from garrison duty in Japan. Seoul had been captured within a matter of days, in late July Taejon had fallen, and by early August defeated American and ROKA ground forces had retreated to the southeast and were hemmed inside an extended defensive perimeter—defined in large part by the Naktong River—around the key port of Pusan. Possession of less than a tenth of the South Korean landmass and a series of fierce North Korean attacks made some observers wonder if American troops might continue to withdraw all the way off the peninsula. Based in Tokyo as overall commander of the United Nations war effort to repel the invaders, General of the Army Douglas MacArthur had been worried enough that a 'general debacle' might occur to pay a personal visit to Eighth Army headquarters at Taegu in late July to impress upon Lieutenant General Walton H. Walker that no Dunkirk-style evacuation should be contemplated.[2]

Concept

The situation was not in fact by this point as grim for the American-led allied effort in Korea as it seemed. In the face of fierce KPA assaults and localized successes the Pusan perimeter was successfully defended through August and into September. Ongoing resistance, along with

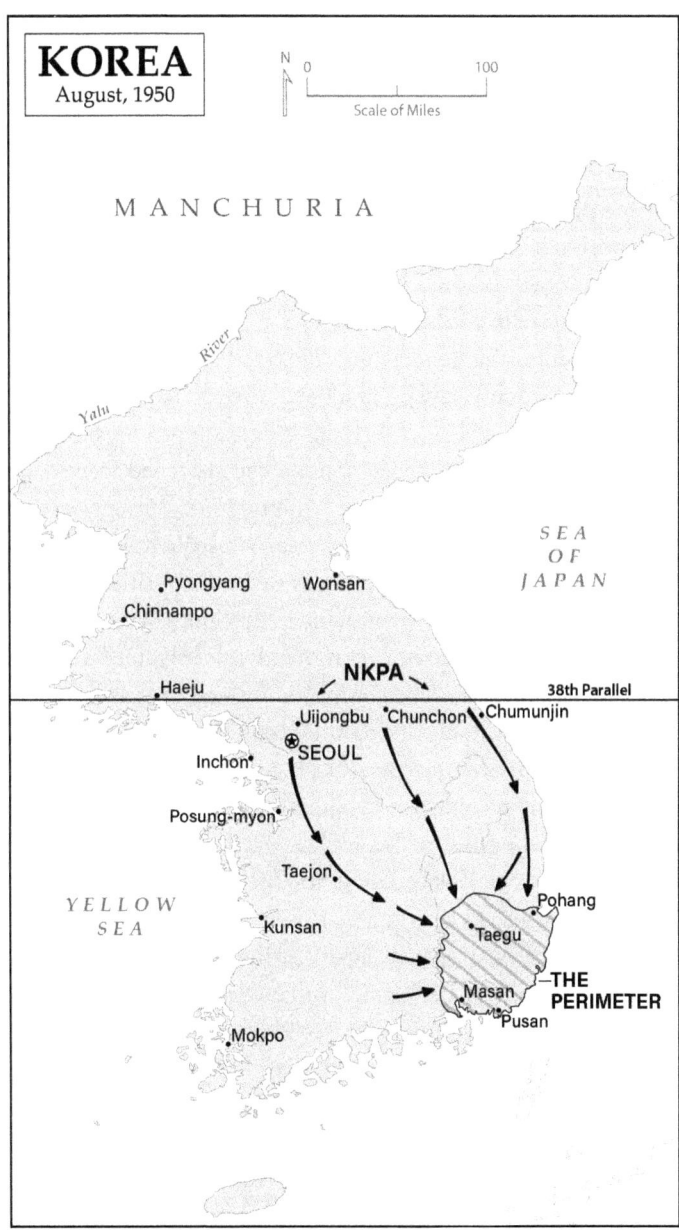

Map 2.1 Korea: August 1950.

an increasingly tenuous supply situation due to the distances involved and the effects of an American aerial interdiction campaign, meant that North Korean units were becoming steadily weaker. Conversely, complete American control of the sea and air meant that American and ROKA combat forces within the relatively compact perimeter could be easily supported and built up in size and strength through Pusan's port facilities. By the middle of September, the KPA was outnumbered two to one. Douglas MacArthur, however, by this point had his gaze fixed elsewhere.[3]

At age seventy, the general was by far the most senior serving officer in the US Army, having graduated first in his class from West Point as far back as 1903. Since then, his military accomplishments and consequent promotions and decorations had stretched from combat leadership positions on the Western Front (1917–18) through serving as US Army chief of staff in the early 1930s, to subsequently advising and commanding forces in the Philippines in various capacities, all the way to tri-service wartime theatre command in the South West Pacific Area (1942–45) and finally supreme command on behalf of the Allied Powers in postwar Japan. The soundness of some of the operational decisions MacArthur made during the Second World War, as well as on earlier occasions, was questionable. But thanks to a combination of titanic ego, media savviness, and politics—the high regard in which he was held by the opposition Republican Party as well as his service seniority made it nearly impossible for the ruling Democratic Party administrations or Pentagon mandarins to rein him in—MacArthur emerged from the war against Japan in the eyes of many ordinary Americans as a military demigod comparable to Julius Caesar. There was therefore no question that he would be given overall command once the decision had been made in Washington to fight the North Korean invasion in the summer of 1950, nor that he would seek to operate thereafter as he saw fit from his headquarters in Tokyo.[4]

Among the general's signature moves in the Second World War had been amphibious landings designed to bypass enemy concentrations. Within a week or so of the start of hostilities on the Korean peninsula

MacArthur was having his staff think along similar lines, and a plan was concocted to insert a substantial force through the port of Inchon. This, along with an alternative project for a landing at Kunsan, soon had to be abandoned as the designated units, principally from the 1st Cavalry Division, were urgently needed in the effort to shore up resistance to the North Korean thrusts in the southeast.[5] A major move from sea to shore, however, remained firmly lodged in MacArthur's consciousness even as he badgered the Pentagon for reinforcements to meet the current emergency.[6] Brigadier General Edwin K. Wright, head of his joint strategic plans and operations group, was directed in the third week of July to 'think of a couple of end runs around each coast', and with the help of his team quickly presented his chief with a shortlist of five potential landing sites. Of these, it was Inchon on the west coast that held MacArthur's attention.[7] From his perspective the port was ideal, being located less than 30 miles from the capital city. A landing at Inchon immediately followed by the capture of Seoul would sever the main lines of communication and supply to the KPA units fighting far to the south, and then open up the chance to catch enemy forces in the jaws of a pincer movement north-westward from Pusan and south-eastward from Seoul. Though he did not articulate them, there were also personal factors to consider. MacArthur understood that a speedy operation with good press coverage that culminated in the liberation of the capital would be heralded as decisive and further reinforce his public identity as a strategic genius.[8] The need to divert reinforcements to the ongoing Pusan perimeter fight meant that the 2nd Infantry Division could not be employed as originally hoped, but in the third week of July MacArthur was confident that if given the 1st Marine Division, then assembling in the United States, his chances for a successful amphibious assault on Inchon in September would be 'excellent'.[9]

Those whose job it was to assess Inchon as an actual landing site rather than a convenient entrepôt for Seoul did not share the general's optimism. Intelligence on everything from hydrographic conditions to shore defences was often speculative at best. The port was nestled behind more than a dozen islands, and the approach, Flying Fish Channel, was narrow, winding, and filled with shoals. Immediately offshore of Inchon was Wolmi-do, an islet connected to the shore by a causeway, which dominated the harbour in all directions. There were seawalls rather than beaches on much of the shoreline, and the huge tidal range meant that even under spring-tide conditions, landing craft and ships would only have a short window of opportunity to offload before the sea ran out and left them stranded on a vast expanse of mudflats. 'We drew up a list of every natural and geographic handicap,' an officer on the amphibious planning staff of Rear Admiral James H. Doyle famously quipped, '—and Inchon had 'em all.'[10]

As the dangers involved in any Inchon operation became obvious, a pair of west-coast alternatives were suggested. The port of Kunsan, 100-odd miles to the south, had far fewer natural obstacles, while the shoreline at Posung-myon, also to the south but still within 30 miles of Seoul, offered excellent landing beaches. MacArthur, however, remained unswervingly committed to Inchon and expressed his faith in the ability of technical experts to overcome the various obstacles it presented. He appointed Major General Edward M. Almond, his chief of staff and a personal acolyte, to oversee the planning process, thereby sidelining doubters lower down the chain of command, while employing a certain amount of subterfuge as well as his famous rhetorical skills in exchanges with his nominal superiors on the Joint Chiefs of Staff (JCS).[11]

MacArthur had first mentioned Inchon to a somewhat sceptical US Army chief of staff, General J. Lawton Collins, in the middle of July during a visit by the latter, accompanied by the US Air Force chief of staff, General Hoyt Vandenberg, to assess the military situation in the Far East. In the weeks that followed MacArthur kept pressuring Washington for reinforcements while concealing the specifics of his developing plan. The risks involved in the choice of Inchon as a landing site were nonetheless obvious enough that the JCS decided to send Collins back to Tokyo in the third week of August, this time accompanied by the chief of naval operations, Admiral Forrest Sherman, along with Vandenberg's deputy. A briefing was arranged for the evening of 23 August 1950 at which the outlines of the prospective operation would be revealed by the senior planners, giving the visitors from Washington a chance to focus attention on the inherent dangers of Inchon and propose alternatives. That a landing at Inchon was a risky proposition from a naval perspective could not be glossed over, and after the initial presentations Collins took the opportunity to make the case for a landing further south. MacArthur then rose to his feet and delivered a lengthy dramatic peroration on the virtues of Inchon, arguing with rising intensity that precisely because of its drawbacks an attack on his chosen target would take the enemy by surprise and have a strategic impact that a landing elsewhere would simply lack. 'We shall land at Inchon,' the general affirmed, 'and I shall crush them.'[12]

As even the sceptical Collins admitted, the general's oratorical brilliance left everybody present spellbound. The following day MacArthur delivered another lengthy verbal riposte when Lieutenant General Lemuel C. Shepherd, Jr., in administrative charge of the Fleet Marine Force Pacific and representing the views of various more junior dissenters, argued in the general's office that his chosen landing site was too risky compared to the alternatives. The prospect of a bold seizure of the Korean capital via Inchon, the general declaimed, was worth a high-stakes gamble since taking Seoul 'would quickly end the war'.[13]

On 28 August, the JCS formally authorized MacArthur to prepare for a landing at Inchon if intelligence reports confirmed weak defences in the vicinity or somewhere more promising if they did not. The alternative landing site proviso was simply ignored in Tokyo, as were efforts by Washington to get the general to reconsider in light of renewed KPA assaults on the Pusan perimeter in the first week of September. 'There is no question in my mind as to the feasibility of the operation', MacArthur reaffirmed in a cable to the JCS a week before the landing, 'and I regard its chances of success as excellent.'[14]

Plan

Gaps in intelligence about enemy forces were hastily filled through photoreconnaissance by the US Air Force and information garnered through special operations involving anti-communist Korean observers.[15] Amidst uncertainty over everything from the availability and strength of participating forces to the accuracy of charts and weather reports, as the mid-September tidal deadline for a landing at Inchon loomed ever closer the main features of what had been dubbed 'Chromite' and its presumed aftermath began to take shape.[16]

From locations near and far an armada totalling more than 260 vessels and a force of over 71,000 soldiers, sailors, and marines was assembled as Joint Task Force 7 under the command of Vice Admiral Arthur D. Struble, mostly American in makeup but including warships from Britain, Canada, Australia, New Zealand, and France, along with a considerable number of Korean and some Japanese personnel.[17] Feints and demonstrations elsewhere on the coastline would be mounted in order to sow confusion as to the principal target.[18] There would be two days of preliminary bombardment by carrier-launched aircraft and naval gunfire in order to do as much damage as possible to identified or suspected North Korean defences located in or around Inchon and, in particular, on Wolmi-do. On D-day itself, scheduled for 15 September, Task Force 90, the amphibious group under the direction of Rear Admiral James H. Doyle, with fighter-bombers and rocket-firing vessels to hand as well as the guns of cruisers and destroyers in support, would utilize various types of specialized landing craft and amphibious vehicles to send in the bulk of the 1st US Marine Division under Major General O. P. Smith. The ship-to-shore assault would begin at dawn with a battalion-strength landing on Wolmi-do (Green Beach), followed on the next incoming tide that afternoon by simultaneous regimental-size landings against the seawalls of the port itself to the north and south of town (Red Beach and Blue Beach). The various units would then link up to create a secure beachhead, and a regiment of Korean marines would come ashore to provide security within the city. The 1st and 5th US Marine regiments, with accompanying tanks and artillery, would then advance eastward towards Seoul under an umbrella of close air support provided by US Marine Corps aircraft launched from escort carriers. Reinforcements would pour in via Inchon, above all the US Army's 7th Infantry Division under Major General David G. Barr, which would strike east and then south to meet up with units of the Eighth Army that would themselves have begun a drive north-westward from the Pusan perimeter.[19]

Other than appointing Ned Almond to command X Corps, incorporating both reinforced divisions as a means of keeping his main objective, the capture of Seoul, to the forefront, MacArthur left the planning details to others.[20] He, meanwhile, continued to assume that the resulting operational plans would work, and went on to assert in a final message to the anxious JCS that 'all my commanders and staff officers, without exception, are confident in the success of the enveloping movement'.[21]

This was in fact far from the case, especially in light of the constricted timetable and uncertainties about an enemy response. The short timeframe available in which to organize the assault increased the chances of serious foul-ups in the intricate approach and landing sequence, especially if bad weather intervened. If news of the operation had leaked, then the key element of surprise would be lost; the narrow approaches to Inchon might be sown with sea mines to catastrophic effect; even if not, the preliminary bombardment might be insufficiently destructive; and intelligence assessments concerning relatively few and weak enemy troop formations in the Seoul region and Inchon itself could prove to have been disastrously over-optimistic. Admiral Doyle, among others, continued to think that there were less risky landing sites.[22]

MacArthur nonetheless remained bullish, telling the courier conveying the final Chromite plan for the chiefs of staff in Washington to stress that the risk involved was small.[23] Only on the eve of the assault, aboard the command ship *Mount McKinley*, did the general exhibit any doubt. MacArthur later wrote that he became acutely conscious that

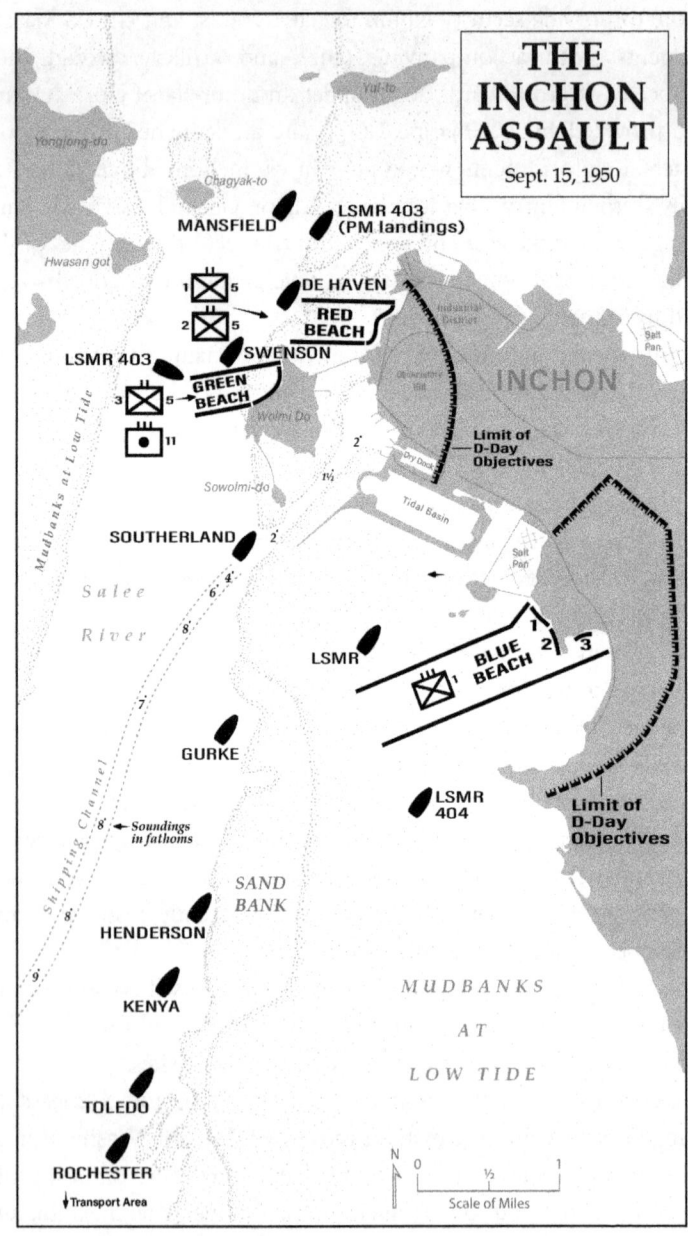

Map 2.2 The Inchon assault: 15 September 1950.

'I alone was responsible tomorrow,' and that 'if I failed, the dreadful result would rest on judgment day against my soul.'[24]

Execution

Chromite did not fail. Instead, almost everything turned out well. Despite being battered by high winds and steep waves on the journey up from Japan, Task Force 90 arrived off Inchon intact amidst overcast and rain squalls rather than typhoon conditions.[25] Despite poor American security measures and a network of informants in Tokyo, the defenders seemed to be taken completely unawares, with trenches along the seawalls left largely untended and troop numbers very much of the limited size and quality estimated.[26] The few floating sea mines encountered were spotted and blown up before they could do any damage, the naval bombardment did its job, and aside from a little confusion on Red Beach and off Blue Beach the landings themselves occurred 'about as planned', as the commander of the 1st Marine Division, O. P. Smith, recorded.[27]

Preceded by an intense naval and air bombardment, the 3rd Battalion, 5th Marine Regiment, came ashore on Green Beach just after 6:30 a.m. to deal with shellshocked remnants from the KPA 8th coastal artillery regiment and with the help of M26 tanks from the 1st Tank Battalion had secured Wolmi-do by 8:00 a.m. Five hours later, as high tide approached and after a preparatory rocket bombardment of the shoreline, the 2nd and 3rd battalions of the 1st Marine Regiment and the 1st and 2nd battalions of the 5th Marine Regiment landed, respectively, at Blue Beach and Red Beach to the south and at the north end of the port; key urban hill objectives then being seized within the space of two hours. By nightfall on 15 September 1950, the assault and follow-on units had secured the Inchon beachhead at a cost of under two-dozen fatal casualties.[28]

The subsequent days were also marked by success, albeit not without difficult moments. Supported by tanks, artillery, and aircraft, the

US Marine Corps infantry units advanced methodically eastward from Inchon against largely ineffective enemy efforts to reorganize and counterattack. Kimpo airfield was seized from enemy air force security units inside the first forty-eight hours, and despite stiffening resistance and occasional setbacks, within five days the 5th Marines had reached the Han River to the northeast. The simultaneous advance directly westward of the 1st Marines was heavily contested by elements of the KPA's 42nd Tank Regiment, 87th Infantry Regiment, and 18th Rifle Division in the hills overlooking the industrial town of Yongdungpo located on the west bank of the Han: but after a series of hard-fought firefights, attacks, and counterattacks, the surviving KPA remnants withdrew eastward on 22 September. Meanwhile US and ROK reinforcements had been coming ashore at Inchon, including the 7th Marine Regiment and the 7th Infantry Division, elements of the latter advancing somewhat haphazardly southeast to secure the X Corps right flank in the vicinity of Suwon while the former marched east to reinforce the 1st and 5th Marines.[29]

Meanwhile as planned, far to the southeast, all four corps of the Eighth Army under Walton Walker had gone over to the offensive the day after the landing against the remaining 70,000 or so KPA soldiers who had been desperately trying to batter their way through to Pusan. At first resistance was fierce and little progress was made, much to MacArthur's irritation. But after a week of grinding combat, North Korean forces in the south simply began to disintegrate, allowing for a breakout in multiple directions, including to the northwest towards X Corps with the 1st Cavalry Division in the lead.[30]

Seoul

Each side sensed that events were approaching a climax in the fourth week of the month. X Corps was now poised to strike the capital, while the Eighth Army was finally on the move northward. Yet though the main North Korean expeditionary force was disintegrating to the south, it was apparent that remaining enemy units in the vicinity of the capital still planned to contest an X Corps advance into Seoul, with troops from the KPA's 25th Rifle Brigade and 78th Independent Brigade occupying strong defensive positions on a series of hills along a ridge west of Seoul on the east side of the Han River while work continued on erecting barricades in the central core of the city.[31]

As commander of the 1st Marine Division, Oliver Smith planned a methodical advance in which the 5th Marines crossed the Han and, in conjunction with the 1st and the 7th Marines in a northern flanking role, then overcame the city's defences. The amphibious crossing of the Han on 20 September, though not without incident, was a success; but the comparatively slow pace of the subsequent fights to break through the enemy's ridgeline and hill positions soon led the tempestuous X Corps commander, Ned Almond, to insist on a major operational change. Thwarted in his desire to send the 1st Marines south to engage in a detached flanking manoeuvre, Almond on 24 September gave this role to the 7th Division's 32nd Regiment and ROKA 17th Regiment. With the help of Marine amphibious tractors these army units crossed the Han the next day and subsequently moved northeastward to gain control of key heights commanding main roads east and south out of Seoul. This, the X Corps commander believed, would force the KPA to abandon the capital, and aerial reports of northward movement led Almond to order the Marines, engaged for days now in house-to-house fighting, to launch an impromptu attack on the night of 25/26 September. This was exactly the point at which the KPA launched a series of energetic counterattacks within the city, resulting in a series of desperately hard-fought street engagements. It was not until 28 September that the fight for Seoul finally came to an end, two days after elements of the Eighth Army's 1st Cavalry Division, advancing from the south, had linked up with elements of X Corps's 7th Infantry Division near Osan, thereby realizing MacArthur's overall vision.[32]

By the end of the month the KPA was estimated to have lost around fourteen thousand men killed in action in attempting to stop the Inchon–Seoul operation. Meanwhile, the overall cost to X Corps had

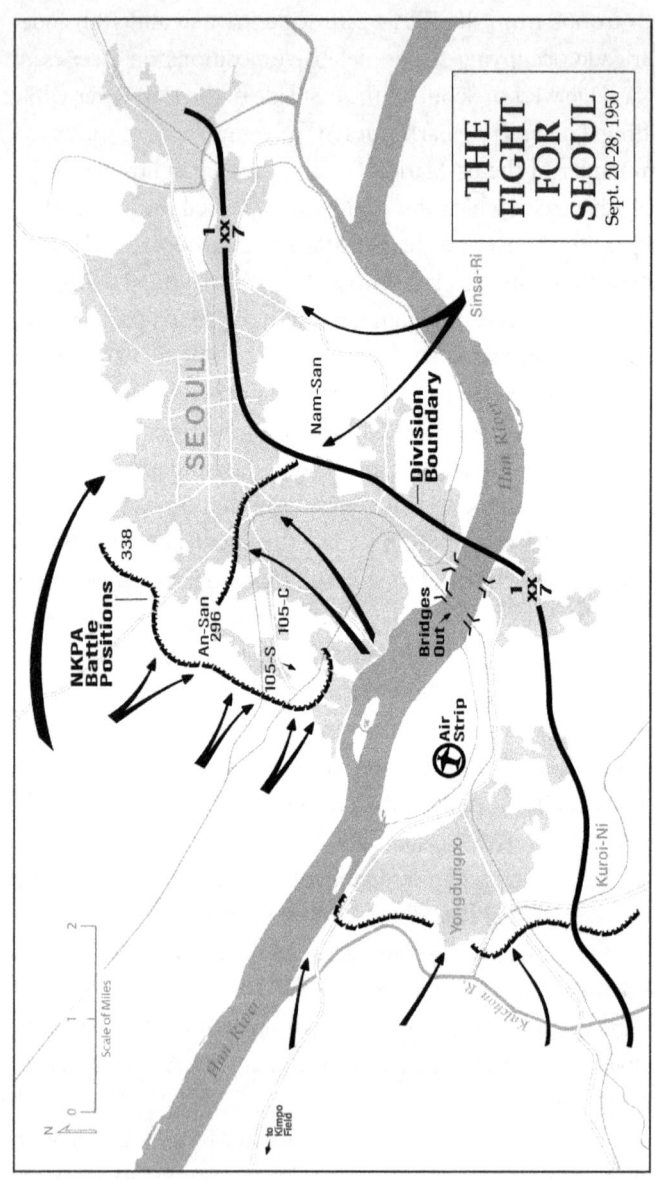

Map 2.3 The fight for Seoul: 20–28 September 1950.

been remarkably small: under six hundred dead and less than three thousand wounded, the majority coming from the Marine Corps units which had borne the brunt of the fighting.[33] The butcher's bill for the Eighth Army on the offensive in the second half of September was significantly greater—around ten thousand casualties in all—but the enemy had been routed.[34]

Aftermath

On 28 September 1950, MacArthur was able to stage a very public restoration ceremony inside the capitol building in Seoul. Amid multiple references to Providence and Almighty God and the formal handover of civil administration back to Syngman Rhee, the general declared Inchon to have been a 'decisive victory'.[35]

The accolades poured in to MacArthur's headquarters in Tokyo. Having feared the worst and hoped for the best, the JCS formally congratulated the general on his 'brilliant and audacious leadership' and his 'magnificently planned, timed and executed' campaign, while the President of the United States, Harry S. Truman, wired his 'warmest congratulations' on a 'brilliant maneuver'. A former US Army chief of staff himself, the current Secretary of Defense, George C. Marshall, sent his 'personal tribute' in honour of 'the daring and perfect strategical operation which [has] virtually terminated the struggle'.[36]

The latter opinion was a view shared by almost everyone in authority on the United Nations side. Thanks to the offensive operations of Almond and Walker, the KPA in the south had been comprehensively defeated by the end of the month, its units pulverized and its troops either killed, captured, taking to the hills, or streaming homeward in disorder through gaps between ROK or US units. All that remained, so it seemed, was to advance across the 38th parallel and deliver the *coup de gras*.[37] MacArthur was therefore authorized by Washington to engage in pursuit and exploitation operations as deep as necessary into a reeling DPRK with the aim of destroying what remained of the enemy force and overthrowing Kim Il Sung.[38]

Reversal

The success of the MacArthur's bid to turn the tables on the enemy in the south meant that he was allowed to conduct the invasion of the northern half of the Korean peninsula pretty much as he saw fit. Growing concerns among JCS staff and some of his subordinate commanders that the general, after having gambled and won handsomely at Inchon, was ignoring their input and running unnecessary risks, were left largely unvoiced.[39] On those few occasions when MacArthur's decisions were openly queried by the Pentagon, moreover, as when in the third week of October he unilaterally chose to override a proviso to his original orders indicating that only ROKA troops should be allowed to advance into territories adjacent to the Yalu River border with China, the JCS quickly backed down.[40]

MacArthur began his invasion of the north by splitting his forces again, laboriously shipping X Corps to the northeast coast at Wonsan while Eighth Army advanced north overland. At first all went well, what remained of the KPA unable to stem the various northward thrusts and Pyongang falling on 19 October. 'This very definitely is coming to an end,' the general commented to reporters.[41]

Such optimism, however, was predicated on the assumption that full-scale armed intervention across the China–Korea border along the Yalu River to save the DPRK was quite unlikely. Even if this did occur, MacArthur told the president in the course of their one and only face-to-face meeting on Wake Island in the middle of October, the forces at his command would easily be able to defeat the Red Chinese. Both these suppositions turned out to be wishful thinking.[42]

Mao Zedong had been preparing communist Chinese formations to enter the conflict with indirect support from the Soviet Union almost from the moment the United States itself had intervened in Korea. In the first week of October, as an appeal from Kim Il Sung and intelligence sources made it clear that the neighbouring fraternal regime was collapsing, he gave the final order to start infiltrating hundreds of thousands of People's Liberation Army soldiers—officially 'Chinese People's Volunteers' (CPV)—into North Korea.[43]

The first encounter battles between the Chinese and MacArthur's troops in late October into early November, in which lightly armed yet tactically adept CPV formations had overwhelmed and forced into retreat various ROKA and American regiments before suddenly breaking contact, suggested that this new enemy required a serious reassessment of objectives and means. There was briefly talk in Washington of issuing a possibly more restrictive set of operational instructions to MacArthur, but the general was having none of it. 'It would be fatal to weaken the fundamental and basic policy of the United Nations to destroy all resisting armed forces in Korea,' he stressed in a cable to the JCS, referencing his plans to resume the drive to the Yalu shortly.[44] In the absence of solid intelligence on what the Chinese were up to and successive underestimates as to the size of the CPV force actually deployed, MacArthur was allowed to respond first with an ineffectual bombing campaign and then, in the third week of November, with what was labelled by the press the 'home by Christmas' campaign: a joint offensive undertaken by Eighth Army and X Corps that was supposed to reach the Yalu and crush all opposition in what was described in an official communiqué as a 'massive compression envelopment'.[45]

This renewed advance was just what Peng Dehuai, the enemy commander, had been waiting for. Chinese units had been deliberately withdrawn northward after the initial encounters in order to lure the Americans and their allies into a trap. The Chinese People's Volunteers south of the Yalu, adept at concealing themselves from aerial observation, in reality now outnumbered their opponents by a factor of nearly two to one. Dispersed advancing UN units were quickly engulfed by CPV flanking and encirclement moves for which they were mostly unprepared, and that collectively forced a general UN retreat through December 1950.[46]

Though certain of its units fared badly, X Corps was able to avoid overall entrapment, the 1st Marine Division managing to sustain a fighting retreat in good order from the Chosin Reservoir and, with the remainder of the formation, eventually be extricated via the port of Hungnam.[47] Significant portions of the Eighth Army, however, notably the 2nd Infantry Division and various ROKA formations, were terribly mauled as they desperately tried to disengage and retire southward.[48] Walker felt he had no option but to abandon Pyongyang and try to establish a defensive line north of Seoul before he was killed in a road accident in the third week of December.[49]

MacArthur's response to this spectacular change of fortune, which he famously characterized as heralding 'an entirely new war', aside from trying to deflect responsibility away from himself, was to lobby Washington to expand the conflict by blockading the Chinese mainland, bombing Manchuria, and allow him to employ Nationalist Chinese troops from Taiwan to counter the Red Chinese in Korea—arguing that, without these measures, Korea might have to be abandoned. But defeat and retreat in the north had dispelled the aura of infallibility that had surrounded the general since Inchon, and none of these demands were accepted by Washington.[50]

Thanks in large part to the actions of Walker's replacement, Matthew Ridgway, to whom the general delegated full operational authority, the situation in Korea began to stabilize in the new year and, after having to abandon Seoul in early January 1951, an Eighth Army joined by X Corps and other reinforcements was able to retake the city in March and establish a viable front extending roughly along the 38th parallel that withstood the last great CPV offensive in the spring. The resulting line would last with only minor alterations through the long months of negotiation and limited though sometimes locally fierce fighting that preceded the armistice agreement of July 1953.[51]

By that stage, however, the general was no longer in charge. Never able to reconcile himself to a mere containment strategy in Korea—there was 'no substitute for victory' in his eyes—he had sounded off publicly one too many times about the need to take the war to mainland China. With JCS concurrence, Truman had finally relieved MacArthur in April 1951 despite the inevitable public and congressional outcry.[52]

The spin which the general tried to put on his decision to push on to the Yalu, namely that the advance was a reconnaissance in force which had prematurely sprung the Chinese trap and thereby saved his forces from complete destruction, proved unconvincing.[53] However, even critics of MacArthur, then and later, tended to accept that Inchon had been a stroke of genius, a risky envelopment move which caused the North Korean invasion of South Korea to collapse. This was at least to a degree due to successful efforts by MacArthur to control the narrative. Even before the landing began, he was taking steps to try and ensure that Western news media coverage of Chromite and its aftermath burnished his image as one of history's great commanders.[54]

3

News Media

By the middle of the twentieth century it had become axiomatic that reportage, either on the printed page or over the airwaves, not only shaped public perceptions of current events but also constituted the first rough draft of history.[1] The need to control the narrative was thus fully understood by those with a stake in how the Inchon landing and the recapture of Seoul were portrayed by journalists. For authoritarian states this was not a problem, insofar as all media were tightly controlled by the regime, and news reports and editorials could be manipulated to meet state desiderata.[2] Within liberal democracies, on the other hand, where freedom of the press was the rule, there were limits to what the authorities could do to mediate the message coming out of Korea.[3]

Party Line

Despite absolute authority over what, how, and when information was disseminated, the propaganda organs in North Korea faced two serious challenges when it came to Inchon. The first was simply lack of information. The second was how to portray a series of defeats.[4]

The first news from Inchon, based on military reports made in the wake of the preliminary naval bombardment the day before the landing, did not indicate trouble. Pyongyang radio announced that four American landing craft and three destroyers had been sunk and all other vessels driven off.[5] Six US Navy destroyers had in fact deliberately sailed in to draw fire from Wolmi-do and thereby identify gun positions for subsequent bombardment; and while one sustained serious damage and two others were hit, none were sunk before they withdrew.[6] Nonetheless, this faulty report would form an important strand in the eventual North Korean narrative of the battle.[7]

For several days thereafter, as the Inchon–Seoul operation proceeded, coverage was notable for its absence. Pyongyang was evidently still trying to work out what was happening and what to do, which in turn meant there was virtually no public response.[8] It took eight days for military communiqués broadcast over Pyongyang radio to admit that the landings and advance had taken place despite 'stubborn resistance'.[9]

The first order of business was then to contest the imperialist narrative of what had happened at Inchon and subsequently proclaim that Seoul was being turned into a veritable street-by-street fortress.[10] Communiqués broadcast by Pyongyang indicated that the struggle was going well. 'Units of the People's Army defending Seoul are repelling the attacks of the enemy,' it was asserted, 'who is attempting to drive a wedge into their defenses.' A day later it was said that counterattacks 'delivered by People's Army units defending the city checked the offensive of the enemy and inflicted on him big losses'.[11] By the middle of the last week of September, though, emphasis was shifting towards the costs imposed on the imperialists in taking the capital and references to an eventual counter offensive.[12]

Things would get a lot worse for the Democratic People's Republic of Korea before the situation dramatically improved around the turn of the year thanks to Chinese intervention. In the meantime Kim Il Sung was personally articulating a perspective on what had happened that would remain the essence of the North Korean view of Inchon for the remainder of the century and beyond. On 11 October 1950 he made a radio broadcast widely disseminated in print around the communist world. Desperate to stave off the defeat of the puppet regime in the South, the American imperialists 'have mobilized the land, sea and air forces in the Pacific area and have brought to Korea part of the Mediterranean fleet, even including the reserve fleet'. Thus 'a tremendous armed force' had been hurled at Inchon with the aim of taking Seoul. The imperialists had expected an easy victory, but helped by the people of the capital city 'the People's Army held back the offensive of the enemy's numerically superior forces' for fourteen days and therein 'displayed exemplary self-sacrifice and heroism in defense of the motherland'. Unfortunately, while a 'decisive blow' would one day hurl them back, the enemy's sheer numerical strength had meant 'the People's Army was compelled to retreat'.[13]

Inner Circle

MacArthur, meanwhile, had been trying to shape how Inchon was reported in the Free World. 'I'm going on a little operation,' he announced to a chosen group of friendly journalists in Tokyo, 'and I'd like to have you boys with me if you'd like to go.' Just in case anyone missed the import of this summons, the general added a clarification: 'I say a little operation—it's a big operation.' Naturally enough, the invitation was accepted.[14] MacArthur was taking care to arrange what amounted to a quid pro quo whereby, in return for privileged access and communications aboard the command ship *Mount McKinley*, he would get the kind of personal press coverage he desired.[15] It was no coincidence that there were photographers of all kinds aboard to record MacArthur observing operations.[16] As for field reporters, the absence of a formal military censorship code was more than counterbalanced by their reliance on the armed forces for transport and filing copy, overlaid by indirect warnings that they could face severe impediments in future if what was published appeared truly unpatriotic in the eyes of General Headquarters (GHQ) Tokyo staff.[17]

That not playing by the implicit rules of the game could lead to trouble was evident in the aftermath of the first published news of the Inchon landing. Members of the inner circle were clearly meant to announce this exclusive jointly, but they were scooped by an enterprising Korean. Able to speak English as well as his native tongue and employed as an Associated Press (AP) stringer, Bill Shinn, like so many others, had known that something was afoot for weeks.[18] On the morning of 15 September, through contacts with various Americans and Korean intelligence officers in Pusan, he learned of the dawn assault on Wolmi-do. Working at great speed, Shinn then obtained de facto confirmation from the Republic of Korea (ROK) naval operations chief, Lee Yong-woon, and afterwards managed to persuade a public information officer that it would be in the interests of ROK Army chief of staff Chung Il-kwan for Shinn to file an announcement ostensibly made by Chung. Commandeering a telephone in the ROK Navy chief of staff's office, the reporter filed his story with the AP Tokyo office, beating the official press announcement by nine hours.[19] Retribution for this display of journalistic initiative was swift: Shinn was denied direct access to all further telephonic communication between Korea and Japan.[20]

The first authorized reports and communiqués, meanwhile, took care to emphasize the complete success of the landings at Inchon and the fact that MacArthur, 'who planned the big amphibious operation, was on hand to direct it'.[21] The next day, individual reports from correspondents aboard *Mount McKinley* appearing in print that had been filed on the day of the assault were unstinting in their praise. 'Inchon Landing Goes like Clockwork with MacArthur in Charge' was a typical headline preceding the story sent in by Russell Brines.[22] 'Today's perfectly timed amphibious landings at Inchon', Percy Wood of the *Chicago Tribune* stated, 'were a high achievement of combined arms guided by the military genius of Gen. Douglas MacArthur.'[23]

Sporting his trademark battered cap and aviator sunglasses the general, one correspondent noted admiringly, 'looked less than his 70 years'.[24] Two days later MacArthur came ashore to inspect and be briefed by Marine commanders on the advancing front, trailed by an entourage of photographers, reporters, and staffers. His cultivated fearlessness was on display and duly admired. Colonel Raymond L. Murray of the 5th Marines suggested that the general not risk his life by getting too close to frontline positions. 'I think we ought to push ahead,' the general replied, 'even if there is sniper fire.'[25] A few days later he was back on land just after the successful crossing of the Han River, driving through areas that had not been fully secured, stopping only a very short distance from frontline positions, and reassuring Murray that resistance outside Seoul would 'evaporate very shortly'.[26]

This assurance proved to be overly optimistic. Confident headlines such as 'Marines Drive Ahead' quickly gave way to 'North Koreans Stall Seizure of Seoul'.[27] The end, though, was not that far off. After several days of intense street fighting, the news services were once again heralding imminent victory. 'Ancient City Totters as Marines Converge' was how the AP report early in the last week of September was interpreted. 'Seoul Fall Near' predicted the United Press (UP), adding, 'Enemy Cracking'.[28] Back in Tokyo, MacArthur issued a communiqué to the press services on Tuesday 26 September heralding the fall of the ancient Korean capital, which immediately prompted headlines such as 'Marines Take Seoul' and 'Seoul Falls'.[29] Given that only about a third of the city had been secured by the following day, the declaration was, as a *New York Herald Tribune* editorial put it, 'evidently premature';[30] but with advancing units from the Eighth Army linking up with elements of X Corps and the enemy in general retreat, after heavy fighting the following night, organized resistance in the capital was rightly reported to have finally ebbed away.[31]

There was extensive media coverage of the carefully stage-managed visit by the general to the liberated city on 29 September 1950.[32] 'Douglas MacArthur, in a triumphant ceremony in Seoul today restored the South Korean capital to President Syngman Rhee of the Korean Republic', as the fairly typical UP report by Frank Tremaine put it, the journalist adding: 'While the Marine band played and flags fluttered in a fresh breeze, MacArthur on behalf of the United Nations formally returned the seat of the South Korean Government to its 75-year-old president.'[33] The impression left by MacArthur's remarks, echoed by pundits in the press, was that the war was all but over.[34]

Figure 3.1 Douglas MacArthur observes the success of Operation Chromite aboard *Mount McKinley*, flanked by Court Whitney and a pointing Ned Almond.

Combat Reporting

In the meantime, accounts by frontline war correspondents who had accompanied the assault waves on D-day rather than remain clustered around MacArthur aboard *Mount McKinley* were starting to appear. James Cameron of *Picture Post*, himself a pacifist, observed what he took to be false bravado on the part of his fellow war correspondents, 'all trying to appear insistently determined to land in Wave One, while contriving desperately to be found in Wave Fifty'.[35] This was doubtless true of some journalists, but there were others who showed commendable courage in reporting on what the frontline Marines encountered as they came ashore and afterwards, a useful corrective to the euphoric tone of reports from the MacArthur entourage.[36]

One of the first civilian journalists to land was Frank Gibney, representing *TIME* magazine, who hitched a ride at dawn with the third wave hitting Green Beach on Wolmi-do. By the time they arrived the assault was virtually over, leaving Gibney to contemplate small groups of dazed, frightened, and often badly injured enemy survivors. 'Going farther along the road towards the causeway, I found a desperately wounded North Korean,' Gibney recorded. '"Salyo chu sio [help me!]," he croaked, waving his hands at his conquerors. Almost all his clothes had been blown off except for a new pair of Russian boots. I watched him grow weaker while he gestured. A minute later he fell back into the dust—dead.'[37]

Harold Levine, going in with the first wave towards Red Beach later that day, noted that the means by which Marines were supposed to get out of their landing craft and over the seawall did not work as planned. 'Now we hit the wall,' he recounted for *Newsweek* readers: 'The men try to dig the big hooks on the ladders into it. They can't. The hooks don't even scratch the stone and are not long enough to reach behind the wall and bite into the dirt of the beach. The men fumble and then—the hell with it. They clamber up the ladder and leap.' Thankfully the unit to which he was attached was able to reach and secure its immediate objective, Consulate Hill, against negligible resistance; a friendly fire incident, though, produced casualties—'an officer and an enlisted man'.[38]

Larry Keighley, going in with the next wave onto Red Beach, experienced more return fire as the remaining defenders recovered from the preliminary bombardment. 'Fifty yards from the sea wall, bullets ping against the high sides of our boat [landing craft],' to which on arrival were added grenades. Heavily laden Marines awkwardly clambered up ladders, only for several to be hit by machine-gun fire and fall backward. 'Four dead, three wounded,' he informed *Saturday Evening Post* subscribers, sardonically adding: 'and we expected "light resistance" at Red Beach.'[39]

It was 'far from the "virtually unopposed" landing the troops had hoped for', Marguerite Higgins wrote for the *Herald Tribune* of her experience aboard a landing craft in the fifth Red Beach wave.

Figure 3.2 US Marines scale the seawall, Red Beach, 15 September 1950.

Enemy tracer fire passed close overhead and bullets spattered the water, leaving 'the men around me with expressions contorted with anxiety'. At the seawall there was still enough enemy rifle and automatic weapon fire to pin down some of the newly landed Marines for a time as landing craft continued to crash in, and when the men then raced forward, ducking and weaving, 'enemy bullets caught a good many in the semi-darkness'.[40] The landing, in short, had involved real fighting and had not been casualty free.[41]

Nor was the advance eastward towards the capital devoid of significant clashes with the enemy. Bill Blair, for instance, travelling with a forward Marine unit, reported for *Baltimore Sun* readers on a night-time North Korean counterattack that occurred after the Marines arrived at Kimpo airfield a few days after the events at Inchon. Infiltrating enemy groups 'were close—very close—when they opened fire and started yelling', Blair recounted. 'The attack was fierce' and there were sharp firefights at close quarters. The dug-in Marines, however, fought back hard for an hour, leaving North Korean bodies strewn around their foxholes. 'By 4.30 [a.m., 18 September] the enemy was silent and the Marines relapsed into uneasy rest, shivering in the early-morning chill.'[42]

The Han River crossing a couple of days later, though a great success overall, was by no means a mere exercise. Hitching a ride aboard a troop-carrying Marine amphibious tractor, AP's Don Whitehead discovered this first hand. 'Bullets began to slam against our amtrack,' he reported. 'Through a slit in the rear door I could see little spouts of water jumping up as bullets hit the water.' As the machine climbed up the opposite bank, he felt the tension mount as the men prepared to disembark under enemy fire. As Whitehead moved out 'the man beside me pitched forward. At the same time we heard the crack of the rifle. Then another Marine screamed and fell from the amtrack. The enemy on the hill above us was shooting straight down into our men as they came out the door. The Marines hugged the embankment as the bullets cracked into the vehicle. The driver fell wounded.' Under covering fire from a machine gun, a rifle squad was able to outflank and eject the North Korean defenders from their immediate position, but the battle continued: 'Above us cracked rifles and machine guns as the fighting moved up the ridge.'[43] Whitehead was not alone in suggesting that getting over the Han was not as trouble-free as the speed of the operation suggested. 'In the communiques the resistance will be described as "medium",' commented Marguerite Higgins after observing from the left bank, 'but it was rough work.'[44]

Covering the advance at or near the tip of the spear was hazardous for journalists, too. Gene Jones, a television cameraman working for the National Broadcasting Company, had been injured by a shell fragment on the day of the Inchon landing and had to be hospitalized. And two days after the Han crossing, Bill Blair suffered serious wounds and had to be invalided home.[45]

The going would only get tougher for all concerned. 'Officers frankly let it be known that this has been the "roughest" battle since they landed at Inchon six days ago,' Michael James of the *New York Times* reported of the stiff fight for Yongdungpo.[46] Marguerite Higgins concurred, noting the increasing risk of death and injury posed by shell bursts as well as rifle and machine-gun fire. 'The enemy is standing his ground better than at any time since the invasion,' she wrote for the *Herald Tribune*.[47] By the last week of the month it was clear to the combat correspondents that clearing Seoul would involve heavy street fighting and lengthening casualty lists.[48] Higgins noted by way of illustration that on the high ground on the northwest outskirts only a single Marine in one rifle squad emerged from one firefight unscathed.[49]

Those reporters who accompanied the Marines all the way into the heart of the capital sent back vivid descriptions of a grinding battle of attrition. 'Every few hundred feet were thick earthen barricades across the street,' wrote Whitehead, 'thrown up by the Reds in the past few days for their defense of Seoul', to which tanks equipped with bulldozer blades seemed the only answer.[50] Much of the fighting was of necessity at very close quarters. Homer Bigart wrote of the 'vicious snap of high-velocity shells' as a North Korean crew fired a 37 mm anti-tank gun down a boulevard towards a barricade which the Marines had taken, and of the effect of an accompanying American tank firing back. 'We could feel the heat of its muzzle blast as it fired down the road at the enemy emplacements,' he recounted, adding: 'Our ears ached from the concussion.'[51] In clearing the city the Marines were, as Michael James cautioned readers of the *New York Times*, moving slowly and 'taking serious casualties from innumerable snipers'.[52] For those engaged in the climax of the battle, involving the repelling of a fierce, tank-led North Korean night counterattack, the fighting had been—in the words of a Marine company commander with whom Higgins spoke—'hell on earth'.[53]

Wages of Destruction

There is evidence to suggest that elements in the press corps were racially insensitive and willing to turn a blind eye to evidence of the brutalities of the war in the name of anti-communist patriotism.[54] Marguerite Higgins of the *Herald Tribune*, for instance, witnessed communist suspects being summarily executed by ROK security forces but stressed the difficulty of telling genuine civilians from North Korean soldiers since the latter quickly disguised themselves as the former once the port city fell.[55] Even Reginald Thompson of the *Telegraph*, who would write a memoir of his experiences that was immensely sympathetic to the plight of ordinary Koreans, confined himself to the big picture in his dispatches on the advance from Inchon to Seoul.[56]

Yet at least some correspondents were willing to report how catastrophic the campaign was for the Korean population living on contested ground and question the official ROK position to the effect that the people were not bitter or depressed despite the death and destruction brought on by American forces using firepower more or less indiscriminately to blast their way ashore and inland.[57] 'The people certainly do not look happy,' AP's Relman Morin pointedly commented, going on to record uncomfortable sights such as 'two men wheeling the frightfully mangled body of a young girl through the streets to some lonely burial place. They had a kind of wheelbarrow. One was pushing, the other held a rope and pulled.' His impression, though it went against the liberation narrative, was probably close to the truth: 'you got the feeling that the people of Inchon were intensely apathetic to the whole business. They looked as though all they wanted was to be left alone.'[58] James Cameron, reporting for *Picture Post*, also thought the surviving population of Inchon the day after the landing looked shell-shocked rather than contented. 'As we edged into the charred town they came stumbling out, some of them sound, some of them smashed, one or two of them quite clearly driven into a sort of bomb-happy dementia by the night of destruction.' Cameramen took pictures that confirmed this.[59]

Much of the subsequent advance was through countryside; but as Morin noted a week later, this put peasant families in extreme peril. 'The fighting is like a scythe as it moves down the roads and fertile Korean valleys, where the fields are fat with rice and corn. It is like a

Figure 3.3 Photo taken by Pfc. Ronald L. Hancock, Inchon, 16 September 1950.

rolling cloud of fire, burning out villages and homes, knocking down the rice-empty little shops.' The inhabitants, meanwhile, had to get on with life as best they could, trying to avoid the destruction of the crops on which their lives depended.[60] Closer to the front, on the outskirts of the capital, Higgins to her credit reported the same day how 'artillery duels were taking a terrific toll of Korean civilians' as a steady stream of injured 'women, little children and old men' were being brought in to a Marine aid post, where their 'pathetic hope' for medical assistance was as often as not dashed by the overworked staff having to tend to wounded Americans.[61]

As for the climactic battle inside Seoul—'a flaming, smoke-filled city of horror', to quote Whitehead[62]—while MacArthur claimed that the 'liberation of the city was conducted in such a manner as to cause the least possible danger to civilian installations', AP stressed that the extent of resistance meant 'the attackers had to use more fire power than they had hoped'.[63] Several correspondents vividly conveyed what this had meant for the hapless inhabitants of the capital city. Tom Lambert, for example, made sure to illustrate one of the most 'pitiful aspects' of the struggle: civilian inhabitants caught in the crossfire. They brought their wounded to a room in the central prison. 'There was little oriental impassivity here. Women crouched on their heels and crooned over an injured child or husband. One old man sat silently holding the hand of his elderly wife, whose lower left leg was almost blown off.' White phosphorous burns were particularly horrible.[64]

Little wonder that, a few days later, after the dust had settled a bit and MacArthur flew in for his ceremonial restoration of President Rhee, the population gave him a somewhat subdued welcome. UP correspondent Ernest Hoberecht was struck by how, despite some flag waving, hand clapping, and occasional cheering, the general's motor cavalcade 'was by no means greeted by the riotous enthusiasm which one might expect'.[65]

MacArthur's Triumph

This sort of gritty reportage was, at least for the moment, more or less acceptable at GHQ Tokyo given how the success of the Inchon–Seoul campaign as a whole was being celebrated by the media not only in the United States but also in Western Europe.[66] 'The invasion to end the war quickly is pulled off,' the narrator for the *British Pathé* newsreel produced ten days afterwards intoned over the first footage of the assault from the sea.[67] 'From now on the United Nations should win in Korea,' Michael Davidson of the *Observer* was not alone in predicting.[68] The landing had been a gamble, but a bet made by the general that had paid off handsomely. 'MacArthur's leadership must be placed at the head of the column of elements contributing to this victory,' retired air force general Carl Spaatz wrote for *Newsweek* magazine.[69]

The media, moreover, deliberately left out an aspect of the Inchon landing which had the potential to embarrass the United Nations cause. The communist press had been trying for some weeks to score a propaganda coup by claiming that the Americans had been importing soldiers from Japan, the supposedly demilitarized former colonial power, into the fight. Japanese seamen did in fact participate at Inchon through manning a goodly number of transports; but this was never mentioned by Western reporters, presumably to avoid giving aid and comfort to the enemy.[70]

Efforts to shape the story of Inchon by no means ended with contemporary media reports. In the war's aftermath the emphasis would shift from such first drafts of history towards something less ephemeral and much more enduring: the creation of officially sanctioned and thereby supposedly authoritative print narratives.

4

Official Histories

In the wake of the 1953 armistice there arose strong institutional imperatives among the major erstwhile belligerents for the development of state-sponsored accounts of the war. On both sides of the Iron Curtain it seemed important to present not only to the armed forces but also to the general public supposedly rigorous and impartial histories based on official records. In all cases military intervention would be portrayed as defensive in nature and the eventual outcome described as a victory of sorts. In the East, these and other works would buttress the established party line.[1] In the West, they would provide authoritative narratives of a more objective and scholarly nature than the necessarily subjective and sometimes contradictory memoirs and authorized biographies being published in the decades after the fighting ceased. Especially while access to official records was limited to authorized personnel, the material contained in such histories would become a major source of information for scholars. These volumes would, in effect, determine what, officially, had happened in the Korean War, and why: not least with reference to Inchon.[2]

United States

Despite the rise in overall defence spending that was occurring as a result of the deepening Cold War in the 1950s, each of the armed services had a vested interest in generating publicly available official histories that emphasized the operational success and importance of their particular branch in the Korean fighting. This had been the first conflict in which the air arm had operated as a fully independent service, and it was thus a priority to stress the achievements of the United States Air Force (USAF).[3] The press had not been kind to the US Army when in retreat in the first year of the conflict, so it was thought important to sponsor a detailed narrative based on official documents that would provide a more objective assessment of the American ground effort on the peninsula.[4] As for the US Navy (USN) and US Marine Corps (USMC), it was clearly in their interest to remind all concerned that operations in Korea, contrary to assertions made in certain quarters after the Second World War, had demonstrated conclusively that neither had been rendered strategically superfluous by the advent of the atomic bomb.[5]

Once the Korean armistice had taken effect military writer and First World War veteran Lynn Montross was tasked, in collaboration with Nicholas A. Canzona, a United States Marine Corps captain who had fought in Korea, with compiling the official multi-volume history of US Marine operations in the war.[6] The second part, *The Inchon-Seoul Operation*, complete with footnotes citing documents and interviews, was published in 1955 through the historical branch of the Marine Corps and laid out in great detail the central role of the service in the landing and subsequent advance. It was a chronicle of virtually unalloyed success, designed to highlight the critical role that the Marines had played in events which had opened up opportunities that 'would have resulted a complete victory for our arms in Korea' if the Chinese had not intervened.[7]

These official USMC volumes were aimed squarely at the professional military fraternity. This meant, among other things, liberal use of acronyms and terminology; which in turn, according to the *Atlanta Constitution*, would 'slow down all but the most technically informed reader'. This was 'a military monograph', as the reviewer for the *Hartford Courant* admitted; but it was nonetheless 'a good job'. And it is noteworthy that the review in a British military periodical counter-argued that *The Seoul-Inchon Operation* could be 'thoroughly recommended to all classes of reader'.[8]

Next in line was the USN naval history division, which helped James A. Field, an academic historian based at Swathmore College, gather as much original documentation as could be found and enabled interviews with key senior USN players. *History of United States Naval Operations: Korea* in theory did not 'express an official view' insofar as the author's work was not directly censored. In fact, however, this volume was the closest the service would get to a fully official account. It was not inconsequential that Field had been a naval officer during the war, and that—while the director of the naval history division, Rear Admiral (retd.) E. M. Eller, claimed that 'the author made only the changes he thought justified' and Field himself stated that 'I have had full liberty to express my own opinions'—a variety of senior officers had not hesitated to weigh in critically on various drafts before the work was given the imprimatur of the government printing office in 1962.[9]

Field devoted a good deal of space to the course of the Inchon landing and its aftermath. Despite the huge hydrographical and logistical difficulties involved and the doubts of various senior figures, the US Navy had risen to the occasion in organizing and carrying out the hazardous operation that MacArthur insisted on. Its success, followed by the liberation of Seoul and coupled with the breakout from the Pusan perimeter, had produced a collapse in enemy resistance and thereby 'changed the entire Korean picture'.[10]

With its formal title and Pentagon provenance, *History of United States Naval Operations: Korea* was more often reviewed in academic circles than in the popular press, but it nonetheless garnered respectful and sometimes laudatory assessments from some impressive names. Stephen Roskill, official historian of the Royal Navy in the Second World War, for example, commented that Field wrote 'with vigour and clarity' and had produced a 'very competent study'.[11] Unencumbered by British understatement, American naval historian and navy veteran Paolo E. Coletta hailed the book as 'excellent' and indeed 'superb'.[12] A leading US military historian, Louis Morton, agreed that the volume was written with 'clarity, wit, and verve', and added that it contained 'the best account of the Inchon invasion' he had ever read.[13] Veteran diplomatic scholar F. C. Jones added that the narrative was sufficiently succinct and clear that, although *History of United States Naval Operations: Korea* remained primarily a book for service specialists, 'it is also of value to the lay student'.[14]

Of the three services directly involved in the Inchon–Seoul campaign—the operational role of the USAF being confined to support for the Pusan breakout and pursuit—the US Army had the most difficult task in terms of chronicling the first year of the Korean War in an official history. Wartime media coverage of the Marines and US Navy had been almost universally positive, but the sometimes poor performance of various army units in combat had generated a good deal of negative comment in the press.[15] The advance on Seoul and the breakout from the Pusan perimeter were, to be sure, victories involving the 7th Division within X Corps and the soldiers of the Eighth Army respectively; and of course the man in charge had been a five-star general of the army. The latter fact, however, could be problematic, insofar as Douglas MacArthur, after a few years in retirement, proved every bit as anxious to protect and burnish his reputation as he had been while in uniform.[16]

The author of the first volume of a projected five-volume set, *United States Army in the Korean War*, was Roy E. Appleman. A commissioned combat historian who had served in the Pacific and been reactivated for Korea, he had been tasked with gathering material within twelve months of the first American troop deployments with a view to eventually compiling a chronicle of US Army operations in 1950. An initial draft was complete by the middle of the decade, at which point Appleman, still holding a commission in the US Army Reserve, returned to civilian life and a job as a staff historian with the National Park Service.[17]

Unfortunately, not everyone who read this and subsequent drafts was happy. In particular, the general himself took exception to any implicit or explicit criticism of his operational decisions in the period under review. Mostly this involved arguing over how the advance

Figure 4.1 Roy E. Appleman.

deep into and subsequent headlong retreat out of North Korea was being portrayed. Yet he also took issue with the claim that the Eighth Army estimates of enemy strength in the South had been too high in the weeks leading up to the Inchon–Seoul campaign. That needed to be challenged because of the implication that the Korean People's Army would soon have been forced into a general retreat and that therefore Operation Chromite was in, effect, strategically marginal rather than decisive. 'His position is supported by only the most doubtful and flimsy calculations,' MacArthur claimed.[18] For his part Ned Almond, early on in the revision process, bluntly argued that 'an official Army history is no place to compare Marine Division idiosyncrasies with the wisdom of an Army Corps Commander's [i.e. his own] exercise of command'.[19] As result of the need to respond to the critics, *South to the Naktong, North to the Yalu* was not published until 1961.[20]

The revised volume was not welcomed by all when it was finally made public. A more prominent combat historian, S. L. A. Marshall, possibly jealous at not having been given the task of writing it himself, damned Appleman's effort with faint praise in the pages of the *New York Times*, calling into question among other things the idea that the North Korean Army was already on the verge of collapse before Inchon.[21] Other critics, however, were more appreciative. Another combat historian, Riley Sunderland, described *South to the Naktong, North to the Yalu* as an 'excellent account' replete with compelling detail.[22] Theodore Ropp, a well-established historian of military and naval affairs based at Duke University, wrote that it was 'a fine combat narrative', while Michael Howard, the young founder of War Studies at King's College London, did not hold back in judging the Appleman version of events 'one of the most readable and convincing works of military history that the present writer has ever encountered'.[23]

The final volume of the *United States Army in the Korean War* series dealing with Inchon appeared in print just over a decade later, eight years after MacArthur had died at Walter Reed Army Medical Center.[24] *Policy and Direction: The First Year* was authored by another retired US Army historian, James F. Schnabel, who had served in Tokyo during the conflict and was by this point working as a civilian historian with the Office of the Joint Chiefs of Staff.[25] *Policy and Direction*, as the name implied, dealt with strategy and planning, and included several detailed chapters on Operation Chromite.[26] As diplomatic historian Robert R. Simmons noted, Schnabel 'vividly' recounted 'the opposition from within both the army and the administration to General Douglas MacArthur's 100-to-1 scheme for the Inch'on landing: he also carefully describes MacArthur's supreme confidence in his ability to overcome the strong reservations held by most leaders in the American government'.[27] Simmons admired the volume; but with the Vietnam War having supplanted the Korean War in public consciousness for the last seven years, comparatively little attention was paid to the publication of *Policy and Direction* even in academic circles. As Theodore Ropp put it in the *Journal of American History*, the subject matter now 'seems as remote as the Wars of the Roses'.[28]

Eventually, however, long-term commemoration superseded near-term relevance as a reason to resurrect or initiate American official histories of the Korean War. More specifically, several old and some new works appeared in the years surrounding the golden jubilee of the conflict. This time it was the US Army that was the first to act, choosing to issue in paperback ahead of schedule its collection of official histories—including *South to the Naktong, North to the Yalu*—for the fiftieth anniversary.[29] At the turn of the century the Department of the Navy's historical centre reissued, in e-book form, *History of United States Naval Operations: Korea* and sponsored an entirely new illustrated booklet, *Fleet Operations in a Mobile War: September 1950–June 1951*, in which Inchon took pride of place.[30]

It was the USMC, however, true to its reputation for seeking maximum positive publicity, which really took advantage of the fiftieth anniversary. Instead of simply reissuing the *U.S. Marine Corps Operations in the Korean War* series, the History and Museums division decided to sponsor the publication of a total of eleven new, short, and heavily illustrated Korean War narratives written by retired Marine officers with a previous publication record. Of these, two dealt with the Inchon–Seoul campaign: *Over the Seawall: U.S. Marines at Inchon*, by Edwin H. Simmons, who had commanded a weapons company during the landing, and *Battle of the Barricades: U.S. Marines in the Recapture of Seoul*, by Joseph H. Alexander, familiar to the public not only through his various books but also from his appearances in television documentaries.[31] 'Both of these pamphlets [*sic*]', concluded the reviewer for the *Journal of Military History*, himself a USMC reserve officer, 'are good history and good reading.'[32]

North Korea

In a totalitarian state like the Democratic People's Republic of Korea (DPRK) all publications dealing with the past can be a viewed as forms of official history designed to bolster the legitimacy of the regime in general and the leader in particular.[33] From the start this has been true

Figure 4.2 Kim Il Sung.

in relation to chronicling the history of what was dubbed the Fatherland Liberation War, consistently portrayed ever since as a conflict started by the wicked American-led imperialists which ended in their humiliating defeat at the hands of the Korean People's Army (KPA) thanks to the brilliance of Kim Il Sung.[34]

Such a perspective, so radically at variance with reality, presented the Institute of History of the Academy of Sciences with a wide range of challenges when it was tasked in the latter 1950s with compiling a volume explaining the origins, course, and outcome of the Korean War. Among them was interpreting what happened at Inchon in a way that overcame the undeniable fact that the enemy landing had not been repulsed. This was achieved by portraying the battle in general, and the defence of Wolmi-do in particular, as a heroic holding action which had succeeded in delaying MacArthur long enough for North Korean forces in the South to make a successful temporary strategic withdrawal.[35]

In the *History of the Just Fatherland Liberation War*, key aspects of the North Korean version of Inchon were spelled out. Desperate to avoid being driven from Korea, the Americans had mobilized their vast resources and those of their puppet allies from around the world in order to assemble a truly massive invasion force that would land and cut off the Korean People's Army units fighting their way towards Pusan to the south.

Marshal Kim Il Sung had given orders to prepare for such an attack, but traitors led by Yi Sŭng-yŏp—leader of a rival southern communist faction purged by the Great Leader in 1953[36]—'wilfully obstructed' efforts 'to mobilize manpower and secure sufficient arms for the defence of the Seoul-Inchon area'. Nonetheless those units that were present when the landing occurred 'fought heroically in defence of Inchon'.[37] This was particularly true of the outnumbered and out-gunned artillerymen on Wolmi-do, who, alongside their commander, 'Li Dai Hoon', pledged to Party and Marshal that they would give their lives rather than retreat from their posts. Over the course of two days a variety of enemy vessels were sunk and repeated assaults driven back thanks to their combined efforts. Only on 15 September 1950, after what remained of the garrison under massive bombardment had 'fought heroically to the bitter end', was the island finally taken. 'With a small force', it was emphatically stated, 'they delayed the enemy's landings for three days.'[38]

Once the enemy was ashore at Inchon the American timetable for the advance on Seoul was disrupted by redeployments and uniformly fierce resistance. 'Our sappers laid obstacles to bar the advance of enemy tanks, and our infantrymen fought furiously under cover of the artillery fire inflicting heavy losses on the enemy.'[39] By the time MacArthur's men reached their objective the city had been turned into a veritable fortress in which 'not a street, not a single house was given away to the enemy without a fierce battle'. It was true that since the Americans had more men and more firepower at their disposal the battle for Seoul was ultimately lost; but 'our units succeeded in winning time by holding the invaders at bay' long enough to help

KPA units under attack further south—themselves under immense pressure and subject to betrayal by traitors—avoid entrapment and, in the words of Kim Il Sung himself, 'retreat in a planned way'.[40]

Hence the Inchon–Seoul battles were represented from the official North Korean perspective as models of heroic self-sacrifice in which the Great Leader displayed his exceptional military acumen and thanks to which the mighty forces under MacArthur, though greatly aided by turncoats, failed to trap their righteous opponents. The people's army would live to fight another day and, ultimately, completely vanquish its imperialist foes.[41]

Over subsequent decades, in everything from hagiographies of Kim Il Sung to lengthier chronicles of the Fatherland Liberation War and histories of the Korean People's Army, this was the line on what had transpired that would be repeated and expanded on.[42] In a multi-part history of the war published three decades after the conflict had ended, for example, special emphasis was placed on the role of Japanese militarists, the hated former colonial occupiers of Korea, in providing large-scale logistical and manpower support to the invasion.[43] At the same time the wise decisions of the Great Leader were highlighted at considerable length, while the achievement of the Wolmi-do garrison only seemed to grow over time. 'Although there are many instances in the history of warfare when coastal batteries fought with enemy naval vessels,' commented the author of the second volume, 'never has there been an instance where one infantry company and one artillery company equipped with just four cannons stood up to such a massive force of over one thousand planes and multitudes of vessels for three entire days while inflicting such heavy casualties.'[44]

South Korea

The view of the war in general and Operation Chromite in particular has been rather different in works published inside the Republic of Korea (ROK). Here too publications were subject to varying degrees of censorship down to the final decade of the last century and beyond.[45]

Figure 4.3 Park Chung-hee.

In comparative terms, however, efforts to explain what was known as the Six-Two-Five conflict have tended to be much more heterodox and evidentiary in nature in the ROK than in the DPRK.[46]

The first attempt at an official account appeared under the auspices of the Korean Military Academy at the end of the 1950s largely based on published American sources. While the introduction dutifully reflected the visceral anti-communist sentiments of President Syngman Rhee, the bulk of *A History of the Korean War* was devoted to a factual account of events from an operational perspective aimed at an audience of service professionals. The origins and course of Operation Chromite and its aftermath were thus chronicled without editorial comment; but it was nonetheless made clear that the successful landing and advance on the capital were justifiable as a means of attacking 'the enemy's rear', thereby cutting his supply lines, and, in conjunction with a breakout from the Pusan perimeter, enabling friendly forces to 'encircle the enemy troops south of Seoul'.[47]

A second and much more ambitious dual-track effort at producing official history began a decade later during the authoritarian presidency of Park Chung-hee. In all, nearly twenty substantial volumes would be produced by the Ministry of National Defense for domestic or foreign consumption between the latter 1960s and the beginning of the 1980s.[48]

At a time when North–South tensions were particularly high and the prospect of renewed conflict loomed large, the government sought to provide younger ROK citizens with an 'objective' account of Six-Two-Five 'free of [North Korean propaganda] lies' that would 'instil awareness of the brutal reality of communism' and underline the need for 'preparation and vigilance against another invasion'.[49] Though relations between the two competing Korean states underwent a brief tactical thaw in the early 1970s, Park Chung-hee with good reason remained deeply suspicious of Kim Il Sung, and the official history volumes continued to be published by the ROK defence ministry until a total of eleven substantial tomes were in print in South Korea by the end of the decade that still garner some respect.[50]

Meanwhile, the regime also sought to respond to critics among the populations of the republic's wartime allies who 'fail to recognize the facts about the Korean War'. The aim in this case was to 'clarify many points that have been in question' and foster international support by reminding various free-world nations, across a half-dozen separate volumes produced in English, of the contributions they had made in stemming the international communist menace two decades earlier.[51]

In the third part of the Korean-language series, which appeared thirty years after the events described, nearly two hundred pages of detailed narrative and commentary were devoted to the Inchon–Seoul campaign as a major turning point in the war. Not surprisingly a good deal of attention was paid to the South Korean contribution, with a great many quoted recollections of ROK participants incorporated. The wider focus, however, was on the planning, course, and significance of the campaign as a whole. In the end MacArthur had been utterly vindicated in pushing through Operation Chromite, with its potential to produce 'a complete reversal of fortunes and snatch victory from the jaws of defeat'.[52] The campaign had succeeded brilliantly, thereby allowing 'liberation from a living hell'.[53] Inchon was covered much more succinctly two years later in the first volume of the English-language series; but readers were left in no doubt that the general had conceived and carried through 'a most masterly and strategic stoke' that had saved the Republic of Korea.[54]

The cautious opening up of various archives in Russia and China in the post-Cold War years around the end of the twentieth century, in combination with the transition from authoritarian rule to liberal democracy already well under way in South Korea, allowed the Six-Two-Five conflict to be looked at from a broader perspective by historians. In response the Korea Institute of Military History, successor to the War Compilation Committee of the Ministry of Defense, decided to update the official history of the Korean War in six new volumes that appeared in Seoul between 1995 and 1997, which were then translated and edited into a trio of English-language volumes. 'While based on the old edition,' Um Sub Il, president of the KIMH, explained in a foreword, 'this work will reflect subsequent findings—in particular the newly declassified documents made available to the public by the countries that participated in the war.'[55]

Though American scholars were not always impressed with the translated results, there were indeed differences between what appeared in print under official auspices during the 1970s and what was published in the latter 1990s.[56] The mid-September 1950 landing and its chief architect, however, continued to be subject to largely unalloyed admiration. Chromite was 'a master stroke' that 'suddenly changed the entire course' of events thanks to the strategic brilliance of Douglas MacArthur. 'It is difficult to find any event in the history of modern warfare where every step of conceptualization, planning, preparation, and execution can be so clearly attributed to the leadership of any one individual.'[57] The Inchon–Seoul operation also saved time and lives, since simply advancing north out of the Pusan perimeter towards Seoul without the amphibious thrust in the enemy's rear would have required an extra month in which the North Koreans would have been able to slaughter a hundred thousand more civilians.[58]

For participants and witnesses with reputations at stake or perceived allegiances to uphold, official histories were not the only means of asserting claims to authenticity. Of equal importance in the decades after the war were attempts to score points before the general public through published memoirs.

5

Memoir Battles

Despite its fame, relatively few of those who fought in the Inchon–Seoul campaign published narrative accounts of the landing and subsequent fight for possession of Seoul. In the Democratic People's Republic of Korea, this was in large part because of the near-exclusive focus on Wolmi-do, whose defenders were said to have died to the last man.[1] In the Republic of Korea, the limited scale of South Korean service involvement in Chromite reduced the odds of there being participants with subsequent literary ambitions.[2] As for America, the smaller overall size of the United States Marine Corps and lower proportion of wartime volunteers to regulars and reservists during the Korean War as compared to the Second World War lessened the likelihood of the sort of widely esteemed combat memoir penned by Pacific campaign veterans.[3]

Meanwhile published accounts from those once at the top, aiming to explain and justify, became comparatively numerous. Some of the senior figures involved in orchestrating or overseeing the Inchon–Seoul campaign, to be sure, were more or less content to let history judge their thoughts and actions through official records and scholarship; hence their opinions only became fully public decades after the events concerned as historians gained access to documents and conducted postmortems.[4] There were plenty of others, however, who during their lifetimes proved anxious to make their case before a contemporary audience. In North Korea only the words of the Great Leader mattered; and towards the end of his life Kim Il Sung embarked on an epic autobiographical project. At the time of his death, however, while six hefty volumes of *Reminiscences: With the Century* had appeared in print, the narrative had not extended beyond the latter stages of the anti-Japanese struggle.[5] Meanwhile in South Korea the leading figures had mostly been simply onlookers as Chromite unfolded.[6] But in America, a fair number of those directly involved worked to see their remembrances appear in print between hard covers; a lasting form of public communication impelled, as often as not, by the published recollections of others with which they took issue.[7]

MacArthur

In view of the multiple controversies surrounding the conduct of the Korean War at the time and after, it was not at all surprising that both civil and military leaders devoted themselves in retirement to often lengthy and necessarily subjective accounts of their careers in which wartime events such as Inchon played a major part. A few of the participants in the actual landing would eventually publish their war memoirs with minor presses; but in the second half of the twentieth century, it was the movers and shakers or witnesses to their actions that readers, and therefore trade publishers, were most interested in hearing from. In reference to the Inchon–Seoul campaign as well as later events this meant replaying the internal debates of the past on the printed page, hindsight having done little to change minds in the intervening years. In the resultant battle of the memoirs, the attitudes and actions of Douglas MacArthur came under scrutiny.[8]

The great man himself, comfortably ensconced with his family in a suite at the Waldorf Towers in New York, generally relied on others to make his case in print in the mid- to late 1950s. Among other things this took the form of memoir biographies by two of his former senior staff officers and remaining devoted admirers that were supervised and on occasion rewritten by the general himself.[9]

The first to appear, in the autumn of 1954, was *MacArthur: 1941–1951*, by Charles Willoughby, his former chief intelligence officer, after it had been given some needed professional polish by wordsmith John

Chamberlain. With reference to Chromite the strategic and operational boldness of the general were contrasted, via liberal quotation from eyewitness statements and staff documents, with the recurring doubts and general vacillation of the Washington mandarins, not least US Army chief of staff Lawton Collins. In the end the bold Inchon–Seoul campaign, as conceived and overseen by MacArthur, turned out to be 'an astounding success' of providential proportions.[10]

While there were some positive responses to Willoughby's effort in friendly papers, some reviews could be problematic from his subject's point of view. 'This book should be entitled "MacArthur on MacArthur"' was the verdict in the *New York Times*; it was a work which contained much of interest but was in the end a compilation of 'partisan pleading' that was 'marred by generalities, distortions, omissions and inaccuracies'.[11] Even one of his former staffers argued in the pages of the *Washington Post* that Willoughby's account was so bitterly prejudiced that 'the chief victim of this slanted and doctored story' was the general himself and that it would do MacArthur 'more harm than good'.[12]

Once it became clear that Truman was in the process of writing his memoirs, the general decided to try again. This time his chosen author was none other than Courtney Whitney, the longtime confidant who had served MacArthur in various official and personal capacities down to and beyond retirement. The preface to *MacArthur: His Rendezvous with History* indicated the author's desire to 'record my impressions... of MacArthur's role in the climactic events which have surged across Asia since the advent of World War II'. Yet as Whitney hinted—'I have sought to let his own voice and pen speak for themselves'—much of the book was dictated by the general himself.[13]

Inchon was therefore treated as a decisive victory planned and executed by MacArthur in the face of recurrent timidity on the part of Washington pen-pushers, with far more space devoted to the opposition Chromite faced in the late planning stages than to the North Korean response once the operation was underway. Whitney's previous writing had lacked flair, but with a good deal of help from

Time-Life—which had purchased the serialization rights to a work which would be published by Knopf—he managed to convey in eyewitness terms over the span of five pages the high drama surrounding the crucial top-level meeting in Tokyo during the third week of August in which MacArthur's dazzling expository rhetoric at one stroke turned the tide of Pentagon opinion towards authorizing his bold but brilliant plan: 'A great voice in a great cause,' Admiral Forrest Sherman, the US Navy chief of naval operations, was overhead murmuring to himself as the general finished speaking.[14] Whitney also revealed publicly for the first time that the outwardly one-hundred-per-cent self-confident MacArthur fell prey to all-too-human second thoughts in the privacy of his cabin aboard *Mount McKinley* on the eve of the landing as he debated with himself out loud the potential pitfalls versus the rewards of Chromite in front of a silent but sympathetic audience of one. 'Finally he stopped his pacing,' Whitney recorded. 'He stood before the desk and looked at the pictures of his family while he spoke, still as if to himself. "No," he said, "the decision was a sound one, the risks and hazards must be accepted."'[15]

When *Rendezvous with History* was published in early 1956 it seemed obvious to reviewers that the listed author had worked as a de facto ghostwriter for his subject. 'Whitney has used MacArthur's personal papers, and there is little doubt that large parts of the manuscript—perhaps the book in its entirety—were examined, revised or even written by MacArthur himself,' Hanson Baldwin wrote for the *New York Times*.[16] The fact that MacArthur was portrayed as 'always right—never wrong' in his clashes with higher authority stretched credulity, and even a rather more supportive Walter Simmons in the *Chicago Daily Tribune* admitted that the book was 'a broadly partisan view of men and events; a chronicle that often exceeds friendly comment and becomes a lawyer's brief'.[17]

MacArthur, nonetheless, had achieved his main aim of putting his version of events before the public in advance of those of Truman, whose memoirs covering the Korean War, *Years of Trial and Hope*, came out a couple of months later. What was more, there was an aspect of

Rendezvous with History, despite its questionable provenance and partisanship issues, which made for highly engaging reading. 'Whitney paints a graphic behind-the-scenes picture of a man of extraordinary warmth and charm heretofore little known except to his intimates,' observed Howard Handleman of the International News Service—a humanizing touch that doubtless helped in turning the book into something of a bestseller.[18]

Truman, as it happened, while highly critical of other, mostly subsequent, words and actions emanating from MacArthur, was in his own memoirs unqualified in accepting Operation Chromite and the part it played in the general's overall strategy as a demonstration of great military acumen. The former president did, however, reproduce in full the congratulatory message quoted only in part by Whitney that he had sent to Tokyo in its wake. The laudatory sentence 'Few operations in military history can match either the delaying action where you traded space for time in which to build up your forces, or the brilliant maneuver which has resulted in the liberation of Seoul' was quoted in both memoirs; but it became obvious that Whitney had elided other parts of the presidential message that suggested the campaign had been an inter-service team effort in order to make it appear that Truman accepted MacArthur alone as responsible for victory.[19]

Finally, confronting mortality around the start of his eighth decade and wanting to provide his wife and son with a solid monetary legacy, MacArthur agreed to present his story 'penned by my own hand'.[20] First serialized in *LIFE* and then appearing in hard copy with McGraw-Hill in the early autumn of 1964, the resulting memoir certainly reflected the author's sense of his own importance. 'The greatest difficulty confronting me', he admitted, 'was that of recounting my share in the many vital decisions involved without giving my acts an unwarranted prominence.'[21]

Reminiscences, as a longtime observer of the general noted, did not reveal much that had not already appeared in print through, say, works ostensibly authored by Willoughby and Whitney.[22] Nonetheless this

Figure 5.1 Cover of the initial 1965 paperback edition of *Reminiscences* (1964).

was at long last the unmediated and unfiltered first-person voice of MacArthur himself on the printed page, complete with occasional examples of his trademark melodramatic style and constant desire to highlight his omniscient infallibility against a backdrop of error and weakness by those who had sought to constrain or undermine him.[23]

As far as Inchon was concerned, that meant indicating that within five days of the outbreak of the Korean War in late June 1950 he had begun thinking about 'a counter-stroke that could in itself wrest victory from defeat' through amphibious means, and how he had proceeded over the next couple of weeks to choose Inchon as the site of 'a turning movement deep into the flank of the enemy that would sever his supply lines and encircle all his forces south of Seoul'.[24] The Joint Chiefs of Staff, lacking in boldness and vision, had sent a delegation to Tokyo in August to argue that a landing at Inchon was too risky; but he had used his rhetorical skills to argue forcefully that a landing elsewhere would not generate the decisive results he was seeking and convince at least one of the doubters that, as he concluded, 'Inchon will not fail. Inchon will succeed.'[25] Preparations for Chromite were thereby allowed to continue, but 'at the eleventh hour' doubts were again expressed in a cable from the chiefs that exhibited unwarranted 'timidity' and which he had to counter by stating in reply that the chances of success were in fact excellent.[26] He admitted that aboard *Mount McKinley* the night before the landing he was very conscious of the gamble he was taking, but the next morning everything went according to plan and a 'decisive pincer movement' thereafter ensued.[27]

MacArthur was not shy about naming those in far-off Washington whom he believed had tried to thwart him over Chromite. The list included President Harry Truman, as Commander in Chief; George Marshall, the Secretary of Defense; Omar Bradley, Chairman of the Joint Chiefs of Staff; and Lawton Collins, the army chief of staff.[28] Truman, not surprisingly, did not like what MacArthur had to say concerning his handling of various, albeit mostly post-Inchon, aspects of the Korean War; yet having already published his memoirs the former president confined his immediate public reaction to a televised rebuttal.[29] By this point Marshall was already in his grave; but the remaining two eventually responded in their own published works.[30]

Joint Chiefs

In a trade press narrative of the Korean conflict, *War in Peacetime*, which appeared five years after MacArthur's last words, Lawton Collins prefaced his account of the lead-up to Operation Chromite by acknowledging that 'the brilliant counteroffensive, spearheaded by the amphibious assault at Inchon, was the masterpiece of one man'; but went on to explain why, especially in light of the restricted waters and tidal problems, he and other senior officers had maintained serious doubts about Inchon as a landing site. MacArthur—'discounting the obvious dramatics'—had given a 'masterly' if not 'brilliant' exposition of the reasons for choosing Inchon at the famous Tokyo meeting of 23 August 1950, and thereby changed several minds. But Collins himself retained 'reservations' and 'many of the naval and marine officers were still dubious', including the US Navy's chief of naval operations and especially the commander of the 1st Marine Division, Oliver Smith; but MacArthur remained obdurate and refused to consider less risky alternatives to Inchon. Back in Washington the assembled chiefs had given their conditional authorization for a landing, but thereafter had been kept out of the loop by MacArthur, who had to be prodded to produce a copy of the Chromite plan and reminded of the risks he was running. As for the suspicion voiced in *Reminiscences* that the president had tried to prevent the landing, there was no truth to this at all. Truman had been kept informed, but it was the joint chiefs alone who had tried to inject a note of realistic caution into the general's grand design: 'We accepted full responsibility for our own actions in querying MacArthur on his plans, expressing to him our concern about their feasibility, and giving our final approval.'[31]

In short, the joint chiefs 'were fully justified in raising the questions regarding Inchon that we did'. If they were to be faulted, it was because

Figure 5.2 Cover of *War in Peacetime* (1969).

of what transpired in the wake of Chromite. 'The success of Inchon was so great, and the subsequent prestige of McArthur so overpowering', Collins recalled, that the Pentagon 'hesitated thereafter to question later plans and decisions of the general, which should have been challenged'.[32] This was a point he would repeat twenty years later in his autobiography, *Lightning Joe*.[33]

It was also the key issue for Matthew Ridgway, a deputy chief of staff under Collins at the time of Inchon and the man who would eventually replace MacArthur. In the aftermath of the conflict he had shied away from commenting on the period before he took command in Korea;[34] but in a later book on the war Ridgway admitted of Chromite that, after attending a meeting with MacArthur and others in Tokyo in early August, 'the brilliance of this plan, the logic of its conception, and the extreme care with which the finest detail had been dealt with persuaded me quickly to support it'.[35] The trouble was the negative effect the against-the-odds success of the Inchon landing had on necessary oversight of subsequent operational plans emanating from Tokyo. 'A subtle result of the Inchon triumph was the development of an almost superstitious regard for General MacArthur's infallibility. Even his superiors, it seemed, began to doubt if they should question *any* of MacArthur's decisions and as a result he was deprived of the advantage of forthright and informed criticism, such as every commander should have—particularly when he is trying to "run a war" from 700 miles away': the end result was a near-total rout at the hands of the Chinese.[36]

A decade later another voice was added to those defending the joint chiefs in the run-up to Inchon when Omar Bradley, their former chairman, cooperated with writer Clay Blair on *A General's Life*. 'The swiftness and magnitude of the victory' achieved by MacArthur in the second half of September was obviously 'mind-boggling'; but it was nonetheless 'the luckiest military operation in history'. The military chiefs had been fully justified in querying various aspects of the theatre commander's intended strategy in light of the myriad dangers involved and in the context of his evident reluctance to keep them informed. 'It was the riskiest military proposal I had ever heard of,' the retired five-star general bluntly asserted. Given the doubts expressed by various navy and marine commanders to his face, MacArthur's claim that his staff and commanders were enthusiastic to a man about Chromite 'was not true'. As for the president, Bradley's recollection was that Truman was ultimately more willing to let MacArthur have his way over Inchon than were the joint chiefs themselves.[37]

The former chiefs-of-staff chairman went on to observe that MacArthur's grand vision to trap the bulk of the enemy's forces between two pincers did not in fact happen despite the capture of Seoul and the breakout from Pusan. 'By October 1 (two weeks after Inchon) it was clear that MacArthur's victory in South Korea had not been as decisive as we had hoped or been led to believe,' Bradley noted. 'Too many North Koreans had slipped through the trap, perhaps a third of the 90,000 North Korean troops in South Korea, including some of the most senior commanders.'[38]

Witnesses

Meanwhile the senior US Marine Corps officers involved in the operation remained more or less silent in public, confining themselves to in-house commentary or post-service interviews. The year after *A General's Life* appeared, however, retired United States Marine Corps (USMC) general Victor 'Brute' Krulak, published *First to Fight*, which contained some incisive commentary on his mid-career experiences as operations officer for the Fleet Marine Force, Pacific, in the context of the Inchon landing.[39]

Krulak related that as early as 10 July 1950, in a meeting in Tokyo between his boss, Lemuel Shepherd, and MacArthur, the former had encouraged the latter to request from Washington a full division of US Marines in order to carry out an amphibious landing at Inchon.[40] Though assembling and equipping this formation in a matter of weeks was a major challenge in light of USMC cutbacks over the previous five years, as all the senior Marine Corps leaders realized a

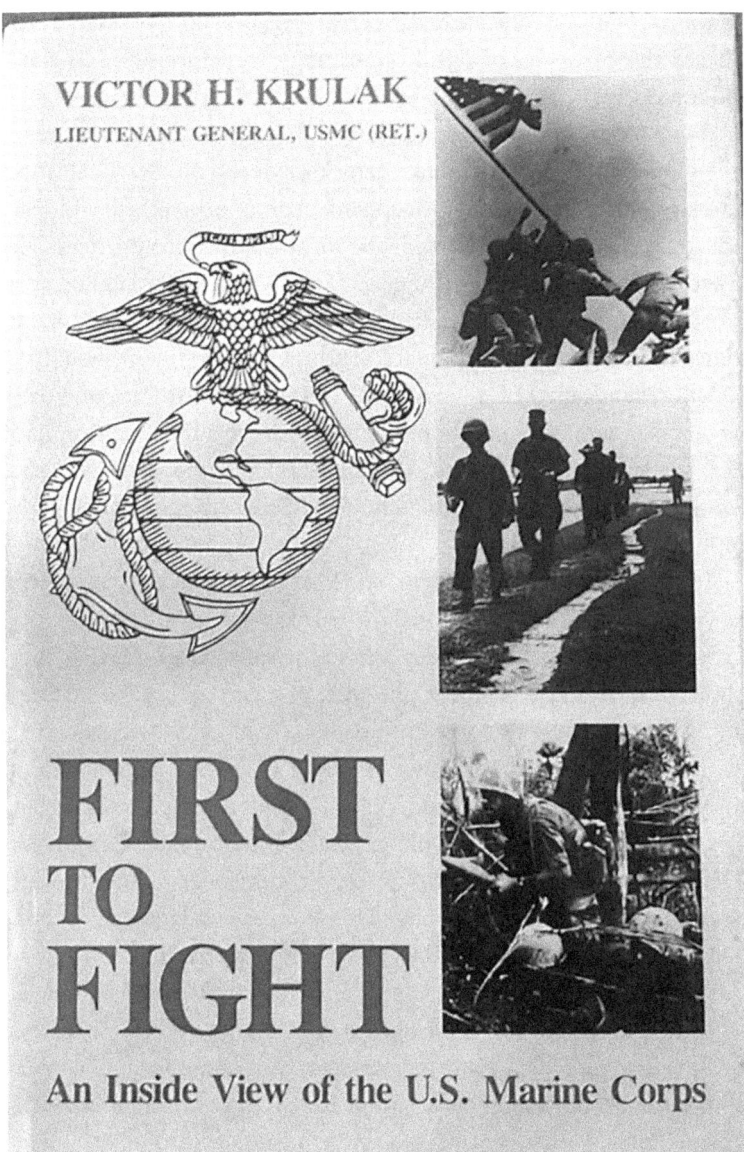

Figure 5.3 Cover of *First to Fight* (1984).

major amphibious operation in Korea spearheaded by the Marines offered the corps a wonderful opportunity to demonstrate its continuing operational relevance.[41]

On closer examination the only problem was MacArthur's desire to stage a landing at a place with so many known and unknown hazards. 'In early August, as General Shepherd became acquainted with the unusual problems involved with the Inchon area,' wrote Krulak, 'he asked me to study the region and to try and find another landing area nearby that offered less formidable obstacles.' The resulting document indicated that a landing 30 miles south at Posung-myon would be equally significant but a good deal less hazardous. 'The alternate landing site would avoid the forbidding hydrography of Inchon harbor, yet it would not sacrifice the benefits of an envelopment and would still be near enough to Inchon and Seoul to permit their early capture.'[42]

According to Krulak, all the senior Marine and Navy commanders had agreed at a preliminary conclave in Tokyo on 21 August 1950 that Inchon posed too many hazards. But in the subsequent meeting with MacArthur, Admiral Sherman, the chief of naval operations, according to the amphibious force commander, Admiral Doyle, had succumbed to the general's rhetoric in favour of Inchon. Shepherd and Krulak continued to advocate for Posung-myon with Sherman, but at a meeting on 24 August the general's chief of staff, Edward M. Almond, had, as the Fleet Marine Force commander reported to his operations officer, 'dismissed the idea summarily, saying that Inchon had been decided upon, and that was where it would be'.[43]

The choice of Ned Almond as landing force commander came as something of a shock to the USMC staff officers involved. 'Shepherd was the logical landing force commander,' Krulak opined: 'The bulk of the forces, air and ground, came from his command, the Fleet Marine Force, Pacific, and he had the requisite depth of amphibious experience.'[44] Almond had no such experience, kept challenging the 1st Marine Division commander, Oliver Smith, who did, and wasted time by trying to arrange a last-minute wargame and a commando-style raid on Kimpo airfield.[45] Present with his boss for some hours alongside a chatting MacArthur-plus-entourage while waiting to board the *Mount McKinley* on 13 September, Krulak was struck by the lack of attention being paid to the risky business at hand. 'In the space of three hours', he noted, 'Inchon was never mentioned.'[46]

Krulak sympathized with Admiral Doyle when, once *Mount McKinley* was at sea, the amphibious force commander angrily turned on MacArthur's US Army G-3 operations officer, 'Pinky' Wright, whom he thought was verbally assuming the lion's share of credit for Chromite planning. 'Get this straight,' the Marine colonel from the pages of his personal diary quoted Doyle testily informing Wright, '... we wouldn't be here today, if the operation hadn't been in the hands of Navy and Marine professionals who knew exactly what they were doing.'[47] Krulak himself was deeply shaken on D-day itself when Almond said something which suggested he, the officer in overall charge of the landing force, did not realize that a Landing Vehicle Tracked was an amphibian.[48]

On the basis of publication dates it might be assumed that the case for MacArthur and loyal deputies like Almond had, not least in relation to Inchon, passed away alongside the men themselves from the mid-1960s through to the latter 1970s, with critics holding forth unimpeded thereafter. Yet, sometimes long after the general and key members of his wartime circle had departed the scene, there remained participants of greater or lesser importance who proved willing in print to defend unequivocally how MacArthur had set about reversing the tide of war in Korea at Inchon. Not all of them, what was more, had been members of his own staff.[49]

Arthur Radford, in 1950 commander-in-chief of US naval forces in the Pacific, in memoirs written from the latter half of the 1960s and published at the start of the 1980s, was forthright in his support. 'I favored the plan,' as did Admiral Turner Joy, commanding naval forces in the Far East, convinced by MacArthur's 'brilliant exposition' at an earlier Tokyo meeting held in mid-July. The only problem with Chromite was that the joint chiefs kept hesitating, and only gave it more or less unequivocal support a few days before it started.[50]

A dozen years later, in his autobiography *Inner Circles*, it was the turn of Alexander Haig, best known for his White House roles in the Nixon and Reagan administrations but at the start of the Korean War a junior aide to MacArthur's then chief of staff and soon-to-be X Corps commander, Ned Almond. 'I vividly remember MacArthur tapping the map in Almond's office, and describing his plan,' wrote Haig. 'Our troops would fall back on the deep-water port of Pusan, establish a defensive perimeter, build up strength by feeding divisions and matériel into the perimeter, and then, when the time was right, turn the enemy's flank and cut his lines of supply with an amphibious landing.' A thrust towards Seoul from the coast in combination with a breakout from Pusan in the south would, as the general put it, 'crack the North Korean Army like a walnut between the jaws of an American pincers'.[51] Haig, who admired the general immensely, subsequently listened in from behind closed doors on the climactic debate on 23 August, and distinctly recalled in his memoir that MacArthur had ended by threatening to resign if Operation Chromite was not approved: 'Gentlemen, we will land at Inchon on September 15 or you will have a new Supreme Commander in the Far East.'[52] And, of course, as events were to prove, 'he was right when everyone else was wrong'.[53]

A rather more senior and experienced officer attached to the staff in Tokyo at the time, though equally smitten—'I succumbed to the charm and persuasiveness of MacArthur'[54]—was Edward Rowny. Sixty years after the armistice, this aged witness would have the last word through the publication of his account of his experiences working for MacArthur early in the conflict under the title *An American Soldier's Saga of the Korean War*.[55] Involved in the planning for an amphibious counterstroke, he remembered that right from the start it was the general who counselled boldness and pushed his staff to come up with a plan to land at Inchon rather than any point further south. Present in the room for the August confrontation with the emissaries from Washington, Rowny was mightily impressed: 'MacArthur's lecture was a tour de force that I thought outdid John Barrymore.'[56] Chromite had been without a doubt a gamble on MacArthur's part given the obstacles involved and restricted time frame, but one that paid off handsomely: 'We achieved complete surprise and the invasion was a resounding success.'[57]

As for Almond, whom he knew well and admired, he had witnessed several instances in the advance on the capital in which the commander of X Corps had been forced to order his USMC subordinates to pick up the pace and act with less deliberation in order to maintain momentum: 'Almond kept pushing the Marines to move rapidly,' he remembered.[58] It had been the X Corps commander's relentless focus on improvisation and exploitation, often in the face of Marine Corps obstinacy, that ultimately caused the enemy to end their fight for Seoul.[59]

By the third decade of the twenty-first century the passage of time had brought the publication of new memoirs to an end as the number of living participants dwindled away. Meanwhile, from the moment they became accessible, the unpublished accounts and papers of those who were witnesses to the planning and execution of the Inchon–Seoul operation had become an important source for professional historians in and out of uniform in assessing the nature and meaning of Chromite.

6

Analysis Wars

Given his consistent refusal to admit any errors of command in his lifetime, MacArthur would have thoroughly disapproved of the postmortem verdicts passed by biographers and other writers in subsequent decades. The overall tendency was to portray him as a flawed genius, one of history's great captains capable of making both inspired choices and terrible mistakes. In particular there emerged a widespread consensus that he had blundered badly in Korea between the capture of Seoul and his dismissal almost seven months later.[1]

To be sure, the general might have taken solace in how he continued to receive top marks for Operation Chromite in both popular and professional circles. In successive trade press and other histories of the Korean War this 'twentieth-century Cannae' was hailed as a 'spectacular success'; a 'masterstroke'; an 'outstanding' victory; an achievement 'without parallel'; and as a complete vindication of its architect's 'vision, careful planning, and his courageous stand against many of his military peers and superiors'.[2] According to one prominent American journalist historian, writing over fifty years after the landing, 'Inchon was Douglas MacArthur at his best: audacious, original, unpredictable, thinking outside of the conventional mode.'[3] Popular volumes which focused more narrowly on the Inchon–Seoul campaign also sang his praises, noting his 'brave' decision to undertake against the odds 'the most daring amphibious landing in history'.[4]

Service analysts in and out of uniform also continued to applaud what MacArthur had accomplished. Three years after the old warrior's death, retired US Army captain and Korean War veteran Pat Tomlinson concluded in the pages of *Military Review* that 'Inchon has to be recorded as one of the great battles of military history, and General MacArthur's brave decision earned him a place among the great captains of the past'.[5] While keen to stress the importance of amphibious warfare veterans such as James Doyle and Oliver Smith in helping turn the idea for Chromite into a reality, retired Marine colonel Robert Heinl, Jr., in writing a book-length study published in 1968 which is still considered a standard work on the campaign, acknowledged that 'MacArthur conceived and planned Inchon, and resolutely defended it against all comers, and in this lies his glory'.[6] Soldiers too could express admiration. James Totten, a commissioned veteran of the Vietnam War, penned an article published in a US Army periodical in the mid-1970s in which he concluded that Chromite had been 'an incredible gamble taken by a courageous commander to achieve unequalled success'.[7] At the start of the following decade Clark Reynolds, who among other things had taught at both the Naval Academy and the Merchant Marine Academy, wrote an article for the *Naval War College Review* in which he analysed the general's maritime strategic thinking and confirmed with regard to Chromite that 'of course, MacArthur was correct; the assault in mid-September took Inchon by surprise, broke the back of the North Korean Army, and sent it reeling back across the 38th parallel'.[8] Two years later it was the turn of Major Bruce Pernie, a former military history instructor at West Point writing for the Armed Forces Staff College journal, to praise MacArthur for his 'acuity, foresight, and intuition' in insisting on an early landing at his chosen site.[9] In the middle of the final decade of the twentieth century recently retired Colonel Wilson Heefner, a graduate of the US Army War College, in an article on Chromite— 'MacArthur's finest hour'—for *Military Review*, concluded that 'the Inch'on invasion must be ranked as one of the most audacious and successful amphibious invasions of all time'.[10]

The golden jubilee of the operation prompted further service accolades. John Ballard, a professor at the Naval War College, in a piece published in *Joint Force Quarterly*, argued that only MacArthur, based on his unusually long operational experience, possessed the vision to organize and deploy his forces for a landing 'in the right place at the right time for maximum effect'.[11] Major Jeffrey Bradford, attending the School of Advanced Military Studies, echoed such sentiments in the conclusion to another *Military Review* article on the subject of Inchon: MacArthur's 'judgment in determining the critical place to act and his ability to integrate joint forces in a decisive blow testified to his greatness as a battle commander'.[12] This was followed by an article in the *Journal of Military History* written by Russel Stolfi, a former Marine officer and retired professor at the Naval Postgraduate School, that was critical of the pace of the advance on Seoul but labelled the landing as conceived by MacArthur 'a strategical masterpiece' so great as to negate any possibility of re-evaluation.[13] And a year after that, Jim Dorschner penned an article for *Military Historian* that once again made the case for the general's supreme sagacity. 'MacArthur identified a strategic opportunity,' this retired US Army colonel wrote, 'managed to cobble together forces to execute a plan and then permitted his commanders and troops to pull it off.'[14] And so the hosannas continued as the sixtieth and then the seventieth anniversary approached.[15]

Yet in certain service-related circles even the general's triumph at Inchon came to be called into question as time went by.[16] A quarter century after the start of the war, the journal *Army* published a letter from a retired US Army colonel, Don Curtis, in which he pointed out that staffers in the Pentagon had developed a prewar plan for a landing at Inchon that Tokyo had borrowed and used to develop Chromite. 'This is where Gen. MacArthur got his idea of the Inchon landing,' Curtis asserted, adding: 'Let's set the record straight.'[17] Around the time of the thirtieth anniversary the chief historian at the Office of Air Force History, Stanley Falk, wrote a response to the laudatory piece by Clark Reynolds in the *Naval War College Review* in which he itemized various ways in which MacArthur had run unnecessary risks in insisting on a landing at Inchon. The operation was, to begin with, 'hastily planned and mounted, with incomplete intelligence, and incredibly poor security arrangements'. Quite apart from all the hydrographical and geographical dangers highlighted by the amphibious experts, Chromite could easily have turned into a catastrophe if the enemy had not 'fortuitously delayed' laying a proper minefield in the approaches to the harbour. The alternative sites recommended by the experts—Kunsan and Posung-myon—were far better suited to an amphibious assault, and each had strategic advantages: the former was close enough to the Pusan perimeter to offer direct support for the planned breakout, while the latter 'would have provided the ready access to Seoul that MacArthur demanded'. Falk pulled no punches in his concluding remarks on Chromite. 'I suggest', he wrote, 'that Inchon reflected MacArthur's penchant for flamboyance, needlessly grand gestures, and unsound risks.' All in all it was 'an unnecessary gamble that subordinated the principles of maritime strategy to the personal ambitions of MacArthur'.[18]

These, it turned out, were not the only critical voices. Karl Larew, a former historian for the US Army signal corps with a PhD from Yale, penned an opinion piece for *Army* eight years later in which he argued that Operation Chromite 'was extremely risky on the one hand and yet not really necessary on the other'.[19] Members of the Joint Chiefs of Staff and others were not being faint-hearted in pointing out the multiple hazards involved in staging a landing at a place like Inchon, and MacArthur himself was running a risk in building up X Corps in reserve in late August and early September when the Pusan perimeter was under greatest threat. A reversal of United Nations (UN) fortunes could have been achieved, albeit less spectacularly, with a more conventional amphibious operation or even a general offensive by Eighth Army reinforced with the two divisions comprising X Corps. 'A slower advance to the 38th Parallel just may have brought about truce talks before the intervention of the Chinese,' Larew opined, adding: '—or at least might have tempered our enthusiasm for a headlong dash toward the Yalu.'[20]

A few years on, D. Clayton James, based at Mississippi State University and latterly the Virginia Military Institute—who also held temporary positions at the Army War College and the Army Command and General Staff College—and author of the standard three-volume biography of MacArthur published between 1974 and 1985, revisited his subject's role in a coauthored book entitled *Refighting the Last War: Command and Crisis in Korea, 1950–1953*.[21] While still admiring the boldness of the Inchon choice and dismissing the alternative landing sites as being too obvious and lacking the element of surprise, James wondered if it might not have been wiser to forgo a landing and concentrate available forces for an offensive out of the Pusan pocket given how brittle the opposing Korean People's Army (KPA) had become by mid-September. 'In view of all that happened adversely in the wake of Inchon, especially the invasion of North Korea that led directly to the war's escalation,' he concluded, 'it might have been discreet to have considered striking northward solely through a Naktong breakout.'[22]

Then early in the new century Michael Pearlman, a retired Army Command and General Staff College history professor, published a well-regarded study, *Truman and MacArthur: Policy, Politics, and the Hunger for Honor and Renown*.[23] In it Pearlman argued that, while a considerable tactical accomplishment, the Inchon landing 'was also a failure, at least at a strategic level'.[24] It had been sold as part of a hammer-and-anvil concept in which the vast bulk of the KPA forces in the South would be trapped as the Eighth Army advanced northwest from the Pusan perimeter once X Corps established itself deep behind enemy lines. But in reality 'X Corps, a little less than 70,000 men, could barely stretch to Seoul, let alone constitute an anvil 200 miles across Korea.' The resulting gap of 175 miles included four major mountain passes through the 38th parallel, allowing around fifty thousand enemy soldiers to flee northwards and potentially fight another day. Given the extent to which the KPA forces besieging the Pusan perimeter had been worn down so thoroughly through battlefield attrition and interdiction of supplies, it would have been possible to have achieved success through a conventional ground offensive alone: in short there was 'no need for a deep envelopment at all'.[25]

Finally, two years after that, came the considered verdict of Allan Millett, a retired US Marine Corps Reserve colonel and leading academic authority on the military history of the Korean War then based at the University of New Orleans. In his magisterial tome, *The War for Korea, 1950–1951*, Millett argued that despite its fame the Inchon–Seoul campaign 'did little to defeat the North Korean army', and through making MacArthur look infallible, and thus unchallengeable, 'sowed the seeds of a strategic disaster' when the Chinese entered the war against his badly positioned forces in the far north of the peninsula a couple of months later.[26]

Such revisionism was bemoaned by the general's most recent sympathetic popular biographer, Arthur Herman.[27] But in fact MacArthur's oracular reputation surrounding Chromite remains largely intact, especially in the public sphere. In the *Encyclopaedia Britannica*, for example, the entry on Inchon reads as follows: 'A daring operation planned and executed under extremely difficult circumstances by U.S. General Douglas MacArthur, the landing suddenly reversed the tide of the war, forcing the invading North Korean Army to retreat in disorder up the peninsula.'[28]

There are a variety of likely reasons why the critics have failed to make much of a dent in MacArthur's reputation for strategic brilliance at Inchon. To begin with, word that staff officers in Tokyo had drawn on Pentagon contingency plans took nothing away from the manner in which the general had pushed through Chromite.[29] Then there was the simple fact that the operation and the campaign of which it formed a seemingly crucial part at least superficially appeared to deliver everything that the general had promised in terms of cause and effect. The landing at Inchon was a great success; Seoul was liberated; the breakout from Pusan occurred; and KPA unit cohesion and fighting power in the South then crumbled away.[30]

There was also the rather defensive manner in which former Joint Chiefs of Staff figures like Collins and Bradley responded in their memoirs to the audacity-versus-timidity narrative created by MacArthur himself and reinforced by the likes of Willoughby and

Whitney in print. In addition there was the way in which the revisionists had to rely on counterfactual arguments to make their case: that other landing sites would have been much safer *if* the enemy had managed to sow all the mines they had stored to protect the harbour approaches around Inchon;[31] that *if* Kim Il Sung had not been so fixated on attacking Pusan then likely enemy foreknowledge of MacArthur's amphibious target through intelligence sources in Japan, on top of a cautionary warning from Beijing, could have led to a potentially fatal reinforcement of the Inchon garrison;[32] that the KPA was so severely weakened that it would have disintegrated *if* assaulted without Chromite;[33] and that Chinese intervention might have been avoided *if* a less spectacular means of turning the tide in the South had been adopted.[34]

Another likely reason for the longevity of the MacArthur legend is the sheer dramatic appeal of the high-stakes nature of choosing Inchon that the general himself had promoted rather than downplayed in selling his plan to the various visiting dignitaries from Washington. This made the story attractive not only to filmmakers but also to skilled biographers and others writing for trade presses who produced books with print runs running into the tens of thousands, thereby reaching vastly bigger audiences than a few revisionist articles in niche journals or strictly limited-edition university press monographs.[35]

The virtually bulletproof general perception of the Inchon landing as the work of a genius, however, had a paradoxically negative effect on the overall military reputation of MacArthur in the Korean War. Though both the general and his acolytes tried their best, it was much more difficult to portray MacArthur's subsequent moves as militarily brilliant or even sound. From the insistence on staging what turned out to be a time-wasting and essentially pointless landing at Wonsan in October to the resumption of an under-resourced and dispersed drive towards the Yalu in the wake of initial Chinese intervention that abruptly ended with UN forces being driven into often highly disorganized and precipitous headlong retreat in late November, the general's strategic intuition seemed to have deserted him.[36] For those who believed that Inchon had been a clairvoyant masterstroke—the majority, as already noted—a common way to frame this sudden decline in good judgement was through reference to hubris.[37] The problem with Chromite, or so it seemed in a broader context, was that the success of MacArthur's great gamble had simply gone to his (and everyone else's) head, thereby allowing him to roll the dice ever more recklessly and without impediment to the point of disaster.[38] Inchon thus became a 'Pyrrhic victory'.[39]

Almond vs. Smith

MacArthur, however, though of course well to the fore in every respect, was not the only figure who came to be judged before the bar of history in the context of the Inchon–Seoul campaign. There were also the two leading players under him: Edward M. Almond, whom the general chose to lead X Corps, and Oliver P. Smith, commanding the principal assault formation, 1st Marine Division. Their papers and interviews made it clear that the relationship between the US Army two-star and the US Marine Corps two-star had been fractious, each implying that the other lacked competence at various junctures before, during, and after Chromite. It was a feud that a junior participant in the Inchon landing later described as 'the stuff of legends'.[40]

Twenty-first century biographers of the two men have tended to side with whichever general they were profiling. But the lack of retrospective consensus concerning the relative merits of Almond and Smith has been on public display ever since a pair of trade books specifically on Inchon were published within a couple of months of each other fifteen years after the war.[41]

Hell or High Water, written by Walt Sheldon, a former air force combat historian, made heavy use of interviews conducted by the author. Interviewees included Ned Almond, whose recollections were used extensively; but, for reasons unknown, not O. P. Smith.[42] The

Figure 6.1 A helmeted Oliver Smith in conversation with Ned Almond.

result was that fractious encounters between the two tended to be viewed through a perceptual lens offered by the X Corps commander. At their initial meeting after the Marine general's arrival in Tokyo in the third week of August, Almond, 'buoyant and energetic as usual', found Smith to be chilly and standoffish.[43] They took opposite positions in the subsequent debate among their superiors on possibly substituting Posung-myon for Inchon as the landing area; but, after some give and take, the two generals and others involved had agreed on plans to ship the 5th Marine regiment fighting in the Pusan perimeter to bolster the strength of the Marine division in the assault on Inchon and, subsequently, reached agreement on not diverting any Marines for a Commando-style raid to seize Kimpo airfield that Almond was planning.[44] Once the landing had succeeded and the advance on Seoul began, Almond kept up a busy schedule of going forward to meet regimental commanders from both the Marine division and the army division under his command to make sure everyone understood his plans for a pincer movement to seize Seoul in the latter weeks of September and to make tactical decisions in order to keep up the momentum of the offensive as and when necessary: 'If this habit disturbed Smith,' Sheldon observed, 'he said nothing about it.'[45]

Just over a week after the landing, Almond met with Smith at Yongdungpo to go over the plan which the corps commander believed would liberate the capital from the enemy within a couple of days. This operation would involve one regiment of Marines striking from the west while another swung round to the southeast, crossed the Han River, and captured vital high ground to the southeast, flanking the defenders and forcing them to withdraw from the city. Smith demurred, since the plan would mean splitting his forces and he doubted that the North Koreans would withdraw from Seoul without a serious fight. He proposed instead a more localized flanking movement to facilitate a combined two-regiment assault from the west of the city, with a third newly arrived Marine regiment deploying to the northwest to block an enemy retreat once the battle swung against them. A tightly wound debate ensued, towards the end of which the divisional commander remarked on the corps commander's habitual hands-on visits to his regimental commanders. 'I'm not handling your regiments,' Sheldon quoted from Almond's recollection of his response, 'I'm just seeing how they do after you handle them. It's my idea that Seoul can be captured by crossing the Han, southeast of the city. I'm going to visit your regiments tomorrow, and if no advances have been made I propose to narrow your sector so that South Mountain will be within the area of General Barr's 7th Division. I'll be here tomorrow by 2:00 P.M. and General Barr will meet me here when I make this decision.'[46]

On the following day—24 September—Almond announced that instead of separating the 1st and 5th Marines he would use the 32nd Regiment from the army's 7th Division, then coming up towards Seoul from the direction of Suwon, to carry out his favoured southeast flanking manoeuvre. Smith again seemed upset about the army corps commander visiting Marine regimental headquarters, and did not like the idea of handing over amphibious tractors that were Marine Corps property to allow an army regiment to cross the Han River. 'That doesn't concern me a particle,' Almond remembered responding firmly. 'They are necessary to the operation.' Happily the Marine Corps major in charge of the vehicles proved much more flexible, indicating that his Marines could crew each Amtrac while sixteen soldiers rode along as passengers.[47]

According to Walt Sheldon, the overall assault plan insisted on by Almond worked, the enemy garrison commander deciding to begin a partial evacuation of Seoul when South Mountain fell to the Americans on the 25th. Receiving reports of enemy columns trekking northwards out of the city, Almond in the evening issued an order over the radio to 1st Marine Division headquarters for an immediate night attack to pressure an enemy on the brink of cracking. Smith, whose units were then engaged in fierce close-quarter combat, queried this order, but was given no leeway by X Corps headquarters. The end result was even fiercer fighting with little or no ground gained; but Sheldon, while conceding this, did not editorialize on this episode beyond a footnote in which he wrote: 'controversy over the actual need for this attack still rages whenever higher ranking veterans of the Inchon-Seoul operation gather'.[48]

Assessing the fraught relationship between the two men, Sheldon found it 'unfathomable' that they had not gotten along better given that each man had previously worked more or less harmoniously with officers from the other's service. His conclusion regarding their first, ill-starred, interaction in Tokyo, which he thought set the pattern for the future, was that while Almond found Smith reservedly orthodox, Smith misperceived Almond to be a lightweight extrovert.[49]

That their interactions could be interpreted in a radically different way was evident in *Victory at High Tide*. As a retired Marine colonel, its author, Robert Debs Heinl, Jr., was likely predisposed to look more askance at an army general than at an officer of equivalent rank from

Figure 6.2 Cover of *Hell or High Water* (1968).

his own service: *Semper Fidelis*, as the Marine Corps motto goes. He drew on interviews with, among others, Oliver Smith, but apparently was unable to meet with Ned Almond. What also set Heinl apart from Sheldon was the former's access to various US Navy and US Marine Corps records, which helped undergird his often quite different interpretation of the relationship in general and his versions of the key encounters between the two commanders as presented in *Hell or High Water* in particular.[50]

In his description of their first meeting on 22 August, based on a written account penned by the 1st Marine Division commander shortly after the event, Heinl explained that the X Corps commander made a number of unfortunate gaffes. 'Major General Almond, fifty-eight years old, addressed Major General Smith, age fifty-seven, as "Son."' More significantly, Almond minimized the complexity and danger of the landing phase by referring to it as the 'purely mechanical' aspect of the projected campaign.[51] The following day Almond, in conversation with Smith, refused to debate the possibility of substituting Posung-myon for Inchon as the landing site; the latter recording that the corps commander simply cut him off with two words: 'Not interested'.[52] The raid Almond wanted the Special Operations Company to mount against Kimpo airfield, among other crackpot schemes, was thoroughly ill-conceived, and Smith was quite right to demur at the last-minute idea of Marine reinforcements.[53] As for the decision to release the 5th Marines from helping defend the Pusan perimeter in order to take part in the landing at Inchon, Almond remained obstinately against this move at a tense conference of 3 September until the commander of Joint Task Force 7 came up with a face-saving compromise.[54]

After X Corps headquarters became operational ashore in the third week of September in the wake of a successful landing and exploitation therefrom, Almond began to press for more speed in the advance on the capital in order to meet the deadline for the liberation of Seoul he had promised MacArthur. At a meeting with his division commanders on the 23rd, he pushed Smith, in the latter's recollection, 'to guarantee that the 1st Marine Division would capture the city by 25 September'.[55] Smith refused to make such a promise. He also did not like the corps commander's plan to split up his regiments to manoeuvre into the capital, as this would not allow for mutual support at a time when enemy resistance was stiffening and would likely not lever the enemy into leaving a city they seemed determined to fight for street by street. Almond's verbal reaction—that he would use elements of his other division, the US Army 7th, to envelop the enemy if the Marines did not make immediate headway—did not elicit any immediate riposte. 'If General Almond thought it was necessary to goad Marines into fighting,' Smith reflected some years later, 'he displayed a complete ignorance of the fighting qualities of Marines.'[56]

The next day Almond abruptly announced that the 32nd Infantry would undertake the flanking operation, and ordered the 1st Marine Division to arrange for the necessary transport across the Han River. It was his mention of having visited the relevant Marine regimental commanders to explain his intentions and ginger them up rather than the passing over control of the amphibious tractors that caused Smith to warn, as he may have apparently done the previous day as well, against the corps commander's tendency to micromanage divisional affairs. 'I told General Almond that I would appreciate it if he would not give orders direct to my regimental commanders,' Smith wrote in his log, adding 'that if he would issue his orders to me, I would see that they were carried out'. Almond claimed that he had never issued orders directly to the regimental commanders, and when Smith pressed him said he would correct any such impression. 'There the matter rested,' the latter wrote.[57]

Heinl went on to argue that Almond's plan to manoeuvre the enemy out of the city by having the 32nd Infantry move against South Mountain failed, insofar as occupation of the heights evidently did not persuade the defenders to evacuate the central districts of the city, where the Marines continued to suffer heavy casualties in bitter house-to-house fighting.[58] Moreover, Almond, in his view, without a doubt blundered badly in first ordering, and then insisting on via his

Figure 6.3 Cover of *Victory at High Tide* (1968).

staff, an immediate Marine night assault on 25 September during the street battle for Seoul. The aerial intelligence report on which he based his assumption that the North Koreans were pulling out was flimsy and inaccurate, and the corps commander evidently refused to accept that the Marines were facing strong enemy resistance and counterattacks inside the city at the time. To add insult to injury, Almond issued a press release before midnight claiming that Seoul had been liberated while hundreds of Marines were still fighting desperately for their lives.[59]

The author of *Victory at High Tide*, in short, had little good to say about the 'impetuous and impatient' Edward Almond; someone who, not surprisingly, 'expressed vigorous dissent with many of my conclusions'.[60] Oliver Smith, on the other hand, was shown behaving with consistent professionalism and prescience, proving that the commandant of the Marine Corps had known exactly what he was doing in appointing this atypically undemonstrative major general to command the 1st Marine Division bound for Korea.[61]

More recently, knowledgeable military historians have pointed out that the discordant relationship between Amond and Smith was partly a matter of training and experience in different organizational cultures and not just a question of contrasting personalities.[62] Nonetheless, especially among those writing for a general audience, the tendency has been to sympathize with the calm and collected 'O.P.' Smith rather than with the ill-tempered and intolerant 'Ned' Almond. Other contrasts aside, Almond's utterly unyielding racism regarding African Americans, placed in counterpoint to Smith's evolving tolerance, made it clear which part each would play in major popular accounts published in the past few decades.[63]

Striking leaders though they were, especially set in juxtaposition, among the American public Almond and Smith remained obscure figures in comparison to the larger-than-life Douglas MacArthur. In translating the dramas of the first year of the Korean War onto the big screen, as often as not Hollywood screenwriters would focus their attention on the general.

7

Projecting History

It was through contemporary newsreels that the public first experienced assembled moving images of the Inchon landing and the fight for Seoul. Later in the war and in subsequent decades there would be more to watch as filmmakers of varying political hue sought to influence popular perceptions of the event and the people involved through documentaries. It was in big-screen cinematic dramas, however, that assorted stakeholders invested the most concentrated effort in the postwar decades when it came to manipulating the popular image of Operation Chromite.[1]

United States

Given the starring role played by the 1st Marine Division in the Inchon–Seoul battle and the service's well-deserved reputation for cultivating positive publicity, it was predictable that the first Hollywood feature aiming to recreate it should be made in collaboration with the United States Marine Corps (USMC).[2] In *Retreat, Hell!*, released by Warner Bros. a mere fifteen months after the events being chronicled, the climactic third act of the movie involved the dramatic recreation of the heroic fighting withdrawal of the Marines from the Chosin Reservoir to the port of Hungnam in North Korea in the face of Chinese efforts to entrap them amid the depths of winter a couple of months after the Chromite landing. The first and second acts, however, covered preparations for and the carrying out of the Inchon operation and the subsequent fight for Seoul.[3]

Based on a story by producer Milton Sperling, the monochrome *Retreat, Hell!* involves a half-dozen or so fictional members of a Marine battalion made up of veteran regulars, young recruits, and recalled reservists who participate in the actual doings of the 1st Marine Division, from assembly and stateside training at Camp Pendleton down through Inchon–Seoul before jumping forward to Chosin-Hungnam. As was to be expected in a motion picture made with a good deal of technical assistance from the Pentagon, the Marine Corps is shown to be highly competent and effective, the emotional flaws exhibited by a couple of the main characters—a callow new recruit played by Russ Tamblyn and a cautious reserve officer played by Richard Carlson—being ironed out over time under the professional oversight of a stern but fair battalion commander played by Frank Lovejoy. The landing at Inchon, complete with scaling ladders at the front of landing craft, is recreated over a ten-minute span, with the help of intercut documentary footage from the battle and shots of landing craft beaching, as a well-executed operation in which only light casualties are suffered in overcoming moderate resistance. Subsequently scenes lasting about ten minutes depict the street fighting in Seoul, with the screen Marines once again prevailing through a mixture of bravery and firepower. A more taxing set of circumstances awaits the battalion in the second half of the film set in northeastern Korea; but it is noteworthy that Chromite-as-prelude is depicted as a series of sharp fights rather than a walkover, beginning with a Marine getting mortally shot as he scales a ladder and comes tumbling back into a landing craft, and ending with line of poncho-covered dead Marines on stretchers. Film critics found the characters and dialogue a bit formulaic; but a solid plot, strong cast, competent direction by Joseph H. Lewis, and high production values courtesy of the USMC meant that *Retreat, Hell!* did solid business at the American box office.[4]

As a Hollywood subgenre the combat film set during the Korean War had largely died out within a dozen years of the end of the conflict.[5] Filmmaker interest in the drama inherent in the words and actions of MacArthur, though, remained strong more than two decades later.[6] In early 1976, Hollywood producer Frank McCarthy announced that Gregory Peck had committed to play the lead in a major big-screen biopic of the general.[7]

MacArthur, though not his life story, was nonetheless broad in scope, covering the title character from the siege of Corregidor down through his farewell address to Congress nine years later, plus the last great speech at West Point the following decade. The dramatic potential of the Inchon decision was not lost on scriptwriters Hal Barwood and Matthew Robbins and was covered at comparative length—eleven minutes—by director Joseph Sargent.[8]

The landing is introduced ninety-three minutes into the two-hour epic as MacArthur, in an exterior scene set within the Pusan perimeter, explains to Eighth Army commander Walton Walker, played by Gary Walberg, that he cannot spare him any reinforcements since he is preparing an amphibious assault at Inchon. The scene then shifts to the White House, where the Joint Chiefs of Staff are shown briefing the president, played by Ed Flanders, on the tidal and other difficulties involved in staging a landing there. The case in favour of the landing site is made by an unidentified civilian secretary played by Art Fleming, who says that MacArthur is counting on the element of surprise. When asked by Truman what he thinks of the plan, soon-to-be Secretary of Defense George Marshall, played by Ward Costello, sagely observes, 'It's daring; it's brilliant; and it's dangerous.'[9]

Stock footage of air and naval bombardment is then inserted to represent the pre-landing bombardment of Wolmi-do and thus indicate that Chromite had in the end been given the green light; immediately followed by an extended nighttime scene on the bridge of the command ship *Mount McKinley* in which MacArthur suddenly starts to question his own wisdom, admitting to confidant Court Whitney, played by Dick O'Neill, that it could all go horribly wrong. But these doubts are instantly put to rest by the appearance from below of Fleet Marine Force Pacific commander Lem Shepherd, played by Warde Donovan, announcing that 'Wolmi-do is ours.' The general is instantly reinvigorated: 'Good work…now let's go!' The biopic

MacArthur then quickly shifts away from Inchon—'a hell of a job', Truman concedes—and towards Chinese intervention and the events that would eventually lead to the general's dismissal.[10]

The scriptwriters thought of the title character as someone who was 'frequently brilliant' but also exhibited 'a great capacity for self-delusion', the scenes involving Inchon being meant to convey the former rather than the latter.[11] Overall, the finished picture cast the general in a more positive than negative light; in no small measure this was due to changes insisted on by the star, Gregory Peck, regarding how his character appeared, what he said, and how he said it.[12] When *MacArthur* premiered in the summer of 1977, a representative from the United States Military Academy—where some of the shooting had taken place—remarked that the film was 'excellent P.R.' for West Point.[13] The press critics, moreover, were mostly positive in their assessments, especially regarding Peck in the title role.[14] The public, though, proved much less enthusiastic. The $13 million picture, which the filmmakers had hoped would replicate the huge success of *Patton* seven years earlier, made barely over $8 million in its initial run.[15]

The Worst Movie Ever Made?

What turned into the most notorious and expensive big-screen representation of Operation Chromite was in theory a Hollywood product but in reality a truly multinational effort involving a production team, crew, and cast hailing from Britain, Italy, Japan, and Korea as well as America: the whole thing being secretly bankrolled, it eventually emerged, by Sun Myung Moon, leader of the controversial Unification Church.[16] What was at first titled *Oh! Inchon*, then *Inchon!*, and finally *Inchon* without the exclamation mark, remains on many lists of the most awful feature films ever released.[17]

Wanting to see a cinematic epic produced which would counter the idea fashionable in leftist circles questioning whether North Korea was entirely responsible for the outbreak of the war while paying homage to a personal hero, Douglas MacArthur, but doubtless aware that direct participation might scare off the requisite talent, the Reverend Moon initially outsourced the project.[18] Thus it was Mitsuharu Ishii, head of a Japanese conglomerate (as well as, as it happened, a Unification Church member), who set up the offices of One Way Productions in Hollywood and grandly announced in March 1978 that plans were well underway towards an on-location epic motion picture focused on the September 1950 landing. In association with Toho Studios of Japan and with a budget quoted as high as $20 million, the production would feature Hollywood stars, major Korean actors, and as many as one hundred thousand Korean extras. Supported by the South Korean authorities, a twelve-week shoot was set to begin on location in the late spring of 1978, with Andrew V. McLaglen directing a screenplay written by Robin Moore and Paul Savage.[19] Then, after it became clearer which organization was behind the production, Toho and McLaglen pulled out and Ishii was forced to begin again. After about a year of public silence, One Way announced that location shooting on what was still called *Oh! Inchon* would now begin in late spring of 1979 under the direction of Terence Young.[20]

On paper all the elements of success had been assembled by the time actual location shooting started at the end of June 1979. South Korean forces with their heavy equipment had been lent to play both sides in invasion and battle scenes which would climax in a large-scale recreation of the Inchon landing itself. An experienced crew had been brought together under a respected action-film helmsman who would be directing an international big-name cast that included American players Ben Gazzara, David Janssen, and Richard Roundtree, Toshiro Mifune from Japan, Jacqueline Bisset for the female lead, and—in the starring role of MacArthur himself—none other than the great English thespian Laurence Olivier. Such talent, however, came at a high price. Olivier ended up pocketing $1.25 million, Bisset's fee was $1.65 million, and director Terence Young asked for and got $1.8 million.[21] Customs glitches, last-minute cast changes, and script doctoring all caused delays and pushed up the costs of a location shoot that dragged on into September, dogged by bad luck—a villager was accidentally run over and killed—and swirling rumours of Unification Church involvement.[22]

The production then moved to Rome to shoot various interior scenes, and then back to South Korea in May 1980 to expand on key battle sequences. There followed yet more changes and delays, with the film's score now being undertaken by Jerry Goldsmith rather than John Williams as previously announced, one of the stars—David Janssen—suffering a fatal heart attack, and Sun Myung Moon arguing with Terence Young over screen credits and a revised ending. By the time the film was complete it ran to 140 minutes at a cost of somewhere between $38 million and $48 million.[23]

Inchon, for which Robin Moore, Laird Koenig, and Paul Savage all eventually received writing credits, involved a variety of melodramatic, periodically intertwining, plot lines set during the course of the first three months of the Korean War.[24] These included the adventures of interior decorator Barbara Hallsworth (Jacqueline Bisset) as she flees by car from an unprovoked, bloody, and generally destructive North Korean advance in the company of a group of orphaned Korean children; the efforts of her estranged United States Marine Corps (USMC) husband, Major Frank Hallsworth (Ben Gazzara), to locate and save his wife with the help of Sergeant Augustus Henderson (Richard Roundtree) while still emotionally involved with Lim (Karen Kahn), the daughter of a retired Japanese admiral, Saito-san (Toshiro Mifune); the trials and tribulations of a betrothed Korean couple played by Lydia Lei and Nam Goon Won, separated by the blowing of a bridge across the Han River during the southward retreat; the efforts of MacArthur (Laurence Olivier) to get Chromite approved, sometimes while being watched by cynical American journalist David Feld (David Janssen); a nighttime special operation involving, among others, Frank, Saito, and Lim to secure and operate a lighthouse on the approaches to the port while destroying floating sea mines in order make Chromite possible; the landing itself; and MacArthur entering Seoul in triumph to deliver his address in the capitol building. A significant amount of screen time was devoted to contrasting the boldness and vision of the general against the caution and orthodoxy of flag-rank American officers outside his own circle, with scripted speeches clearly drawn from sympathetic sources, not least the recollections of MacArthur himself.[25]

Sun Myung Moon had reason to be pleased with the finished picture despite its eventual cost. It featured an international star cast, had been directed by someone who had contributed greatly to the success of the early James Bond films, and—most importantly from his perspective—not only portrayed the North Koreans as heinous invaders but also made multiple explicit references to MacArthur's faith in and reliance on God as well as his strategic acumen and anticommunism.[26] Yet his admiration for the general was so boundless that, against the strong objections of Terence Young, he insisted on inserting footage of the actual Douglas MacArthur delivering his farewell address to Congress after Olivier's final scene.[27]

One Way Productions then set about launching *Inchon* with a splashy premiere in Washington, DC. An honorary committee made up of Korean War veteran congressmen and both retired and serving senior officers was set up by the film's technical advisor—and actual USMC landing participant—General (retd.) Samuel Jaskilka to organize a special benefit performance at the Kennedy Center to be staged on behalf of Carl Vinson House, a retirement home for US Navy, Marine, and Coast Guard officers. Even before the performance occurred, however, the Moonie connection was generating waves. With Sun Myung Moon by this stage linked to political bribery efforts as well as what many saw as a religious cult, committee members and prominent invitees, including the commandant of the Marine Corps and many congressmen, stayed away in droves as the press made evident just how much the Unification Church had been involved with *Inchon*.[28]

Taking place on the evening of 4 May 1981, the premiere itself was something of a fiasco. Outside, the event was picketed by two dozen or so protesters with placards who objected to what looked like politico-military support for the Moonies. Inside, as a Marine drum and bugle corps played patriotic tunes, attendees were presented with brochures about *Inchon* which claimed that in a séance the spirit of MacArthur himself had given his blessing to the production. With the involvement of the Unification Church made clear, pointed questions were asked in the wake of the premiere as to how the Pentagon had allowed itself to be duped into de facto cooperation with Moon by allowing, for instance, off-duty American servicemen in Korea to serve as extras.[29]

Reaction to the film itself after this first showing was, to put it mildly, rather mixed. 'I thought it was remarkable,' commented E. Clay Shaw, a Republican congressional representative from Florida, adding that *Inchon* was 'a tremendous bit of patriotism'. It was ominous, however, that a fellow Republican congressional attendee wondered aloud if Laurence Olivier had been spoofing General MacArthur and would only rate the movie itself as 'quite good'.[30] The review in the influential trade paper *Variety* in the wake of the premiere was decidedly negative. Various players were ludicrously miscast, the plot featured 'an abundance of corn and silly situations' that generated laughter, there were too many 'overacted battle scenes', too much 'contrived dialog', and the whole thing was 'woefully long'.[31] Ishii had predicted that the premiere would be 'a good sales pitch for the movie'; but in its aftermath no company would agree to distribute *Inchon*.[32]

After whittling the running time down to 106 minutes (by, among other things, cutting any scene involving the deceased David Janssen), One Way tried again to promote *Inchon* as a commercial feature a year later at the 1982 Cannes Film Festival, employing a public relations firm and spending $250,000 on exposure. Distribution talks with Twentieth Century-Fox fell through, but eventually Metro-Goldwyn-Mayer stepped in as US distributor and the movie was released for the first time commercially in September.[33]

Newspapers across America panned the revised *Inchon*. It was 'a total disaster' (*Atlanta Constitution*); 'funny when it should be moving, ludicrous where it should be intense' (*Baltimore Sun*); 'overproduced' yet 'muddled' (*Boston Globe*); 'a lost cause' (*Chicago Tribune*); 'simpleminded'

Figure 7.1 M-G-M publicity poster for *Inchon*.

(*Hartford Courant*); 'insultingly awful' (*Minneapolis Star and Tribune*); 'ridiculously sloppy' (*Philadelphia Enquirer*); and 'simply a bore' (*Pittsburgh Post-Gazette*).[34] As for Olivier as MacArthur, complete with very odd makeup job and unique American accent, critics were divided as to whether his performance was a brilliant over-the-top satire or just a truly awful acting effort.[35] It was contemporary reviewers who were the first to opine that *Inchon* was the worst film ever made.[36] 'War is hell and so is this movie', read the damning final verdict in the *Washington Post* weekend section.[37]

Even more unflattering were the audience figures. Over its opening weekend *Inchon* earned only $2,326,112; and despite efforts by Ishii to boost numbers by offering ticketholders the chance to take part in a lottery for a free Rolls Royce plus $100,000 in cash and church members handing out promotional flyers on city streets, the numbers only went downhill from there. In the end *Inchon* recouped a mere 11 per cent of its estimated total production cost through ticket sales in North America.[38] The embarrassment was such that the film was not released in South Korea and Sun Myung Moon, after publicly complaining that foreign film critics were expressing their religious prejudices rather than judging *Inchon* on its artistic merits, in later years totally ignored the whole episode in his memoirs.[39]

North Korea

Plans for *Inchon* had not gone unnoticed north of the demilitarized zone. Commenting on what was known of the storyline, the Workers Party newspaper, *Rodong sinmun*, denounced it on 15 May 1979 as a 'vicious slander of the people's army' and a 'distortion of history'.[40] It seems plausible that news of a film about Chromite being made with the help of the South Korean authorities prompted Kim Jong Il, heir presumptive to his father Kim Il Sung and something of a film aficionado, to order development for propaganda purposes of a cinematic version of the Inchon story as it was understood in the Democratic People's Republic of Korea (DPRK).[41]

Figure 7.2 Kim Jong Il gives on-the-spot film-shoot guidance.

Scripted by Li Jin U and directed by Cho Gyong Sun, *Wolmi Island* appeared in North Korea in the same year *Inchon* was released in North America. Ninety-three minutes in length and in full colour, it dramatized the Alamo-like party line on the landing in which the defenders of the island, inspired by Kim Il Sung, fight to the last man and last round in order to hold up MacArthur long enough for the North Korean People's Army to engage in a 'strategic retreat' and thereby escape the Yankee trap. The official English-language catalogue description is as follows:

> In September 1950, 50,000 US imperialist troops led by the warmonger MacArthur carry out landing operations at Inchon. This turns Wolmi Island into a cauldron of fire. Men of the coast battery commanded by Li Tae Un [alternatively Romanized as Li Dai Hoon, and played by actor Choe Sang Su] fight the enemy with only four guns and the strength of one company. They check the enemy's landing for three days by displaying unexcelled bravery, mass heroism and a high degree of self-sacrificing spirit.[42]

In the course of their delaying efforts, Li and his men capture a dishevelled, red-haired, shifty-eyed USMC officer engaged in reconnaissance who, before expiring miserably, writes a despairing note to a friend stressing that 'I've never seen such true men as these people who love their motherland so much. We can't beat them. America may win a battle but not the war.'[43]

Even in communist agitprop terms *Wolmi Island* was far from original, the script piggybacking on an earlier Soviet screenplay as well as elements of 'The Island in Flames', a celebrated DPRK short story by Hwang Gon. But, as one otherwise unimpressed outside observer conceded, 'it definitely hammered home the usual points about reverence for the Leader, love for the motherland, and self-sacrifice as a noble concept in life'.[44] And that, of course, was the whole point. When the film was first released in North Korea in 1982 an entire issue of *Rodong sinmun* was dedicated to explaining the plot and significance of the events depicted, followed by a variety of promotional events around the country in which cast members met with Party youth groups.[45]

Buttressing the idea that the people's forces had seriously impeded the imperialist landing was *Don't Wait for Us*, once again scripted by Li Jin U but this time directed by Kim Yu Sam. Released two years after

Wolmi Island, the plot of *Don't Wait for Us* portrayed North Korean air operations against the American supporting fleet. 'The film deals with the feats of the death-defying airmen who ensure the strategic retreat of our troops by plunging themselves into enemy ships as human bombs,' as an official catalogue put it.[46]

Through the remainder of the twentieth century and on into the twenty-first, *Wolmi Island* would be revived in the DPRK whenever Pyongyang wanted to whip up anti-American sentiment or mark a particularly important anniversary from the Fatherland Liberation War.[47] As for *Don't Wait for Us*, it was still considered important enough to serve, under the watchful gaze of Kim Jong Il's son and successor, Kim Jong Un, as one of the films used to test an experimental '4D' audience experience thirty years after it was made.[48]

South Korea

Inchon was referenced in several war film dramas made in the Republic of Korea under the authoritarian rule of Park Chung-hee. *Five Marines* (dir. Kim Ki-duk 1961) opens with a brief stock-footage depiction of the landing, while *The Marines Who Never Returned* (dir. Lee Man-hee 1963)—a commercial success and considered something of a classic—begins with a longer version of the landing staged with the help of the Republic of Korea Marine Corps that shows Korean rather than American marines storming ashore and taking the port. *Inchon Landing Operation* (dir. Cho Gung-ha 1965) is the story of a female North Korean spy who is won over to the South Korean cause by an information officer and sends bogus details on the location of the landing to her superiors in Pyongyang. *A Glorious Operation* (dir. Koh Yŏng-nam 1969) recreated the preliminary seizure of the Palmi-do lighthouse, again dispensing with US involvement entirely. And the epic, full-colour *Testimony* (dir. Im Kwon-taek 1973) features the battle briefly as background detail in the story of a female refugee escaping southwards in the first months of the war.[49]

Figure 7.3 Press conference for *Operation Chromite*.

The return of democratic government in the latter 1980s ushered in several decades of more nuanced South Korean cinematic and televisual representations of the conflict in which participants were presented more ambiguously than had been possible under Park.[50] This did not mean, however, that more traditional good-versus-evil big-screen war dramas were no longer made, as co-producers Jeong Tae-won and Lee Kyu-chang demonstrated with *Operation Chromite* (dir. Lee Jai-han 2016).[51]

As written by Lee Man-hee (not to be confused with the film director of the same name referenced above) the plot of *Operation Chromite*, inspired by actual events while incorporating a lot of fictional elements, contains two major intercut storylines. The primary one involves a battle of wits—and eventually a huge amount of gunplay—between, on the one hand, a former communist turned anti-communist officer (played by Lee Jung-jae) and his team of disguised South Korean spy saboteurs, and on the other, the ruthless but intelligent Inchon garrison commander (played by Lee Beom-su) and his minions, for control of secret plans that will determine the fate of the upcoming operation. The secondary storyline involves the efforts of MacArthur (performed by a miscast Liam Neeson) to organize the Inchon landing in the face of opposition from Washington mandarins. The stories ultimately converge as the two central figures fight to the death on Wolmi-do just as the landing takes place and the general steps ashore. Costing nearly $13 million and lasting over 110 minutes, *Operation Chromite* sought to highlight heroic sacrifices made by South Korean agents in ensuring that MacArthur met with success at Inchon.[52]

Not surprisingly, it was denounced in Pyongyang.[53] But reaction among critics in Seoul was also largely negative, the film being faulted for, among other things, its 'simplistic patriotism' and 'worn-out anti-communism'.[54] Nonetheless as a big-budget, big-name domestic action feature *Operation Chromite* proved a huge draw in the Republic of Korea. Over 2.6 million tickets were sold between its release in the last week of July 2016 and the end of the month, and a total of seven million within two months, generating the equivalent in won of $49.92 million.[55]

Though the end results might vary in terms of mass impact, reconstructing the Inchon landing in the comparatively new medium of feature film was thus a significant means through which stakeholders sought to refresh, reinforce, or reshape popular perceptions within the countries concerned.[56] However, nothing projected on celluloid compared in terms of longevity to the much older visual tradition of seeking to memorialize people and the battles they fought in bronze and stone.

8

Commemoration Sites

As might be expected of a three-year conflict which drew in citizens hailing from at least twenty-seven countries, there exist hundreds of memorials and dozens of museums devoted wholly or in part to commemorating national or unit participation in the Korean War. Among the contributing states from the United Nations, a global survey conducted in the first decade of the twenty-first century counted over eight hundred of the former.[1] As for museums, among the major participants these have ranged from the privately run (and now defunct) Korean War National Museum in the United States to China's state-sponsored (and still operating) Memorial Hall of the War to Resist US Aggression and Aid Korea.[2] But it is in the two Koreas that the largest concentration of commemoration sites can be found, including, among other things, atrocity memorials in various locations and major museums located in the respective capitals dedicated to explaining the conflict for the benefit of both domestic and foreign visitors.[3] As one of the central events in the struggle, the landing at Inchon has been memorialized by the three main participating states through everything from text and photo displays to larger-than-life statues.[4]

South Korea

Since the port remained part of the Republic of Korea (ROK) after the armistice agreement was signed in late July 1953, it is not surprising that Inchon itself became the focal point of commemorative activity surrounding Operation Chromite not long after the war. How it was memorialized, however, would eventually become a matter of considerable public controversy.

In the eyes of the first president, Syngman Rhee, the Inchon–Seoul campaign had saved the republic and opened a fleeting opportunity to unify the country under his own leadership. And for him, nobody was more responsible for this than Douglas MacArthur. Hence forty-three months after the fighting stopped it was announced that a bronze statue of the great man was to be cast in time for the commemoration of the seventh anniversary of the landing, to be paid for in part through compulsory donations from government employees. The work of Kim Kyuk-sung of the Seoul art college, the 12-foot statue cost over 3,000,000 won, and was unveiled at Inchon atop a 20-foot plinth in International Park—subsequently rechristened Freedom Park—facing Wolmi-do, with a host of dignitaries in attendance, on 15 September 1957. At the base of the statue were inscribed the words: 'The savior of our Nation and the Protector of Freedom for All Mankind'.[5]

This was an accurate representation of how the general and the landing operation he had championed were generally venerated by even youthful South Koreans in the immediate postwar decades.[6] For example, after a student-led uprising finally drove the aged Rhee from power in the spring of 1960, some of those involved placed flowers in homage at the base of a statue widely adopted as a shrine to liberation and freedom.[7] It also became the focal point for commemorative events involving Korean veterans. On 15 September 1970, for instance, a press release announced that the Republic of Korea 'Marine Corps will celebrate the 20th anniversary of the Inchon Landing during the Korean War with a street parade of honor guards and a band through downtown Inchon Port today. In Freedom Park in the center of the city will be shown pictures of the famous amphibious operation in which the Korean marines fought together with the U.N. forces.'[8]

The role of Inchon as commemorative site expanded literally as well as figuratively in the first half of the 1980s. Added to the MacArthur

Figure 8.1 Douglas MacArthur statue in Freedom Park, Inchon.

statue and associated plaques in Freedom Park were the Monument to the Inchon Region Battle in Sudong Park, approximately three miles to the southeast, and the even more imposing Inchon Landing Operation Memorial Hall, roughly four miles south on the slopes of Mount Cheongnyangsan.

To mark the thirtieth anniversary, a new state-sponsored memorial to the landing and the subsequent advance was built. At an unveiling ceremony attended by government dignitaries and several hundred veterans, the Monument to the Inchon Region Battle, with construction costs drawn from the Ministry of Transportation budget, was seen to incorporate among other things a trio of armed and advancing Marines in bronze below a fourth bronze figure—an ROK Marine—holding aloft a torch of freedom atop a stone tower that drove the whole thing more than 52 feet skyward. The new monument aimed to memorialize 'the soldiers who fought for the freedom and peace of this land'.[9]

Four years later, the Inchon Landing Operation Memorial Hall, a joint venture of the city authorities and the Ministry of Defense, was opened on a site over 8 acres in extent. With a bas-relief archway entrance and an exterior resembling a seawall, the main structure was bisected by a stone staircase leading up to an 18-metre ornamented pillar, fronted by three advancing Marines, contained within a bas-relief semicircular wall depicting MacArthur directing the invasion. The interior of the hall was given over to photo–text display cases containing dressed-up dummies, documents, weapons, and other relics pertaining to Operation Chromite, along with a diorama depicting the landing. Though a fair amount of space was devoted to the contributions of Korean servicemen, MacArthur featured prominently both in photographs and in three dimensions via a bust and a three-figure mannequin replica of a famous snapshot of the general seated on the exterior bridge of *Mount McKinley*, field glasses in hand, flanked by a pointing Ned Almond on one side and Court Whitney on the other. The general thus seemed to be as venerated as ever.[10]

However, by the following decades perceptions of the American role in the conflict were starting to shift from positive to negative among certain segments of the South Korean population. Since pro-Americanism was the default position of the repressive rightist-authoritarian regimes that had governed the country more or less continuously for forty-odd years, and the US forces stationed in the

Figure 8.2 Exterior of Inchon Landing Operation Memorial Hall.

country had conspicuously failed in 1980 to stop ROK army paratroopers from bloodily crushing the Gwangju Uprising launched against yet another ex-military president, when multi-party democracy took hold via the sixth republic from the latter 1980s through the 1990s and on into the new century, there was a tendency among those of more left-wing inclination, particularly among the young, to question the traditional view of the USA as South Korea's benign protector. This was in the context of anti-American sentiment arising from the deaths of civilians at the hands of US troops: both contemporaneously, as in the Yangju highway incident in June 2002; and historically, as with the newly revealed events at No Gun Ri during the American retreat towards Pusan in July 1950.[11] In fact something of a generational divide seemed to be developing, with a survey of Seoul residents a few years into the new millennium indicating that while roughly three quarters of those polled who were in their fifties approved of the Americans, approximately three quarters of those polled who were in their twenties disliked the United States.[12]

This divide in turn affected what the MacArthur statue in particular was thought to represent in South Korea as the sixth republic continued to unfold. For many older and/or conservative citizens, the central feature of Freedom Park remained at the millennium an emblem of deliverance.[13] Meanwhile, for some younger and/or more radical citizens, it had become a symbol of both persistent American hegemony and of the wonton destruction wrought on the country during the Six-Two-Five War. This was the context in which calls began in 2005 for the statue to be removed. 'MacArthur is a war criminal,' one anti-American group claimed in a petition to the National Human Rights Commission. To teach that he was 'a great figure is a national disgrace'. This sort of thing, however, particularly accompanied as it was by loud demands from Pyongyang that the statue of the 'cutthroat war criminal' and 'chieftain of aggression' be torn down, only made older patriotic South Koreans more determined to keep the statute in its current location in Freedom Park. 'Around the statue are numerous invisible soldiers that fought with him,' argued one war veteran: 'To take his statue down is to eliminate their souls.'[14]

The most passionate believers in these two utterly irreconcilable points of view began to rally in Inchon and elsewhere, with police having to intervene to prevent the two sides from coming to blows in Freedom Park by mid-July 2005. Though himself left of centre politically, then-president Roh Moo-hyun decided that removing the statue would place too much strain on already fractious US–ROK relations. The public on the whole seemed to agree, a poll of the time indicating that only 10 per cent of respondents wanted the MacArthur bronze dismantled.[15]

And so the MacArthur statue remained standing in Inchon's Freedom Park, becoming less of an emotional lightning rod as time passed, even though there were still occasional smaller-scale public demonstrations and a couple of isolated acts of vandalism.[16] Despite condemnation emanating from North Korea, a planned recreation of the Inchon landing involving ROK forces and veterans to mark the fifty-seventh anniversary went off without serious incident.[17]

Meanwhile, left–right differences of opinion regarding the Six-Two-Five War were being played out through the War Memorial of Korea in Seoul. Built on the grounds of a former army headquarters during the liberal presidency of Kim Dae-jung in the early 1990s, the underlying theme of many of the museum's displays when it opened with regard to the Korean War was one of remembrance and reconciliation rather than condemnation and confrontation, a reflection of Kim's policy of positive engagement towards North Korea, and symbolized outside the building by a striking Statue of Brothers depicting a wartime ROK officer embracing a wartime Korean People's Army soldier as a younger sibling.[18] Within a few years, however, the political pendulum had swung rightwards, and with the so-called Sunshine Policy formally abandoned moving into the 2010s under the conservative presidencies of Lee Myung-bak and his immediate successor, Park Geun-hye, the interior exhibits took on a more robustly bellicose hue; they now included, for example, a multimedia representation of the Inchon landing that was thoroughly conventional in terms of content but comparatively high-tech in delivery.[19] North Korea angrily took note when in 2019 yet another memorial—a ROK–US Alliance sculpture, the central tower of which featured a South Korean and an American helping each other surmount the Inchon seawall, funded by the American

Chamber of Commerce in Korea—was opened at the big American base near Pyeongtaek.[20]

North Korea

The importance Kim Il Sung attached to visually reinforcing his counterfactual version of the conflict in order to buttress his legitimacy as leader of the Democratic People's Republic of Korea (DPRK) was evident through the setting up of an 'Exhibition in Commemoration of the Victory in the War' immediately after the 1953 armistice. A year later, what was dubbed the Fatherland Liberation War Memorial Museum opened in central Pyongyang, moving a few miles north within the city early the following decade to a purpose-built courtyard facility mixing occidental with oriental architectural elements, complete with a triumphal entry arch, on the banks of the Pothong River. As a brochure proudly indicated, it contained over four thousand individual items, including photographs, paintings, sculptures, war kit, and over forty models of military operations spread over sixteen gallery halls.[21]

The overall goal was to illustrate to visitors how the armed forces, people, and workers party led by Kim Il Sung had, with assistance from China and other states in the socialist camp, inflicted a 'crushing defeat' on the American imperialists.[22] With respect to the Inchon–Seoul campaign, with the help of suitably heroic if somewhat crudely drawn renditions of events, it was explained that: 'Our soldiers defending the coast put up a stiff resistance. Especially a company of coast-battery [troops] under the command of Hero of the D.P.R.K. Li Dai Hoon which was defending Wolmi Island fought to the last man against the enemy.' Unfortunately, the imperialists proved too strong in numbers to be contained at Inchon, but when they moved on to Seoul, they encountered massive resistance. 'Our units defending Seoul put up heroic fights and held the enemy's advance at bay for a fortnight. The citizens of Seoul fought valiantly along with the People's Army units against the invading enemy.' Along with successful delaying efforts further south this had allowed the Korean People's Army (KPA) to make a successful 'strategical temporary retreat' and prepare for the next round of attacks.[23]

Over time the exhibits and descriptions at the Fatherland Liberation War Memorial Museum changed, with mention of Chinese help being omitted and the role of the Great Leader greatly expanded as Kim developed his personality cult. Thus, the English-language guide produced at the end of the 1960s admitted of only one true hero. 'Under the pre-eminent leadership of Comrade Kim Il Sung, the military strategist-genius,' it was explained, 'men and officers of the Korean People's Army, at the unexpected turn of the situation [the Inchon invasion], honorably pulled through the stern trial of the strategic temporary retreat that was designed to get ready for a new decisive blow at the aggressors.'[24]

In the early 1970s the museum was rebuilt and expanded along socialist classicism lines and 'Victorious' inserted in the title.[25] Further expansion took place to mark the fortieth anniversary of the

Figure 8.3 Heroes of Wolmido statue, Victorious Fatherland Liberation War Museum, Pyongyang.

imperialists acknowledging defeat, by which time a vast memorial had been added, consisting largely of a series of colossal bronze ensemble statue pieces composed of figures in heroically aggressive poses outside the main building—including one titled 'Heroes of Wolmido'—facing a solo bronze soldier on a higher granite plinth holding the national banner aloft and calling the nation to arms.[26]

Inside the museum itself the island's garrison appeared equally heroic in a semi-panoramic oil canvas. 'The defenders of Wolmi Island with four guns and the forces of one infantry company fought heroically against the enemy' who possessed 'over 1,000 planes and hundreds of warships', according to the guidebook, and in doing so 'delayed the enemy's landing for three days' to allow for the defence of Seoul to be organized and contribute to Marshal Kim Il Sung's policy of 'strategic temporary retreat' for the main units of the KPA.[27]

After another round of renovation to mark the sixtieth anniversary of triumph over the invaders, the three-storey Victorious Fatherland Liberation War Museum was said to have no less than 51,000 square metres of floor space containing 120,000 war relics. The defence of Wolmi-do and the battle for Seoul continued to be covered in the context of the brilliant grand strategy of the Great Leader, the semi-panoramic paintings reduced to more conventional proportions but now accompanied by photographs, maps, and newspaper headlines, along with examples of the type of 76 mm field piece and wheeled heavy machine gun used at the time, plus, in another location, a diorama rendition of the battle accompanied by headshots of coastal artillery commander Ri Tae Hun (aka Li Dai Hoon) and the platoon leader Chou Son Ju, both posthumously awarded the title of Hero of the DPRK. Most prominent of all, of course, were the wise words of Kim Il Sung.[28]

The Wolmi-do displays in the Victorious Fatherland Liberation War Museum continued to play an important part in how the war was presented in North Korea into the second decade of the twenty-first century. In the summer of 2021, for example, in the run-up to Victory Day, a television news programme included an interview with a museum guide who extolled 'the feats of the defenders of Wolmi Island' and cited a letter pledging allegiance they had sent Kim Il Sung on the eve of 'their last life-and-death battle'. The moral was obvious: 'loyalty to the leader is the basic source of all feats'.[29]

United States

For much of the second half of the twentieth century the conflict in Korea was said by veterans, and the few others who took an interest, to be America's forgotten war. The relative frequency with which this phrase was trotted out in the decades surrounding the millennium suggests that this familiar moniker was becoming an overstatement.[30] Nonetheless there can be little doubt that, sandwiched between the country's global effort in the Second World War and the long and troubled Vietnam experience, the Korean War was overshadowed in American popular memory by the preceding and succeeding conflicts.[31]

Symptomatic of this was the number of memorials built in remembrance of those who had served in Korea as against those who had served in the Second World War and Vietnam. Given the relative scale of United States involvement, it is not surprising that the number of sites across the country relating to the so-called Good War exceeds that for the Forgotten War; yet the number for Vietnam at the end of the century was also about double that for Korea.[32] As for national sites of commemoration located in Washington, DC, it was telling that the American Battle Monuments Commission got around to overseeing the completion of the Korean War Veterans Memorial only thirteen years after the opening of the Vietnam Veterans Memorial.[33]

The relatively scarcity of Korean War commemorative sites within the United States was rendered even more acute in the case of Inchon by the fact that what monuments there were tended to memorialize American participation in the war as a whole rather than any particular action.[34] This held true even for the United States Marine Corps, whose triumph at Inchon had ensured its future. The leathernecks, more than anyone, might have considered building something to commemorate Operation Chromite. The trouble was that the justly famous Marine Corps War Memorial located in Arlington Ridge Park, Virginia, developed during the Korean War and dedicated shortly thereafter to all those Marines who had laid down their lives for their country since the founding of the United States Marine Corps, depicted in striking fashion the flag-raising scene at Iwo Jima in bronze, thereby firmly anchoring the memorial in the island-hopping battles of the Pacific War. There were plaques along the plinth acknowledging other conflicts, but in many cases, including Korea, these referenced an entire war rather than specific battles. In any event, thanks to the sculpture, the monument became popularly known as the Iwo Jima memorial.[35]

To be sure, statues of Douglas MacArthur were erected in the United States in locations as distant from one another as Los Angeles, California in the mid-1950s, West Point, New York at the end of the 1960s, a second casting of the same bronze figure in Norfolk, Virginia a year later, and a different statue in Milwaukee, Wisconsin at the tail end of the 1970s. These, however, were meant to honour the entire military career of the general rather than any one triumph; and in any event represented him as he appeared *circa* 1944. In short, there was no effort to create an equivalent in America to the MacArthur statue at Inchon.[36]

Museum exhibits covering Chromite did eventually make an appearance but tended to be sections of limited space devoted to the Korean War as part of either the nation's military history, or the story of a particular individual, or of an entire branch of the armed services. For despite its aspirational title, the Korean War National Museum, established in 1997, was essentially a small community exhibition in Illinois that turned itinerant and which closed its storefront doors in Springfield for the last time due to persistent funding difficulties in the summer of 2017.[37] There remained a small space devoted to Korea in the context of the Cold War as part of a much bigger—over 18,000 square feet— exhibit, 'The Price of Freedom', that first opened in 2004 at the

Smithsonian National Museum of American History in Washington, DC thanks to a generous donation from a real-estate philanthropist.[38] But Inchon, discussed at moderate length in the defunct Springfield storefront facility, barely got a mention at the Smithsonian.[39]

On the other hand, both the landing at Inchon and the liberation of Seoul continue to receive decent coverage at the MacArthur Memorial in Norfolk, Virginia. Tempted by an offer from the mayor to convert Norfolk city hall into a presidential library-type facility in which his papers and memorabilia could be accessed and displayed, the general had agreed on condition that he and his wife be buried in the rotunda of the memorial, which opened the year he died.[40] A variety of objects, displays, and text panels inside the memorial covered MacArthur's entire military career, but, naturally enough, his 'brilliant amphibious invasion' via Inchon continues to receive due recognition.[41]

Museums dedicated to the individual American armed services are a little more forthcoming than the Smithsonian if the service concerned was involved in Chromite. The relative size of the exhibits and display panels, though, tend to reflect the comparative importance of a particular service branch in the operation.

Given the secondary role of the US Army in the Inchon–Seoul campaign, it is perhaps not surprising that curators at the army's many individual museums have chosen to focus on other aspects of the Korean War, though it is at least touched on at, for instance, the National Infantry Museum, opened eight years into the current century just outside Fort Benning, Georgia, and the National Museum of the United States Army, opened even more recently at Fort Belvoir, Virginia.[42] The effort is greater at the somewhat more venerable National Museum of the US Navy, located within the Washington Navy Yard. Here, in a building devoted to the Cold War, there is an exhibit titled 'Korea 1950–53: The Navy in the Forgotten War', featuring a jeep-laden landing craft as well as other artifacts such as a piece of the Inchon seawall.[43]

All this, however, pales in comparison to the lavish attention paid to Inchon by the United States Marine Corps (USMC). Located in

Triangle, Virginia, near the Marine base at Quantico, the National Museum of the Marine Corps, opened five years into the new millennium, explains and celebrates at length Operation Chromite. The Korean War gallery on the first 'deck' (i.e. floor) includes exhibits through which visitors can vicariously 'ride with Marines to the sea wall at Inchon as part of General MacArthur's end run to attack the enemy's rear' as well as hear a Pershing tank rumbling through the streets of Seoul.[44] The landing is explained at length through a seven-minute documentary as well as via the following tour narrative:

> The surprise U.S. landing at Inchon reflected General MacArthur's strategic vision and the creative flexibility of the 1st Marine Division. The massive, seaborne flank attack enabled the U.S. Eighth Army to break the North Korean's [sic] siege of the Pusan Perimeter and drive the enemy North against MacArthur's newly established 'anvil' along the Han River. At Inchon, the 1st Marine Division faced its most daunting challenge, deploying so hurriedly it still lacked its third infantry regiment. They were ordered to execute an amphibious assault in a city the size of Omaha under the worst tidal conditions the Marines ever faced. Yet MacArthur's prophesy proved correct. The Marines overcame Inchon's notorious tidal surges, mudflats, and seawalls, and indeed 'crushed' the port's defenses. Within two weeks the Leathernecks had fought their way inland and raised the American flag in recaptured Seoul.[45]

Innovative and welcoming, the National Museum of the Marine Corps quickly became a big tourist draw, receiving about half a million visitors each year a within decade after it first opened its doors.[46]

Interior collections and exterior memorials are thus clearly a major aspect of how various authorities have sought to give meaning to Inchon, not only in the present but also for future generations. Yet what is literally set in stone has not always remained fixed figuratively, as the demise of the Korean War National Museum and the controversy surrounding the MacArthur statue in Freedom Park both illustrate.

9

Conclusion

The meaning of Inchon from the start has been contested—usually between, though occasionally within, the major belligerent states involved in fighting the battle. It is almost always represented as significant; but specific national contexts have produced interpretations over time that differ from one another to greater or lesser degrees.[1]

National Narratives

In North Korea, the war narrative has remained essentially the same for over seventy years now, not least with respect to Inchon. The assertion that it was the imperialist United States through its puppets which had initiated hostilities remained sacrosanct in Pyongyang as one century gave way to another. After the initial imperialist attack the subsequent liberation and unification of the peninsula by the Korean People's Army was only prevented through the application of America's global military resources by a warmongering MacArthur. Though ultimately overwhelmed, those who had defended Inchon and Seoul had fought ferociously in a successful effort to delay the imperialist enemy's advance, thereby facilitating a successful withdrawal from the South. Various fighters had demonstrated particular heroism while laying down their lives in order to foil the strategic entrapment planned by the war criminal MacArthur, among them the gunners of Wolmi-do; and, of course, everyone had been inspired by Kim Il Sung, whose wise policy of shifting from general attack to orderly withdrawal had been necessitated by the actions of traitors as well as the mobilization of Yankee resources on a global scale. Whether in party newspapers, between hard covers, carried over the airwaves, shown on screens, or expressed through exhibits and statuary, the story of Inchon in North Korea is still one of exemplary conduct through which MacArthur's aims were thwarted.[2]

In South Korea, however, the Inchon legacy became more multifaceted over time. Under successive authoritarian governments Operation Chromite and what followed were portrayed in multiple forms as events orchestrated by Douglas MacArthur which had reversed the military situation and thereby saved the fledgling republic from imminent destruction at the hands of the communists. Even after the shift to liberal democracy in the final decade of the twentieth century, there were still many South Koreans of right-wing persuasion who thought, wrote, and acted in these terms who strongly objected to what they saw as left-wing revisionist attempts to brand the general a war criminal. That there were indeed citizens who wanted to express a much more jaundiced view of Inchon in particular, and American intervention in general, is most obvious in the periodic efforts to deface the MacArthur statue in Freedom Park. Yet even outside the more conventionally patriotic community there have been ongoing efforts to foreground the specifically Korean contributions to the success of Operation Chromite.[3]

In the United States, meanwhile, Inchon has always had less resonance than on the Korean peninsula but remains inextricably tied to the reputation of Douglas MacArthur. From the planning stage onwards, the general sought not only to control events but also shape how they would be remembered. Thanks in large part to his own flair for the dramatic, buttressed by the loyalty of acolytes, he made Operation Chromite—both at the time and long afterwards—appear a visionary gamble which frightened various Pentagon mandarins but yielded exactly what he had promised: unalloyed strategic victory. Whether in print or on screen, Inchon continues to be portrayed in popular discourse as MacArthur's last great triumph, various caveats and academic critiques notwithstanding.[4]

Corps Beliefs

At the same time the United States Marine Corps (USMC) continues to profit from the general's ultimately successful choice of landing site, most criticism of his insistence on Inchon being displaced onto the subsequent handling of the 1st Marine Division by Ned Almond.[5] MacArthur, after all, had asked for the Marines, and in allowing them to stage a major conventional amphibious operation, had given the corps a hugely helpful demonstration of continuing relevance in the atomic age. In testimony before the House Armed Services Committee four years after the end of the Second World War, Omar Bradley, chairman of the Joint Chiefs of Staff and a US Army general, had famously predicted that large-scale amphibious operations of the sort that had characterized USMC operations in the recent war against Japan in the Pacific would never occur again. The implication was that the Marine Corps had become superfluous to military requirements at a time when a war fought with nuclear weapons seemed the most likely form of conflict America would face in future. After the success of Chromite and the fighting in Korea that followed, however, the future of the Marines was assured, the corps leveraging the resulting positive image into successful lobbying for the creation of Marine amphibious task forces around the globe by the early 1960s.[6]

Through the rest of the Cold War, however, it became clear that, while a sea–land capability of this kind was very useful in responding quickly to developing crises in regions of the world with accessible coastlines, Inchon would probably remain for the United States the last great amphibious assault.[7] This was in large part because the level of surprise achieved was unlikely ever to be repeated, raising the spectre of a vigorously opposed landing in which the costs incurred in the way of casualties might well outweigh whatever strategic advantage was being sought. It was for this reason that plans for major American amphibious landings north of the DMZ during the Vietnam War and on the coast of Kuwait during the Gulf War were abandoned.[8]

Though the ability to project forces from platforms at sea onto hostile coastlines remains at the heart of USMC identity, the growth in the range and precision of shore-based sea-denial missile and other systems meant that, sixty years on, future Inchon-style landings were no longer being contemplated. Nineteen years into the present century, the commandant of the Marine Corps, General David Berger, in calling for a more dispersed and agile approach to sea-to-shore operations, explicitly stated that 'visions of the massed naval armada' launching hordes of amphibious vehicles against defended beaches 'are impracticable and unreasonable'.[9]

On the other hand, amphibious combat landings on a more modest scale than Inchon were still being undertaken by other countries in the second half of the last century, including those staged by Great Britain during the Suez Crisis in the middle 1950s and the Falklands War in the early 1980s. Moreover, in the current century various other states, notably the People's Republic of China with an eye on Taiwan, have increased their amphibious capabilities. Much depends on how contemporary amphibious warfare is conceptualized. If it is thought of in terms of form and scale comparable to Operation Chromite, then Inchon might best be viewed simply as a magnificent coda to the great allied landings of the Second World War.[10] If it is imagined in terms of evolving doctrine and equipment, utilizing smaller and more dispersed yet interconnected elements, then assault from the sea has a future as well as a past. As another USMC general, Jason Q. Bohm, pointed out some years ago, critics have pronounced amphibious warfare obsolete many times—only to be proven wrong by events.[11]

Historical Perspectives

Viewed in isolation, Operation Chromite can be seen as something of a paradox in terms of potential risk and actual gain. On the one hand, if the North Koreans had managed to make real progress on the minefields they were planning to lay to protect Inchon—an unknown variable in opposition naval circles—then the landing might well have been rendered impossible.[12] On the other hand, signals and other forms of intelligence had already revealed to MacArthur that the garrison and supporting units were comparatively weak, which meant that establishing a beachhead ashore was less of a gamble than it might have seemed to those US Marine and US Navy senior officers not privy to top-secret information.[13] As for the wider strategic aim behind the landing and advance on the capital as articulated by MacArthur, while it was true on the one hand that the Korean People's Army fell apart in the second half of the month in the South as predicted, there are plenty of indications on the other that the Eighth Army was accomplishing this even without the aid of X Corps.[14]

But, of course, the larger point is that, whatever it may or may not have amounted to in an operational sense, for over seventy years now Operation Chromite has been presented in ways that satisfy needs other than those of professional officers. These requirements have ranged from leadership legitimation and national pride to burnishing the image of a particular branch of the armed forces or personage. The resulting narratives, be they printed on the page, projected on the screen, cast in bronze, or carved in stone, aim to meet the popular human desire for the conventions of drama rather more (sometimes a great deal more) than they do any objective and accurate ideal of what recorded history ought to be about. And once established in popular discourse, these versions of events become hard to modify even when the opportunity exists—admittedly never the case in North Korea—to set the record straight. As the newspaper reporter famously says at the end of that classic Western, *The Man Who Shot Liberty Valance*, 'when the legend becomes fact, print the legend'.[15]

NOTES

Chapter 1

1. In Britain, for example, the Imjin battle (see e.g. Andrew Salmon, *To the Last Round: The Epic British Stand on the Imjin River, Korea 1951* [London, 2009]); in China, among other engagements, Triangle Hill (see e.g. the 1956 film *Shangghanlin* [dir. Lin Shan]); in North Korea, victories such as the taking of Taejon (see e.g. the photograph of the enormous panoramic display in O Hae-yŏn, *The Victorious Fatherland Liberation War Museum* [Pyongyang, 2014], 116); in South Korea, for instance, the defence of Po'hang-dong (see e.g. the 2010 film *71: Into the Fire* [dir. Lee Jae-han]); and in the United States tough fights for specific locations—see e.g. the 1959 Hollywood film *Pork Chop Hill* (dir. Lewis Milestone) based on the book by S. L. A. Marshall, *Pork Chop Hill: The American Fighting Man in Action, Korea, Spring, 1953* (New York, 1956); and, above all, the Chosin Reservoir battle (see e.g. Thomas McKelvey Cleaver, *The Frozen Chosen: The 1st Marine Division and the Battle of the Chosin Reservoir* [Oxford, 2016]; Hampton Sides, *On Desperate Ground: The Marines, the Reservoir, and the Korean War's Greatest Battle* [New York, 2018]).
2. Inchon, to be sure, is not unique with respect to being celebrated as a victory by each side in Korea: see for instance the way in which the Battle of the Chosin Reservoir, long celebrated as a triumphant fighting retreat in the United States (see e.g. the 1952 Hollywood movie *Retreat, Hell!* [dir. Joseph H. Lewis]), was interpreted as a great Chinese victory in the 2021 state-sponsored film epic *The Battle at Lake Changjin* (dir. Chen Kaige et al.); on which see Matthew Kotowski, 'The Battle at Lake Changjin: The Influence of Korean War Memory on Contemporary Chinese War Films', *Journal of Chinese Military History* 13, 1 (2024), 53–92. Inchon, however, does appear in a class of its own insofar as not two but three states were directly involved on the ground—the two Koreas and the USA—with each recounting either subtly or radically different versions of events thereafter down to the present.
3. On the 2018 VR game see Steam, Operation Chromite 1950, https://store.steampowered.com/app/695490/OperatioSteam, Operation Chromite VRm n_Chromite_1950_VR/ (accessed 26 August 2022); see also Sin Nayŏng, 'Inch'ŏn sangnyuk chakchŏn VR keim ŭro t'ansaeng', *Inch'ŏn ilbo*, 13 September 2017. On the building-block set from Oxford Toy in South Korea see

OM33020, http://oxfordtoy.co.kr/index.asp (accessed 26 August 2022). On the GI Joe Invasion of Inchon action figure see e.g. GI Joe Invasion of Inchon figure review, 9 August 2017, MIB Master Toy Museum, https://www.youtube.com/watch?v=6E19ipdfOqI (accessed 10 September 2022). There have also been various board games over the years, e.g. *Inchon: Turning the Tide in Korea* (1981) from Simulations Canada; *Inchon: MacArthur's Gambit* (1991) from Kokusai-Tsushin.

4. On the opera *Three Days of Wolmi Island* and the evolution of the messages being conveyed see Alexandra Leonzini and Peter Moody, 'From MacArthur's Landing to Trump's Fire and Fury: Sonic Depictions of Struggle and Sacrifice in a North Korean Short Story, Film and Opera', *Korean Studies* 44 (2022), 73–107. On the 'Inchon' symphonic band piece see Robert W. Smith, publications, https://rwsmithcomposer.com/publications/ (accessed 27 August 2022); Inchon, Alfred Music, https://www.alfred.com/inchon/p/00-BDM01012/ (accessed 27 August 2022). On the Inchon March (*In'chŏn haengjin'gok*) see Keith Howard, *Songs for "Great Leaders": Ideology and Creativity in North Korean Music and Dance* (New York, 2020), 17.

Chapter 2

1. On events in Korea following Japanese defeat down to the outbreak of hostilities see e.g. Wada Haruki, *The Korean War: An International History* (Lanham, MD, 2018), 1–75; Alan R. Millett, *The War for Korea, 1945–1950: A House Burning* (Lawrence, KS, 2005); Michael J. Seth, *Korea at War* (Rutland, VT, 2023), 58–82; see also James I. Matray, 'Koreans Invade Korea', in James I. Matray and Donald W. Boose, Jr. (eds), *The Ashgate Research Companion to the Korean War* (Farnham, 2014), 309–20.
2. MacArthur's visit was prompted by an erroneous report from his chief of staff, who implied that a cascading debacle was in the offing: see Roy E. Appleman, *United States Army in the Korean War: South to the Naktong, North to the Yalu* (Washington, DC, 1961), 206–7; Alan R. Millett, *The War for Korea, 1950–1951: They Came from the North* (Lawrence, KS, 2010), 200–1. On the problems of US forces in Japan and the course of the first months of the war see ibid. 75–96, 135–231. On prewar difficulties in Japan see also Thomas E. Hanson, *Combat Ready? The Eighth U.S. Army on the Eve of the Korean War* (College Station, TX, 2010).
3. On the mid-September manpower ratio see Stephen R. Taaffe, *MacArthur's Korean War Generals* (Lawrence, KS, 2016), 83.
4. MacArthur was authorized to respond to the North Korean invasion initially in his capacity as Commander-in-Chief, Far East, and then also as the designated leader of the United Nations Command. For a generally sympathetic summary of MacArthur's career see Tony R. Mullis, 'Douglas MacArthur', in

James H. Willbanks (ed.), *Generals of the Army: Marshall, MacArthur, Eisenhower, Arnold, Bradley* (Lexington, KY, 2013), 63–111. For his questionable operational decisions in the Pacific War see James Ellman, *MacArthur Reconsidered: General Douglas MacArthur as a Wartime Commander* (Essex, CT, 2023), 35–143.

5. See Donald W. Boose, Jr., *Over the Beach: US Army Amphibious Operations in the Korean War* (Fort Leavenworth, KS, 2008), 119–23; James A. Field, Jr., *History of United States Naval Operations: Korea* (Washington, DC, 1962), 102; D. Clayton James, *The Years of MacArthur*, Volume 3 (Boston, MA, 1985), 465.

6. MacArthur stressed his faith in a landing, plus his ongoing preference for Inchon, during visits to his HQ in the second and third week of July by the commander of the Fleet Marine Force, Lemuel C. Shepherd, and the US Army Chief of Staff, J. Lawton Collins. See Boose, *Over the Beach*, 155–6; J. Lawton Collins, *War in Peacetime: The History and Lessons of Korea* (Boston, MA, 1969), 115; Lemuel C. Shepherd interview in Henry Berry, *Hey, Mac, Where Ya Been? Living Memories of the U.S. Marines in the Korean War* (New York, 1988), 34.

7. Edwin K. Wright quoted in Arthur Herman, *Douglas MacArthur: American Warrior* (New York, 2016), 728; see MacArthur Memorial Archive [hereafter MMA], RG-6, OH50, AUD184T, Edwin Wright interview TS, 14–15; Boose, *Over the Beach*, 157; see also Edward L. Rowny, 'Intelligence and the Political Objectives of the War', in Daniel J. Meador (ed.), *The Korean War in Retrospect: Lessons for the Future* (Lanham, MD, 1998), 163.

8. On the narcissistic element in MacArthur's way of thinking see Russell D. Buhite, *Douglas MacArthur: Statecraft and Stagecraft in America's East Asian Policy* (Lanham, MD, 2008).

9. MacArthur response in a 24 July teleconference with JCS quoted in Collins, *War in Peacetime*, 118. On MacArthur turning to the Marines see United States Marine Corps University [hereafter USMCU], Lemuel C. Shepherd, Jr., 55, https://www.usmcu.edu/Research/Marine-Corps-History-Division/Oral-History/Distinguished-Marine-Career-Interviews/; USMCU, Victor H. Krulak, 148–9, https://www.usmcu.edu/Research/Marine-Corps-History-Division/Oral-History/Distinguished-Marine-Career-Interviews/.

10. Arlie G. Capps quoted in Walter Karig, Malcolm W. Cagle, and Frank A. Manson, *Battle Report: The War in Korea* (New York, 1952), 161.

11. On MacArthur's likely reasons for choosing his own chief of staff to head X Corps see Donald Chisolm, 'Negotiated Joint Command Relationships: Korean War Amphibious Operations, 1950', *Naval War College Review* 53, 2 (2000), 81.

12. On the concluding remarks see MMA, RG-32, OH64, U.S. Military History Institute, Senior Officers Debriefing Program, Conversations between Lieutenant General Edward M. Almond and Captain Thomas C. Fergusson, 1977, TS, 41. For the positive impression MacArthur made on the Chief of Naval Operations see MMA, RG-10, Box 10, Folder 24, Sherman to MacArthur, 25 August 1950. On the successful efforts by Almond and MacArthur to keep Inchon as the landing site in the face of criticism see e.g. Millett, *War for*

Korea, 1950–1951, 207–12. On MacArthur's sparring with Washington in gaining authorization for his amphibious landing see, from the JCS perspective, James F. Schnabel and Robert J. Watson, *The History of the Joint Chiefs of Staff: The Joint Chiefs of Staff and National Policy*, Volume 3: *The Korean War, Part I* (Washington, DC, 1998), 85–92; see also *Summary of messages exchanged between CINCFE and JCS concerning the Inchon landing conducted in Korea in September 1950* (Department of the Army, Office of the Chief of Staff, G-3, Operations).

13. Robert Debs Heinl, Jr., *Victory at High Tide: The Inchon-Seoul Campaign* (Philadelphia, 1968), 43; see ibid., 42; Collins, *War in Peacetime*, 126–8.
14. Appleman, *South to the Naktong*, 495; see Collins, *War in Peacetime*, 126–8.
15. See Millett, *War for Korea, 1950–1951*, 241–2, 527 n. 18; Boose, *Over the Beach*, 172–4. For summary accounts of the key human reconnaissance special operation, codenamed Trudy Jackson, see Thomas J. Mitchell, *Winds, Waves, & Warriors: Battling the Surf at Normandy, Tarawa, Inchon* (Baton Rouge, LA, 2019), 114–28; Curtis A. Utz, 'Assault from the Sea: The Amphibious Landing at Inchon', in Edward J. Marolda (ed.), *The U.S. Navy in the Korean War* (Annapolis, MD, 2007), 73–6. See also, on USAF photoreconnaissance, Al Browser in Berry, *Hey, Mac*, 40–1.
16. There was uncertainty until almost the last moment, for example, if the 5th Marine Regiment, diverted to shore up the Pusan perimeter, would be freed to join the 1st Marine Division for the landing: see USMCU, Oliver P. Smith, 200-02, https://www.usmcu.edu/Research/Marine-Corps-History-Division/Oral-History/Distinguished-Marine-Career-Interviews/. On the 5th Marines in action before Inchon see Kenneth W. Estes, *Into the Breach at Pusan: The 1st Provisional Marine Brigade in the Korean War* (Norman, OK, 2012); T. X. Hammes, *Forgotten Warriors: The 1st Provisional Marine Brigade, the Corps Ethos, and the Korean War* (Lawrence, KS, 2010).
17. Korean personnel included various civilian and ROK navy figures as well as several thousand men from the 1st Regiment, ROKMC and the ROKA 17th Regiment plus over 8,600 civilians hastily drafted into American service to bring the US Army 7th Infantry Division up to strength. Up to forty-seven vessels, mostly ex-US Navy landing ships given over to Japan after 1945 for coastal transport but taken back into service for Korea, were crewed by almost four thousand Japanese sailors. Tessa Morris-Suzuki, 'A Fire on the Other Shore? Japan and the Korean War Order', in Tessa Morris-Suzuki (ed.), *The Korean War in Asia: A Hidden History* (Lanham, MD, 2018), 18.
18. In the run-up to D-day, for example, attacks would be launched against Kunsan from the British carrier *Triumph* and a special operations raid hastily mounted from the sea. On the latter see John W. Connor, *Let Slip the Dogs of War: A Memoir of the GHQ 1st Raider Company (8245th Army Unit) a.k.a. Special Operations Company. Korea, 1950–51* (Berrington, VT, 2008), 104–9; Richard L. Kiper, *Spare Not the Brave: The Special Activities Group in Korea* (Kent, OH, 2011), 3–71.

19. On details of the development of the Inchon landing plan see Boose, *Over the Beach*, 162–9; Field, *History of United States Naval Operations: Korea*, 175–81; Lynn Montross and Nicholas A. Canzona, *U.S. Marine Corps Operations in Korea, 1590–1953*, Volume 2: *Inchon-Seoul Operation* (Washington, DC, 1955), 37–71.
20. On MacArthur appointing his chief of staff to command X Corps see MMA, RG-32, OH15, Edward M. Almond 1967 interview TS, 6–7; MMA, RG-32, OH64, Conversations between Lieutenant General Edward M. Almond and Captain Thomas C. Fergusson, 1977, TS, 29; MMA, RG-38, Box 3, Folder 3, Edward M. Almond, How Inchon was Chosen for the X Corps Amphibious Landing of 15 September, 1950, 3; MMA, RG-49, D. Clayton James, Box 11, Folder 17, Edward M. Almond 1971 interview TS, 17.
21. Douglas MacArthur, *Reminiscences* (New York, 1964), 352. MacArthur may have been trying to negate the effect of having been heard to declare earlier that 'I realize that Inchon is a 5,000 to 1 gamble, but I am used to taking such odds.' Heinl, *Victory at High Tide*, 42.
22. See Robert Smith, *MacArthur in Korea: The Naked Emperor* (New York, 1982), 78. On some of the inter-service and intra-service problems encountered in planning see e.g. National Archives and Records Administration, College Park, MD [hereafter NARA], NAID 7408495, RG 127, Smith to Cates, 7 September 1950; USMCU, Oliver P. Smith, 199–202, 204–5, 207, https://www.usmcu.edu/Portals/218/Smith%2C Oliver P_.pdf (accessed 12 May 2022); USMCU, Victor H. Krulak, 150–1, https://www.usmcu.edu/Research/Marine-Corps-History-Division/Oral-History/Distinguished-Marine-Career-Interviews/.
23. Lynn D. Smith, 'A Nickel after a Dollar', *Army* 20 (September 1970), 25.
24. MacArthur, *Reminiscences*, 353.
25. Almond would take credit for developing a study which showed that, historically, the majority of typhoons swung up toward the east coast of Korea rather than the west coast where Inchon was located. MMA, RG-49, D. Clayton James Collection, RG-49, Box 11, Folder 17, Edward M. Almond 1971 interview TS, 11. Disaster still might have struck if Rear Admiral Arleigh Burke, then deputy chief of staff, Naval Forces Far East, had not persuaded MacArthur to allow the task force to set sail a day earlier than planned from ports in southern Japan in order to avoid the worst effects of Typhoon Kezia. Hiroshi Masuda, *MacArthur in Asia: The General and His Staff in the Philippines, Japan, and Korea* (Ithaca, NY, 2012), 261–2.
26. On the prevalence of North Korean spies and lack of secrecy surrounding Chromite see e.g. James Cameron, *Point of Departure: Experiment in Biography* (London, 1967), 92–3; William J. Sebald with Russell Brines, *With MacArthur in Japan* (New York, 1965), 195.
27. O. P. Smith log quoted in Heinl, *Victory*, 120. On neutralizing the few floating mines on the approach see Arnold S. Lott, *Most Dangerous Sea: A History of Mine Warfare, and an Account of U.S. Navy Mine Warfare Operations in World War II and Korea* (Annapolis, MD, 1959), 271.

28. Heinl, *Victory at High Tide*, 90–120.
29. Ibid., 121–89; Appleman, *South to the Naktong*, 509–52.
30. Millett, *War for Korea, 1950–51*, 268–73; Taaffe, *MacArthur's Korean War Generals*, 83–6.
31. Heinl, *Victory*, 201–2.
32. Ibid., 225–51. On the advance from Inchon to Seoul see *Inchon Seoul Invasion: Headquarters X Corps: Operations Instructions: Nos 1-10: 15 Sep – 4 Oct* (U.S. Army Military History Research Collection); NARA, NAID 798007, RG 407, X Corps, War Diary Summary for Operation Chromite, 15 August to 30 September 1950, Periodic Intelligence Reports 3–9, 21–27 September 1950, Periodic Operations Reports 1–10, 19–28 September 1950. On the battle for Seoul see also Eric Setzekorn, 'The Battle for Seoul, September 1950', in Gregory Fremon-Barnes (ed.), *Urban Battlefields: Lessons Learned from World War II to the Modern Era* (Annapolis, MD, 2024), 172–96; Alec Wahlman, *Storming the City: U.S. Military Performance in Urban Warfare from World War II to Vietnam* (Denton, TX, 2015), 128–80.
33. Heinl, *Victory at High Tide*, 257–8.
34. Clay Blair, *The Forgotten War: America in Korea 1950–53* (New York, 1987), 319.
35. NARA, NAID 7384852, RG 319, General MacArthur's statement with reference to the return of the Government of the Republic of Korea to Seoul, 29 September 1950. On MacArthur planning in advance for this public ceremony see Harold Joyce Noble, *Embassy at War* (Seattle, WA, 1975), 194, 198, 203.
36. MacArthur, *Reminiscences*, 356, footnote.
37. On the Eighth Army offensive between 19 and 29 September 1950 see Appleman, *South to the Naktong*, 542–72.
38. Ibid., 607–8. The only serious caveats to MacArthur being given free rein to operate in North Korea were that that operations directed against Chinese or Russian territory were strictly forbidden and that to avoid provoking direct intervention in Korea by either communist power ROK-only troops should be deployed close to their borders with Korea. See Document 453 in *Foreign Relations of the United States, 1950, Korea, Volume VII* (Washington, 1976), 781.
39. See Collins, *War in Peacetime*, 141–2; Matthew B. Ridgway, *The Korean War* (Garden City, NY, 1967), 61–2; Taaffe, *MacArthur's Korean War Generals*, 86–91.
40. See James, *Years of MacArthur*, Volume 3, 499–500.
41. Herman, *Douglas MacArthur*, 763. The landing at Wonsan was delayed for several weeks by the need to clear sea mines protecting the harbour, so that ROKA forces had occupied the port from the landward side before the Marines finally came ashore on 25 October 1950. See e.g. Theodore L. Gatchel, *At the Water's Edge: Defending against Modern Amphibious Assault* (Annapolis, MD, 1996), 180–3; Korea Institute of Military History, *The Korean War*, Volume 1 (Lincoln, NB, 2000), 771–6.

42. If the Red Chinese did come into Korea and tried to advance southward to retake Pyongyang MacArthur remarked that 'there would be the greatest slaughter'. Substance of Statements Made at Wake Island Conference on 15 October 1950 in *Foreign Relations of the United States, 1950, Korea, Volume VII*, 953.
43. On Sino-Soviet-DPRK negotiations and Chinese preparations before and after Kim Il Sung appealed for intervention at the end of September see e.g. Shen Zhihua, *A Misunderstood Friendship: Mao Zedong, Kim Il-sung, and Sino-North Korean Relations, 1949–1976* (New York, 2018), 34–42. On the misplaced retrospective focus in the West on the actual crossing of the 38th parallel as the decisive factor see Richard B. Frank, *MacArthur* (New York, 2007), 157. On Mao's calculations concerning when to begin crossing the Yalu in force see e.g. Michael Sheng, 'Chinese Intervention', in Matray and Boose, *Ashgate Research Companion to the Korean War*, 35–70. On the 'volunteers' see Bin Yu, 'Chinese People's Volunteers Force' in Matray and Boose, *Ashgate Research Companion to the Korean War*, 269–82.
44. MacArthur to JCS, 9 November 1950, *Foreign Relations of the United States 1950: Korea, Volume VII*, 1108; see JCS to MacArthur, 8 November 1950, ibid., 1098.
45. *New York Times*, 24 November 1950, 2. On the press taking up an overheard remark by MacArthur that if all went well some Americans would be home by Christmas see Herman, *Douglas MacArthur*, 774. On friction over the bombing campaign see James, *Years of MacArthur*, Volume 3, 520–4. On erroneous estimates of CPV strength in-country see Appleman, *South to the Naktong*, 769; Bin Yu, 'Chinese People's Volunteers Force', in Matray and Boose, *Ashgate Companion to the Korean War*, 273.
46. See Roy E. Appleman, *Disaster in Korea: The Chinese Confront MacArthur* (College Station, TX, 1989). On the true ratio of opposing forces and Peng's general plan see Li Xiaobing, *Attack at Chosin: The Chinese Second Offensive in Korea* (Norman, OK, 2020), 37.
47. See Roy E. Appleman, *Escaping the Trap: The U.S. Army's X Corps in Northeast Korea, 1950* (College Station, TX, 1990); Roy E. Appleman, *East of Chosin: Entrapment and Breakout in Korea, 1950* (College Station, TX, 1987); Lynn Montross and Nicholas A. Canzona, *U.S. Marine Corps Operations in Korea, 1950–1953*, Volume 3: *The Chosin Reservoir Campaign* (Washington, DC, 1957).
48. See e.g. S. L. A. Marshall, *The River and the Gauntlet: Defeat of the Eighth Army by the Chinese Communist Forces, November 1950, in the Battle of the Chongchon River, Korea* (New York, 1953).
49. On Walker and other subordinate commanders in this period see Taaffe, *MacArthur's Korean War Generals*, 104ff.
50. See Herman, *Douglas MacArthur*, 783, 790. For 'entirely new war' see MacArthur to JCS, 28 November 1950, *Foreign Relations of the United States 1950: Korea, Volume VII*, 1237.

51. See Roy E. Appleman, *Ridgway Duels for Korea* (College Station, TX, 1990); Walter G. Hermes, *United States Army in the Korean War: Truce Tent and Fighting Front* (Washington, DC, 1966); Billy C. Mossman, *United States Army in the Korean War: Ebb and Flow, November 1950–July 1951* (Washington, DC, 1990); Li Xiaobing, *China's Battle for Korea: The 1951 Spring Offensive* (Bloomington, IN, 2014); see also Leo Barron, *High Tide in the Korean War: How an Outnumbered American Regiment Defeated the Chinese at the Battle of Chipyong-ni* (Mechanicsburg, PA, 2015); J. D. Coleman, *Wonju: The Gettysburg of the Korean War* (Washington, DC, 2000).
52. The phrase 'no substitute for victory' was used in a letter from MacArthur to a Congressional supporter, Representative Joseph Martin (R-Maine), who imprudently read it out on the House floor: see *Congressional Record—House*, Proceedings, 97, Part 3, 5 April 1951, 3380. On the resulting decision to fire MacArthur see editorial note, *Foreign Relations of the United States, 1951: Korea and China, Volume VII, Part I* (Washington, 1983), 298–301. For overviews of the deteriorating relations between Washington and Tokyo leading to MacArthur's dismissal see e.g. H. W. Brands, *The General vs. the President: MacArthur and Truman at the Brink of Nuclear War* (New York, 2016), 264–380; Matthew Moten, *Presidents and Their Generals: An American History of Command in War* (Cambridge, MA, 2014), 227–70.
53. MacArthur, *Reminiscences*, 372, 377. On this being unconvincing see e.g. Robert Leckie, *Conflict: The History of the Korean War, 1950–53* (New York, 1962), 232; Richard T. Ruetten, 'General Douglas MacArthur's "Reconnaissance in Force": The Rationalization of a Defeat in Korea', *Pacific Historical Review* 36 (1967), 79–83.
54. On the consensus concerning Chromite see Michael Pearlman, 'The Inch'ŏn Landing', in Matray and Boose, *Ashgate Research Companion to the Korean War*, 333ff.

Chapter 3

1. On the origins of the phrase see Jack Shafer, 'Who Said It First? Journalism is the "first rough draft of history"'. *Slate*, 30 August 2010, https://slate.com/news-and-politics/2010/08/on-the-trail-of-the-question-who-first-said-or-wrote-that-journalism-is-the-first-rough-draft-of-history.html (accessed 7 September 2019).
2. On the highly authoritarian DPRK under Kim Il Sung see e.g. Charles K. Armstrong, *The North Korean Revolution, 1945–1950* (Ithaca, NY, 2003); see also Sydney A. Seiler, *Kim Il-sŏng, 1941–1948: The Creation of a Legend, the Building of a Regime* (Lanham, MD, 1994); Michael J. Seth, *North Korea: A History* (London, 2018), 38–185. On the increasingly dictatorial Syngman Rhee in the ROK—and the role of the United States therein—see e.g. Gregg

Brazinsky, *Nation Building in South Korea: Koreans, Americans, and the Making of a Democracy* (Chapel Hill, NC, 2007), 14–30; Oliver Elliott, *The American Press and the Cold War: The Rise of Authoritarianism in South Korea, 1945–1954* (London, 2018).
3. See Stephen Casey, *Selling the Korean War: Propaganda, Politics, and Public Opinion in the United States, 1950–1953* (New York, 2008).
4. For a sense of the attention paid to narrative control in North Korea see e.g. Sam Bum Kim, 'The Role of the DPRK's Propaganda Office in the Korean War (1946–1953)' (MA thesis, University of Southern California, 2012).
5. Ansel E. Talbert on Pyongyang radio report, *New York Herald Tribune*, 15 September 1950, 2; *New York Daily Worker*, 15 September 1950, 3.
6. See *New York Times*, 17 September 1950, 1, 10.
7. See e.g. O Hae-yŏn *Victorious Fatherland Liberation War Museum* (Pyongyang, 2014), 60–1.
8. Hence the communist press elsewhere had to remain quiet or rely on Western reports. See e.g. AP report, Moscow, 17 September, 'Pravda Reports Inchon landing', *New York Times*, 18 September 1950, 6; Moscow, 17 September, 'Moscow Papers Keep Silent', *South China Morning Post*, 19 September 1950, 12; see also special Hong Kong report, 16 September, 'Peiping Ignores Landing', *New York Times*, 17 September 1950, 43; UP Tokyo report, 'Pyongyang Radio Silent: Communique Does Not Mention Inchon for Second Day', *New York Times*, 16 September 1950, 3; AP Tokyo Report, 19 September, 'Enemy Radio Silent on Seoul Fight', *Los Angeles Times*, 19 September 1950, 2. It is noteworthy that the Soviet ambassador in Pyongyang thought the *Pravda* editor had given aid and comfort to the enemy by publishing news of the landing based on foreign reporting and should have been arrested: see Stalin to Zakharov, 29 September 1950 in Katherine Weathersby, 'New Russian Documents on the Korean War', *Cold War International History Project Bulletin* 6-7 (Winter 1995/1996), 109.
9. AP Tokyo report, 23 September, 'Enemy Line on Landings Changed', *New York Times*, 23 September 1950, 3; AP Tokyo report, 23 September, 'Reds Admit Reverses', *New York Herald Tribune*, 24 September 1950, 5; see, with reference to similar reports in China, Masuda Hajima, *Cold War Crucible: The Korean Conflict and the Postwar World* (Cambridge, MA, 2015), 122, 325 n. 26.
10. This was also true in Moscow: see e.g. Irma Volk and Alexander Chakovsky, 'The Truth about the Interventionists' Landing', *Literaturna gazeta*, 21 September 1950, in *Current Digest of the Soviet Press*, October 1950; see also Harrison E. Salisbury, 'What Russians Are Told about the War in Korea', *New York Times*, 24 September 1950, E5; AP Moscow report, 23 September, *New York Times*, 24 September 1950, 5.
11. London AP reports, *New York Times*, 25 September 1950, 2; *New York Times*, 26 September 1950, 2; Tokyo report, *South China Morning Post*, 26 September 1950, 1, 7.

12. This shift was in turn reflected in the Moscow press. Sergei Borzenko, 'Seoul Fights', *Pravda*, 27 September 1950, in *Current Digest of the Soviet Press*, October 1950, 15–16.
13. 'Appeal by Kim Il Sung', TASS report, *Pravda* and *Isvestia*, 12 October 1950, in *Current Digest of the Soviet Press*, November 1950, 18–19. Meanwhile in Beijing the authorities were adopting a similar line concerning Inchon as Mao prepared the people for direct intervention under the premiss that the Americans were going to keep right on going northwards into China. See e.g. American Consulate General, Hong Kong, *Survey of China Mainland Press*, no. 1, November 1950, 7. On the propaganda campaign see Gary Rawnsley, '"The Great Movement to Resist America and Assist Korea": How Beijing Sold the Korean War', *Media, War & Conflict* 2, 3 (2009), 285–315.
14. Carl Mydans in *TIME*, 25 September 1950, 25.
15. On this inner press circle around MacArthur see Marguerite Higgins, *War in Korea: The Report of a Woman Combat Correspondent* (Garden City, NY, 1951), 31, 57; O. H. P. King, *Tail of the Paper Tiger* (Caldwell, ID, 1961), 384–5; Reginald Thompson, *Cry Korea* (London, 1951), 36.
16. See e.g. Sun-A Kim, 'Life and War in Korea: Photographic Portrayals of the Korean War in LIFE Magazine, July 1950–August 1953' (PhD thesis, University of Missouri, 2008), 102ff.; and on film, National Archives and Records Administration, College Park, MD [hereafter NARA], NAID 79590, RG 428, Naval Photographic Center, Aboard Mt. McKinley on "D" day, Inchon, Korea; ibid., NAID 79594–95, D-day at Inchon.
17. Casey, *Selling the Korean War*, 53–7; Michael S. Sweeney, *The Military and the Press: An Uneasy Truce* (Evanston, IL, 2006), 130. The communications problem was if anything even more acute for radio reporters than it was for print journalists. Paul M. Edwards, *The Mistaken History of the Korean War: What We Got Wrong, Then and Now* (Jefferson, NC, 2018), 96–7, 99.
18. On press knowledge of the impending landing—though not necessarily the specific target—see Mason Edward Horrell, 'Reporting the "Forgotten War": Military-Press Relations in Korea, 1950–1954' (PhD thesis, University of Kentucky, 2002), 54–5.
19. Bill Shinn, *The Forgotten War Remembered: Korea: 1950–1953: A War Correspondent's Notebook and Today's Danger in Korea* (Elizabeth, NJ, 1996), 120–5; see his byline report via AP in e.g. *Boston Globe*, 15 September 1950, 1.
20. See *Chicago Daily Tribune*, 16 September 1950, 5; *Washington Post*, 17 September 1950, M2.
21. AP report in *Los Angeles Times*, 15 September 1950, 1; see e.g. UP report in *New York Times*, 16 September 1950, 1; Ansel E. Talbert in *New York Herald Tribune*, 16 September 1950, 2; see also e.g. NARA, NAID 7384852, RG 319, UN Communique No. 3, 16 September 1950.
22. Russell Brines, *Hartford Courant*, 16 September 1950, 1.
23. Percy Wood, *Chicago Daily Tribune*, 16 September 1950, 3.

24. Ibid.; see also e.g. Philip Potter, *Baltimore Sun*, 16 September 1950, 9; Frank Robertson, *Christian Science Monitor*, 16 September 1950, 1; *New York Herald Tribune*, 16 September 1950, 2; *Manchester Guardian*, 16 September 1950, 7.
25. AP report, *New York Times*, 18 September 1950, 3; see also e.g. Reuters report, *Boston Globe*, 18 September 1950, 2; Philip Potter, *Manchester Guardian*, 18 September 1950, 5. As an unusually sardonic account of the visit put it, 'General MacArthur put on a good show, as always, for a dozen or two photographers who clustered around him.' Frank Robertson, *Christian Science Monitor*, 18 September 1950, 6.
26. *New York Times*, 21 September 1950, 5.
27. *Washington Post*, 23 September 1950, 1; *Washington Post*, 22 September 1950, 1.
28. UP in *Los Angeles Times*, 25 September 1950, 1; AP in *Washington Post*, 26 September 1950, 1.
29. 'Seoul Falls', *Boston Globe*, 26 September 1950, 1; *Los Angeles Times*, 26 September 1950, 1; see also e.g. *Baltimore Sun*, 26 September 1950, 1; *South China Morning Post*, 27 September 1950, 1.
30. *New York Herald Tribune*, 27 September 1950, 26. On holding only a third of the city on 26 September, see AP report, *Los Angeles Times*, 27 September 1950, 1. That fierce street battles were still going on did not escape the editorial team at the otherwise supportive *Chicago Tribune*, so the headline was less exultant: 'M'Arthur Announces Capture of Seoul; Yanks Fight on', *Chicago Daily Tribune*, 26 September 1950, 1; see also editorial and Homer Bigart report, *New York Herald Tribune*, 27 September 1950 1, 26.
31. See e.g. *New York Times*, 28 September 1950, 5.
32. On the stage management of the event see Thompson, *Cry Korea*, 83–9.
33. Frank Tremaine, UP, *Boston Globe*, 29 September 1950, 1; see also e.g. AP report in *Chicago Daily Tribune*, 29 September 1950, 1.
34. See e.g. *New York Times*, 30 September 1950, 1; *New York Times*, 1 October 1950, 4.
35. James Cameron, *Picture Post*, 7 October 1950, 16; see also James Cameron, *Point of Departure: Experiment in Autobiography* (London, 1967), 137.
36. The landing craft Maggie Higgins rode in on, for example, contained not only Marines but also John Davies of the *Newark Daily News* and Lionel Crane of the *Daily Express*. Higgins, *War in Korea*, 141. They only went in with last Red Beach wave at the insistence of 5th Marines regimental commander, Ray Murray: see USMCU, Raymond L. Murray interview TS, 203, https://www.usmcu.edu/Research/Marine-Corps-History-Division/Oral-History/Distinguished-Marine-Career-Interviews/. On Higgins see Jennet Conant, *Fierce Ambition: The Life and Legend of War Correspondent Maggie Higgins* (New York, 2023).
37. Frank Gibney, *TIME*, 25 September 1950, 29–30.
38. Harold Levine, *Newsweek*, 25 September 1950, 25.
39. Larry Keighley, *Saturday Evening Post*, 21 October 1950, 157.

40. Marguerite Higgins report in *New York Herald Tribune*, 18 September 1950, 1, 4; see also John Shaw, *Daily Express*, 17 September 1950, 1. On this story and the problems writing it up and sending it see Higgins, *War in Korea*, 139–50. On Higgins in Korea see also Keyes Beech, *Tokyo and Points East* (Garden City, NY, 1954), 167–83.
41. This was also the media experience on Blue Beach: see e.g. Charles Jones and Eugene Jones, *The Face of War* (New York, 1951), 74.
42. William D. Blair, Jr., *Baltimore Sun*, 19 September 1950, FF1. There had been brisk firefights reported on the road to Kimpo: see e.g. Joseph Alsop, *New York Herald Tribune*, 20 September 1950, 25.
43. Don Whitehead, *Los Angeles Times*, 21 September 1950, 2; see also Keyes Beech, *Boston Globe*, 21 September 1950, 4; Marguerite Higgins, *New York Herald Tribune*, 21 September 1950, 1–2.
44. Marguerite Higgins, *New York Herald Tribune*, 21 September 1950, 2; see also Tom Lambert, *Los Angeles Times*, 25 September 1950. Another crossing on 24 September was less contested. See Don Whitehead, *Baltimore Sun*, 25 September 1950, 2.
45. *New York Times*, 18 September 1950, 3; *New York Times*, 22 September 1950, 6; *New York Herald Tribune*, 22 September 1950, 2. On earlier correspondent casualties see Philip Knightly, *The First Casualty: The War Correspondent as Hero and Myth-Maker from the Crimea to Iraq* (Baltimore, MD, 2004), 369–70.
46. Michael James, *New York Times*, 22 September 1950, 4.
47. Marguerite Higgins, *New York Herald Tribune*, 23 September 1950, 2; see also e.g. Homer Bigart, *New York Herald Tribune*, 22 September 1950, 1–2.
48. See e.g. W. H. Lawrence, *New York Times*, 24 September 1950, 11; Homer Bigart, *New York Herald Tribune*, 24 September 1950, 1–2; Philip Potter, *Baltimore Sun*, 24 September 1950, 1.
49. Marguerite Higgins, *New York Herald Tribune*, 25 September 1950, 3.
50. Don Whitehead (AP), *Los Angeles Times*, 27 September 1950, 2; *Austin Statesman*, 26 September 1950, 1.
51. Homer Bigart, *New York Herald Tribune*, 27 September 1950, 41; see also Max Desfor, 'The Korean War through the Camera of an American War Correspondent', in Philip West and Suh Ji-moon (eds), *Remembering the "Forgotten War": The Korean War through Literature and Art* (Armonk, NY, 2001), 80–1; David Douglas Duncan, 'The City', in *This Is War! A Photo-Narrative of the Korean War* (Boston, MA, 1990); Jones and Jones, *Face of War*, 90–7.
52. Michael James, *New York Times*, 28 September 1950, 5.
53. Marguerite Higgins, *New York Herald Tribune*, 27 September 1950, 3.
54. On the Korea-phobic racism of some American correspondents, mirroring that of American servicemen, see Thompson, *Cry Korea*, 39. For the charge of self-censorship by American reporters see Knightly, *First Casualty*, 389.
55. Higgins, *War in Korea*, 165; see e.g. on whitewashing the behaviour of ROK security forces, Higgins, *Boston Globe*, 18 September 1950, 11. Higgins tended

to portray ordinary Korean civilians as inherently anti-communist and pro-American: see e.g. *New York Herald Tribune*, 18 September 1950, 3; *New York Herald Tribune*, 19 September 1950, 1.
56. Elliott, *American Press*, 142 n. 30. Compare Thompson, *Cry Korea*, passim, with his reports in *Daily Telegraph*, 16 September 1950, 1, 6; *Daily Telegraph*, 21 September 1950, 1; *Daily Telegraph*, 28 September 1950, 1, 6; *Daily Telegraph*, 29 September 1950, 1. On at least some American correspondents being willing to report on atrocities committed by friendly forces see Elliott, *American Press*, 127.
57. Various reports, for instance, repeated an assurance to this effect from a South Korean admiral and stressed that while the US Navy had sought to 'concentrate on the Red gun positions' during the bombardment, the fact that 'the guns were all over the hilly peninsula on which the city is built' meant that two-thirds of the city was blasted or burned to the ground. *South China Morning Post*, 17 September 1950, 1. On the South Korean admiral's assurance that 'the people are happy you are here' see also Frank Goldsworthy, *South China Morning Post*, 19 September 1950, 12.
58. Relman Morin, *South China Morning Post*, 17 September 1950, 5; see also e.g. Imperial War Museums, 11245/7, Frank Goldsworthy; MacArthur quoted in Frank Goldsworthy, *Want You Soonest ...: Memoirs of a War Reporter* (Pittsburgh, PA, 1997), 79.
59. James Cameron, *Picture Post*, 7 October 1950, 17; see also Bert Hardy in 'There Is No Substitute for Victory' episode of television documentary *Korea: The Unknown War* (Thames Television, 1988).
60. Relman Morin, *St. Louis Post-Dispatch*, 23 September 1950, 2.
61. Marguerite Higgins, *Washington Post*, 25 September 1950, 3.
62. Don Whitehead, *Austin Statesman*, 26 September 1950, 1.
63. *Chicago Daily Tribune*, 26 September 1950, 1; see also Frank Tremaine for UP in *Boston Globe*, 26 September 1950, 1.
64. Tom Lambert, *St. Louis Post-Dispatch*, 27 September 1950, 2; *New York Times*, 27 September 1950, 5; see also Rutherford M. Poats, *Decision in Korea: An Authentic History of the Korean War* (New York, 1954), 68; Desfor, 'Korean War', 81–2.
65. Quoted in *Boston Globe*, 29 September 1950, 4; see also, by way of corroboration, the silent crowds mentioned in Thompson, *Cry Korea*, 85.
66. See 'What They Are Saying: Broadcast Comments on the Inchon Landing', *The Listener*, 21 September 1950, 368. On the positive attitude of American reporters at the time see e.g. Relman Morin, *A Reporter Reports* (New York, 1960), 11.
67. 'Inchon Landing: First Pictures', *British Pathé News*, 25 September 1950; for the USA listen to e.g. the 15-minute report, using audio recordings he himself had made on the scene as Wolmi-do was being secured—see Robert D. Taplett, *Darkhorse Six: A Memoir of the Korean War, 1950–1951* (Williamstown, NJ, 2002), 116—by Ensign Jack Siegal, USN, broadcast by

Ed Murrow on CBS radio in America a month after the landing. US Marine Landing at Wolmi Do (Inchon) Korea 1950, YouTube, https://www.youtube.com/watch?v=CRNPQoC8V-0 (accessed 29 September 2018); Korean War Educator, American Notables Who Served in the Military during the Korean War, Jack L. Siegal entry, http://www.koreanwar-educator.org/topics/p_american_notables.htm (accessed 29 September 2018).
68. Michael Davidson, *Observer*, 17 September 1950, 1; see also e.g. *Le Monde* 15 September 1950 as reported in *New York Times*, 16 September 1950, 4; *Times of India*, 20 September 1950, 6; *Life*, 2 October 1950, 23; *Hsing Tao Jih Pao*, 17 September 1950, quoted in American Consulate General, *Review of the Hong Kong Chinese Press*, No. 177/50, 17–18 September 1950, 1; *Zuay Shang Jih Pao*, 19 September 1950 quoted in ibid., no. 178/50, 19 September 1950; and, more cautiously, Hanson Baldwin, *New York Times*, 24 September 1950, E5; editorial, *New York Times*, 25 September 1950, 22; editorial, *The Times*, 25 September 1950, 5; editorial, *Washington Post*, 26 September 1950, 10.
69. *Newsweek*, 9 October 1950, 26. On Inchon as a gamble see e.g. editorial, *Washington Post*, 18 September 1950, 6; Hanson Baldwin, *New York Times*, 21 September 1950, 3.
70. Edwards, *Mistaken History*, 95.

Chapter 4

1. In China, for example, entry into the Korean War was portrayed in terms of defending the homeland from imperialist attack and aiding a weaker socialist regime; see Anon. (ed.), *Eight Years of the Chinese People's Volunteers Resistance to American Aggression and Aiding Korea* (Beijing, 1958); see also Institute of Military History Research, Academy of Military Science (comp.), *War to Resist US Aggression and Aid Korea*, Volume 1 (Beijing, 2020).
2. On Western official histories and their aims see Jeffrey Grey (ed.), *The Last Word? Essays on Official History in the United States and British Commonwealth* (Westport, CT, 2003); Robin Higham (ed.), *The Writing of Official Military History* (Westport, CT, 1999); Robin Higham (ed.), *Official Histories: Essays and Bibliographies from around the World* (Manhattan, KS, 1970). Though British and Commonwealth warships participated in the Inchon operation—either as part of the bombardment or the covering forces—the relevant official histories did not overstate the significance of Royal Australian Navy, Royal Canadian Navy, Royal Navy, and Royal New Zealand Navy involvement in Chromite: see Anthony Farrar-Hockley, *The British Part in the Korean War*, Volume 1 (London, 1990), 150–7; Ian McGibbon, *New Zealand and the Korean War*, Volume 2 (Auckland, 1996), 24; Robert O'Neill, *Australia in the Korean War, 1959–53*, Volume 2: *Combat Operations* (Canberra, 1985), 423; Thor Thorgrimsson, *Canadian Naval Operations in Korean Waters, 1950–1955* (Ottawa, 1965), 17.

3. See Robert F. Futrell, *The United States Air Force in Korea, 1950–1953* (New York, 1961).
4. On army objections to the way in which the press was portraying the American soldier in Korea see Steven Casey, *Selling the Korean War: Propaganda, Politics, and Public Opinion in the United States, 1950–1953* (New York, 2008), 53–5, 149–50.
5. See e.g. with reference to the USMC, Lemuel C. Shepherd, Jr., preface to Lynn Montross and Nicholas A. Canzona, *U.S. Marine Operations in Korea, 1950–1953*, Volume 2: *Inchon-Seoul Operation* (Washington, DC, 1955), iii. Both the USN and USMC sought to generate positive public opinion through sponsoring semi-official as well as official histories. The former included, for the USN, Walter Karig, Malcolm W. Cagle, and Frank A. Manson, *Battle Report: The War in Korea* (New York, 1952), and Malcolm W. Cagle and Frank M. Manson, *The Sea War in Korea* (Annapolis, MD, 1957), as well as for the USMC Andrew Geer's *The New Breed: The Story of the U.S. Marines in Korea* (New York, 1952). On USMC publicity efforts in general see Aaron B. O'Connell, *Underdogs: The Making of the Modern Marine Corps* (Cambridge, MA, 2012), 144; see also Robert George Lindsay, *This High Name: Public Relations and the U.S. Marine Corps* (Madison, WI, 1956). On the budgetary and power struggles of the latter 1940s see Keith D. McFarlane and David L. Roll, *Louis Johnson and the Arming of America: The Roosevelt and Truman Years* (Bloomington, IN, 2005), 168–204, as well as Jeffrey G. Barlow, *Revolt of the Admirals: The Fight for Naval Aviation, 1945–1950* (Washington, DC, 1998) and Gordon W. Keiser, *The US Marine Corps and Defense Unification, 1944–47: Politics of Survival* (Washington, DC, 1982).
6. Canzona had won the Silver Star for 'superb leadership, courage and unrelenting devotion to duty in the face of grave peril' in December 1950: see Korean War Educator, Silver Star Citations submitted to KWE, Names Starting with 'C', http://www.koreanwar-educator.org/topics/silver_star/p_silver_star_citations_c.htm (accessed 19 October 2019). Employed as a writer by the USMC, Montross had among other things written an article praising the achievement at Inchon for the corps's professional journal—see Lynn Montross, 'The Inchon Landing: Victory over Time and Tide', *Marine Corps Gazette* 35, 7 (1951), 26–35—and would go on to write a popular account of the corps, *The United States Marines: A Pictorial History* (New York, 1959).
7. Lemuel C. Shepherd, Jr., foreword to Montross and Canzona, *U.S. Marine Operations in Korea*, Volume 2, iii; see also Allen G. Mainard, review in *Leatherneck*, May 1956, 68.
8. *Journal of the Royal United Service Institution*, 1 February 1956, 631; *Hartford Courant*, 1 July 1956; *Atlanta Constitution*, 22 July 1956.
9. E. M. Eller, foreword and author preface to James A. Field, Jr., *History of United States Naval Operations: Korea* (Washington, DC, 1962), vi–vii, x. More

than one reviewer echoed the idea that it was not an official history (see *Pacific Affairs* 36, 2 [1963], 187; *Philadelphia Inquirer*, 17 October 1962), but others recognized that it was indeed a de facto official account (*International Affairs* 39 [1963], 276; *Pacific Historical Review* 32 [1963], 336).

10. Field, *United States Naval Operations*, 219; see ibid., 171–218.
11. Stephen Roskill, *International Affairs* 39 (1963), 276–7; see also e.g. Richard D. Challenger, *Journal of Modern History* 35 (1963), 336.
12. Paolo E. Coletta, *Pacific Historical Review* 32 (1963), 336–7.
13. Louis Morton, *Mississippi Valley Historical Review* 50 (1963), 151–2.
14. F. C. Jones, *Pacific Affairs* 36, 2 (1963), 188.
15. See Casey, *Selling the Korean War*, 53, 149 ff.
16. When Major Edwin H. Simmons, USMC, was asked in 1958 to write the entry on amphibious warfare for the *Encyclopaedia Britannica*, he decided to leave out the Inchon landing, in which he had participated, because it broke every rule in the book for a successful amphibious operation. MacArthur, shown a draft, was incensed that his masterstroke had been excluded and recommended that the piece be rejected. Only after Simmons had included positive references to Inchon was the entry accepted. Geoffrey Perret, *Old Soldiers Never Die: The Life of Douglas MacArthur* (New York, 1996), 581, 650 n. 39.
17. Author preface to Roy E. Appleman, *United States Army in the Korean War: South to the Naktong, North to the Yalu (June–November 1950)* (Washington, DC, 1961), viii–ix. On the work of US Army combat historians in Korea see Kathryn Roe Coker and Jason Wetzel, *The U.S. Army Combat Historian and Combat History Operations* (Philadelphia, PA, 2023), 103–19.
18. National Archives and Records Administration, College Park, MD [hereafter NARA], NAID 2529125, RG 319, Douglas MacArthur to Richard W. Stephens, 15 November 1957, et al.; see Appleman, *South to the Naktong*, 544–5.
19. United States Army Heritage Education Center [hereafter USAHEC], Roy Appleman Papers, Correspondence from Edward M. Almond to Roy Appleman regrading Chapters XVII and XIII, Almond to Appleman, 15 December 1953, 2. Almond approved of the final product: see MMA, RG-38, Almond Papers, Box 4, Folder 4, Almond to Appleman, 10 October 1975.
20. On the drafting process see NARA, NAID 2385511, RG 319, Background Files to the Study 'North to the Naktong, South to the Yalu, 1951–1961'.
21. S. L. A. Marshall, *New York Times*, 10 September 1961.
22. Riley Sunderland, *Military Affairs* 26 (1962), 34–5.
23. Michael Howard, *Pacific Affairs* 35 (1962), 68; Theodore Ropp, *Mississippi Valley Historical Review* 48 (1962), 740.
24. MacArthur was dead, but Ned Almond remained very much alive and kicking, and was not shy in submitting a detailed critique of the draft submitted to him for review: see USAHEC, Roy Appleman Collection [also MMA, RG-38, Almond Papers, Box 4, Folder 3], Correspondence from Edward Almond to Hal C. Pattison regarding 'Policy and Direction:

The First Year', Almond to Pattison, 7 March 1969, encl. detailed review dated 20 February 1969.
25. James F. Schnabel, *United States Army in the Korean War: Policy and Direction: The First Year* (Washington, DC, 1972), viii.
26. Ibid., 139–72. See NARA, NAID 239848, RG 319, Background Files to 'U.S. Army in the Korean War. Policy and Direction: The First Year', 1951–1972.
27. Robert R. Simmons, *Pacific Historical Review* 42 (1973), 598.
28. Theodore Ropp, *Journal of American History* 61 (1974), 843. Fading interest was even more evident with the relevant volume in the official history of the office of the secretary of defence published in the following decade—Doris M. Condit, *History of the Office of the Secretary of Defense*, Volume 2: *The Test of War, 1950–1953* (Washington, DC, 1988)—though the single academic review was generally positive: see *Journal of American History* 77, 3 (1990), 1091.
29. See e.g. Roy E. Appleman, *United States Army in the Korean War: South to the Naktong, North to the Yalu (June–November 1950)* (Washington, DC, 1992).
30. Joseph H. Alexander, *Fleet Operations in a Mobile War: September 1950–June 1951* (Washington, DC, 2001), 10–24; James A. Field, 'History of United States Naval Operations: Korea', Washington, DC, 2000, https://www.history.navy.mil/research/library/online-reading-room/title-list-alphabetically/h/history-us-naval-operations-korea.html (accessed 10 September 2024).
31. Joseph H. Alexander, *Battle of the Barricades: U.S. Marines in the Recapture of Seoul*, Marines in the Korean War Commemorative Series (Washington, DC, 2000), 65; Edwin H. Simmons, *Over the Seawall: U.S. Marines at Inchon*, Marines in the Korean War Commemorative Series (Washington, DC, 2000), 69.
32. Keith F. Kopets, *Journal of Military History* 65 (2001), 561.
33. See Jae-Cheon Lim, *Leader Symbols and Personality Cult in North Korea: The Leader State* (London, 2015), 79–103; Leonid Petrov, 'Turning Historians into Party Scholar-Bureaucrats: North Korean Historiography from 1955–1958', *East Asian History* 31 (June 2007), 101–19. On the impossibility of unauthorized composition and publication in North Korea see e.g. Jang Jin-sung, *Dear Leader: North Korea's Senior Propagandist Exposes Shocking Truths behind the Regime* (London, 2014), 4.
34. The Great Leader had helped establish the official line through publication of his wartime speeches soon after the armistice: Kim Il Sung, *The Just Fatherland Liberation War of the Korean People for Freedom and Independence* (Pyongyang, 1955). See, on the immediate postwar years, Sanghun Cho, 'Memory as Propaganda: The Molding of Official Memory of the Korean War and Its Employment in the DPRK from 1953 to 1958' (MA thesis, University of Toronto, 2007); see also Chosŏn Rondongang Ch'ulp'ansa, *Cha-ju Toknip eul wihan Chosun In-min ui Cho-kuk Hae-bang Cheon-Chaeng* (Pyongyang, 1959). This line would continue to be propagated into the twenty-first century: see e.g. Jim-min Kang in Daniel Tudor, *Ask a North Korean* (Tokyo, 2017), 124; John Everard, *Only Beautiful, Please: A British*

NOTES

Diplomat in North Korea (Stanford, CA, 2012), 87. Everything from diplomatic histories to school textbooks and children's literature were affected: see e.g. Ho Jong Ho, Kang Sok Hui, and Pak Thae Ho, *The U.S. Imperialists Started the Korean War* (Pyongyang, 1977/1993); Hyok Kang, *This Is Paradise! My North Korean Childhood* (London, 2005), 51; Andrei Lankov, *North of the DMZ: Essays on Daily Life in North Korea* (Jefferson, NC, 2007), 47; Dafna Zur, 'Textual and Visual Representations of the Korean War in North and South Korean Children's Literature', in Rüdiger Frank, Jim Hoare, Patrick Köllner, and Susan Pares (eds), *Korea 2010: Politics, Economy and Society*, Volume 4: *Korea Yearbook* (Leiden, 2010), 287–91.

35. See Sonia Ryang, *Reading North Korea: An Ethnological Enquiry* (Cambridge, MA, 2012), 92–3. This perspective was in line with the interpretation developed in North Korean media after Inchon (see e.g. *Rodong Sinmun*, 11 June 1951), and had been publicly articulated by the Great Leader himself (see Speech at a Consultative Meeting of Provincial Party Committee Chairmen, 27 September 1950, in *Kim Il Sung: Works*, Volume 6 [Pyongyang, 1981], 107–8; Radio Address to the entire Korean People, 26 June 1950, in Kim, *Just Fatherland Liberation War*, 70). It was replicated often, including in illustrative (see e.g. Nicholas Bonner with Simon Cockerell and James Banfill, *Printed in North Korea: The Art of Everyday Life in North Korea* [London, 2019], 220) and literary form (see 1952 short story by Hwang Gon, 'The Island in Flames', in *Korean Short Stories* [Pyongyang, 1966], 5–28; on which see Brian Myers, *Han Sŏrya and North Korean Literature: The Failure of Socialist Realism in the DPRK* [Ithaca, NY, 1994], 81; Alexandra Leonzini and Peter Moody, 'From MacArthur's Landing to Trump's Fire and Fury: Sonic Depictions of Struggle and Sacrifice in a North Korean Short Story, Film and Opera', *Korean Studies* 44 [2022], 80–2).
36. See Dae-Sook Suh, *Kim Il Sung: The North Korean Leader* (New York, 1988), 92, 93, 99, 129, 130–4. On the purges see also Lim, *Leader Symbols*, 22.
37. Research Institute of History, Academy of Sciences of the Democratic People's Republic of Korea, *History of the Just Fatherland Liberation War of the Korean People* (Pyongyang, 1961), 98–9.
38. Ibid., 101.
39. Ibid., 102.
40. Ibid., 112, 108.
41. Though a comparison was avoided by Pyongyang for obvious reasons, North Korean representations of the defence of Wolmi-do were strikingly analogous to American representations of the siege of the Alamo.
42. See e.g. Korean People's Army, *The Heroic KPA, the Invincible Revolutionary Armed Forces* (Pyongyang, 1990), 7; Baik Bong, *Kim Il Sung Biography*, Volume 2: *From Building Democratic Korea to Chullima Fight* (Beirut, 1973), 308–11.
43. Kang Sŏkhŭi, *Chosŏn inmin ŭi chŏngŭi ŭi choguk haebang chŏnjaengsa*, Volume 2 (Pyongyang, 1983), 6–8. Communist accusations of large-scale Japanese

participation, first made during the war, were exaggerated but, with regard to landing vessels at Inchon and later, not completely groundless: see Tessa Morris-Suzuki, 'Post-War Warriors: Japanese Combatants in the Korean War', *Asia-Pacific Journal: Japan Focus* 10, 31 (2012), 1–19; ibid., 'A Fire on the Other Shore? Japan and the Korean War Order', in Tessa Morris-Suzuki, *The Korean War in Asia* (Lanham, MD, 2018), 7–38; see also Reinhard Drifte, 'Japan's Involvement in the Korean War', in James Cotton and Ian Neary (eds), *The Korean War in History* (Atlantic Highlands, NJ, 1989), 129–30; Kazuki Fujiwara, *Han'guk chŏnjaeng esŏ ssaun Ilbonin: ilgŭp pimil konggae ro tŭrŏnan Ilbonin ŭi Han'guk chŏnjaeng ch'amjŏn kirok* (Seoul, 2023). The role at Inchon of the Japanese in American and South Korean official histories was not mentioned at all or only in passing (see Appleman, *South to the Naktong, North to the Yalu*, 501; Chŏnjaeng kinyŏm saŏphoe, *Han'guk chŏnjaengsa kwŏn* 6 [Seoul, 1992], 47) due to a mix of South Korean sensitivities regarding their former colonial overlords and the fact that Japan was supposed to have renounced war and have no armed forces according to the 1947 constitution.

44. Kang Sŏkhŭi, *Chosŏn inmin ŭi chŏngŭi ŭi choguk haebang chŏnjaengsa* 2, 11; see also e.g. Ron Yok Min, *Outstanding Leadership and Brilliant Victory* (Pyongyang, 1993), 32–3; Pak Song Min, 'Loving Memories of Wartime Heroes', Pyongyang Times, 28 July 2008, https://kcnawatch.org/periodicals/pyongyangtimes/ (accessed 23 June 2023).

45. On censorship within the official ROK History Compilation Committee with regard to the Korean War see e.g. Bruce Cumings, *The Origins of the Korean War: Volume II* (Princeton, NJ, 1990), 884 n. 70. On wider ROK censorship see e.g. Yun Sik Hwang, 'Nationalism in Crisis: The Reconstruction of South Korean Nationalism in Korean History Textbooks' (MA thesis, University of Toronto, 2016); Dorian Lange, 'The Republic of Korea's Public Libraries: A Critical Examination of Censorship Practices' (PhD thesis, University of Missouri, 2013); Youngju Ryu, *Writers of the Winter Republic: Literature and Resistance in Park Chung Hee's Korea* (Honolulu, 2015); Kyo Ho Youm, 'Freedom of the Press in South Korea, 1945–1983: A Sociopolitical and Legal Perspective' (PhD thesis, University of Southern Illinois, 1985).

46. See Allan R. Millett, 'The Korean War: A 50-Year Critical Historiography', *Journal of Strategic Studies* 24 (2001), 196, 204–5.

47. Yukkun sagwan hakkyo, *Han'guk chŏnjaengsa* (Seoul, 1959), 175; see also 177, 181. The ROKMC published work around this time in which Inchon was chronicled as a great victory. See Haebyŏngdae Saryŏngbu, *Haebyŏng palchŏnsa: haebyŏng sibinyŏnsa: cha 1949, 04, 15 chi 1960, 12, 31* (Seoul, 1961), 87–133; Haebyŏngdae Saryŏngbu, *Haebyŏngdae chŏnt'usa* (Seoul, 1962), 31–46; ROK Marine Corps, *Marine Album for 10th Foundation Anniversary* (Seoul, 1959). On the militantly anti-communist and pro-MacArthur views of Syngman Rhee and his regime see e.g. Henry Chung, *Korea and the United States through War and Peace, 1943–1960* (Seoul, 2000).

48. These included a pair of Korean-language volumes from 1967 and 1968 that were later revised and merged into a single volume in the mid-1970s (see preface to Kukpangbu p'yŏnch'an wiwŏnhoe, *Han'guk chŏnjaengsa*, Volume 1 [Seoul, 1977]) as part of an eleven-volume set published one volume at a time out of chronological order throughout the 1970s (Kukpangbu p'yŏnch'an wiwŏnhoe, *Han'guk chŏnjaengsa*, Volumes 1–11 [Seoul, 1970–80]), as well as a six-volume English-language set chronicling the activities of UN forces (War History Compilation Committee, *The History of the United Nations Forces in the Korean War*, Volumes 1–6 [Seoul, 1972–77]).
49. Preface and foreword to Kukpangbu p'yŏnch'an wiwŏnhoe, *Han'guk chŏnjaengsa*, Volume 3 (Seoul, 1970). On tensions and crises in Korea in an international context during the 1960s see e.g. Sheila Miyoshi Jager, *Brothers at War: The Unending Conflict in Korea* (New York, 2013), 365–89.
50. See e.g. Il-Song Park, 'Republic of Korea Army', in James I. Matray and Ronald W. Boose, Jr. (eds), *The Ashgate Research Companion to the Korean War* (Farnham, 2014), 242; see also, on the origin of the War Compilation Committee, Mun Hui Sok, 'War History in Korea', in Higham, *Official Histories*, 294–5. Even in 1972, Kim Il Sung publicly made little effort to conceal his position that 'peaceful' reunification would mean the South being politically subsumed by the North. See e.g. Takagi Takeo, *Kim Il Sung: Master of Leadership* (Pyongyang, 1976), 197.
51. Foreword by Yu Gae Hung (Minister of Defense) to War History Compilation Committee, *The History of the United Nations Forces in the Korean War*, Volume 1 (Seoul, 1972). On the brief tactical 'thaw' in inter-Korean relations see e.g. Don Oberdorfer and Robert Carlin, *The Two Koreas: A Contemporary History* (New York, 2014), 9–13, 18–25, 35–6, 47.
52. Kukpangbu p'yŏnch'an wiwŏnhoe, *Han'guk chŏnjaengsa*, Volume 3 (Seoul, 1970), 618.
53. See ibid., 690.
54. War History Compilation Committee, *The History of the United Nations Forces in the Korean War*, Volume 1 (Seoul, 1972), 108. Chromite had been described shortly after the war as 'brilliant' in an ROK Army history aimed at wartime allies: Office of Information, *Republic of Korea Army*, Volume 1 (Seoul, 1954), 69; see also Chung Il-kwon foreword, ibid., 4.
55. Um Sub Il, foreword to Korea Institute of Military History, *The Korean War*, Volume 1 (Lincoln, NB, 2000); see also Allan R. Millett, introduction, ibid., x–xii.
56. On mixed American reviews of the three-volume translated version of *The Korean War* see e.g. John H. Barnhill in *Air Power History* 49, 4 (2002), 61–2; James Matray in *Journal of Asia Studies* 62 (2003), 643–5; Kenneth P. Werrell in *Aerospace Power Journal* 15, 4 (2001), 104.
57. Chŏnjaeng kinyŏm saŏphoe, *Han'guk chŏnjaengsa kwŏn*, Volume 1 (Seoul, 1992), 265; see also ibid., Volume 4, 500.

58. Ibid., Volume 1, 274. The ROKMC, meanwhile, continued to celebrate Inchon in lavish golden jubilee and seventieth-anniversary history volumes: see Haebyŏngdae, *Haebyŏngdae chŏnu 70-yŏnsa*, Volume 1 (Seoul, 2019), 42–9; Haebyŏndae Saryŏngbu, *Sajin ŭro pon haebyŏndae 50-yŏnsa, 1949–1999* (Seoul, 1999), ch. 2; see also along these lines Kim Chae-yŏp, *Taehan Min'guk Haebyŏngdae: segye esŏ kajang kanginham kundae ŭi chopko* (Seoul, 2009), ch. 3.

Chapter 5

1. Hence no participant observations but rather an historical account in a collection of otherwise first-person heroic narratives: Kim Do Yung, 'Heroes of Wolmi Island', in *They Fought for the Fatherland* (Pyongyang, 1963), 151–8. There does exist, in fact, one extant and remarkably frank account by a former KPA political officer, Chang Hak-pong, who was present in Inchon during Operation Chromite, but it was written as part of a collection created after the fall of the Soviet Union of recollections by Russian-trained North Koreans who had managed to return to the USSR before they were purged by Kim Il Sung: see Fyodor Tertitskiy, *The Forgotten Political Elites of North Korea: Woe to the Vanquished* (London, 2024), 74–81.
2. Though there was some South Korean service involvement: see e.g. Sŏk Chŏng-nae, *Pobyŏngdŭl: K'at'usa 6.25 ch'amjŏn hoegorok* (Taegu, 2014).
3. On the comparative lack of, and lower popular profile of, memoirs, novels, and other participant literature for the Korean War as compared to the Second World War and Vietnam see Bruce Cumings, *The Korean War: A History* (New York, 2010), 67; see also William D. Ehrhart, 'Above All, the Waste', in Philip West and Suh Ji-moon (eds), *Remembering the "Forgotten War": The Korean War through Literature and Art* (Armonk, NY, 2001), 40–1. The combatant memoirs that do exist tend to be by former US Marines who focus on experiences later in the year: see Emilio Aguirre, *We'll Be Home for Christmas: A True Story of the United States Marine Corps in the Korean War* (New York, 1959); Morgan Brainard, *Men in Low Cut Shoes: A Marine Rifle Company in Korea, 1950–1951* (Great Neck, NY, 1986); Jesse A. Hand, *The Change Is Forever: Memories, 1931–2022* (Middleton, DE, 2022); Joseph R. Owen, *Colder Than Hell: A Marine Rifle Company at Chosin Reservoir* (Annapolis, MD, 1996); Robert D. Taplett, *Darkhorse Six: A Memoir of the Korean War, 1950–1951* (Williamstown, NJ, 2002). There have been, in addition, versions of personal experiences in the Inchon–Seoul campaign published in semi-fictionalized form: see e.g. Eugene Franklin Clark, *The Secrets of Inchon: The Untold Story of the Most Daring Covert Mission of the Korean War* (New York, 2002) and Edwin Howard Simmons, *Dog Company Six* (Annapolis, MD, 2000). For different forms of fictionalized participant memoir see e.g. James Edwin Alexander, *Inchon to Wonsan: From the Deck of a Destroyer in the Korean War* (Annapolis, MD, 1996),

xiv; Bill Quigley, *Passage through A Hell of Fire and Ice: Korea... The First Five Months: A Marine Epic* (New York, 2015), viii–ix. A further alternative to the first-person participant memoir was the authorized popular biography, where opinions could also be expressed at one remove with any resulting ruffled feathers blamed on the author rather that the subject. Thus, for example, Burke Davis, *Marine! The Life of Lt. Gen. Lewis B. (Chesty) Puller, USMC (Ret.)* (Boston, MA, 1962), on which see Jon T. Hoffman, *Chesty: The Story of Lieutenant General Lewis B. Puller, USMC* (New York, 2001), x–xii. Participant interviews could also be woven into a collective narrative: see e.g. Oscar E. Gilbert, *Marine Corps Tank Battles in Korea* (Havertown, PA, 2003); Patrick K. O'Donnell, *Give Me Tomorrow: The Korean War's Greatest Untold Story—The Epic Stand of the Marines of George Company* (Cambridge, MA, 2010).

4. See Chapter 6.
5. See Kim Il Sung, *Reminiscences*, 1–6 (Pyongyang, 1992–5). Two further volumes were published posthumously, but these only extended the story down to 1945. The original plan had been for a total of thirty volumes: see Kim Il Sung's reminiscences distributed worldwide, Korean Central News Agency, 8 July 1994, http://www.kcna.co.jp/item/2002/200207/news07/08.htm (accessed 18 March 2022). According to a former propaganda cadre member, Kim's memoirs were in fact the product of a top-tier writers' group: see Jang Jin-sung, *Dear Leader: North Korea's Senior Propagandist Exposes Shocking Truths behind the Regime* (London, 2014), 4–5. In the 1980s the published recollections of generals involved in China's military intervention towards the end of 1950 supported the general party line that the American drive to the Yalu was a threat to the nation that had to be confronted (see e.g. Peng Duhai, *Memoirs of a Chinese Marshal* [Beijing, 1984], 473), but might also mention that Mao in August had anticipated the American counterstrike at Inchon that preceded it (see e.g. Nie Rongzhen in Xiobing Li, Allan R. Millett, and Bin Yu [trans. and eds], *Mao's Generals Remember the Korean War* [Lawrence, KS, 1991], 40).
6. Syngman Rhee was not informed about Operation Chromite until after the landing had taken place, though he seems to have guessed what was afoot. See Harold Joyce Noble, *Embassy at War* (Seattle, 1975), 193, 308 n. 3; Bruce Cumings, *The Origins of the Korean War*, Volume 2 (Princeton, NJ, 1990), 896 n. 115. The commandant of the ROKMC was not briefed until two days before the landing and had to sign a pledge of secrecy. Shin Hyun-joon, *Memoirs of an Old Marine* (Chesapeake, VA, 2020), 80.
7. MacArthur, for example, only became truly interested in promoting his case in print in response to news that Harry Truman was soon to publish his memoirs. Geoffrey Perret, *Old Soldiers Never Die: The Life of Douglas MacArthur* (New York, 1996), 580.
8. Trade publishers were above all interested in hearing from MacArthur himself, though promises of huge advances initially failed to entice him. Ibid., 579.

9. See ibid., 580; *Chicago Daily Tribune*, 24 Oct 1954, G12.
10. Charles A. Willoughby and John Chamberlain, *MacArthur: 1941–1951* (New York, 1954), 376, 364–75; see David A. Foy, *Loyalty First: The Life and Times of Charles A. Willoughby, MacArthur's Chief Intelligence Officer* (Philadelphia, PA, 2023), 202.
11. Hanson Baldwin in *New York Times*, 3 October 1954, BR1, 22–3. For more positive responses see e.g. Walter Simmons in *Chicago Daily Tribune*, 3 October 1954, O3.
12. Gordon Prange, *Washington Post*, 3 October 1954, B7.
13. Courtney Whitney, *MacArthur: His Rendezvous with History* (New York, 1956), vii. On MacArthur dictating much of the contents see Perret, *Old Soldiers*, 580.
14. Whitney, *MacArthur*, 350.
15. Ibid., 358.
16. *New York Times*, 22 January 1956, 224; see also e.g. Robert R. Kirsch, *Los Angeles Times*, 24 January 1956, A5.
17. *Chicago Daily Tribune*, 22 January 1956, G1.
18. Howard Handleman in *Washington Post*, 22 January 1956, A8. On the Whitney book becoming a bestseller see Perret, *Old Soldiers*, 580.
19. Harry S. Truman *Memoirs, Volume 2: Years of Trial and Hope* (Garden City, NY, 1956), 360; Whitney, *MacArthur*, 365. Press reviews of *Years of Trial and Hope*, though by no means uncritical of the former president overall, tended to be more sympathetic to Truman than to MacArthur. See e.g. *New York Times*, 4 March 1956, BR1, 39; *Chicago Daily Tribune*, 14 March 1956, I1; *Washington Post*, 4 March 1956, E1.
20. Douglas MacArthur, *Reminiscences* (New York, 1964), v. On the decision to write his own memoirs and the process involved see Perret, *Old Soldiers*, 581; Arthur Herman, *Douglas MacArthur: American Warrior* (New York, 2016), 840–1; D. Clayton James, *The Years of MacArthur*, Volume 3 (Boston, MA, 1985), 670. It is worth noting that MacArthur eight years earlier had already made a more limited but similarly adamant attempt at making his case directly on the page when he had agreed to provide a rebuttal to Truman's version of events in Korea in the pages of *LIFE* magazine. See *LIFE*, 13 February 1956, 95–6, 101–8; see also *New York Times*, 9 February 1956, 25.
21. MacArthur, *Reminiscences*, v.
22. See Hanson Baldwin, *New York Times*, 27 September 1964, BR1; *New York Times*, 3 October 1954, BR1; *New York Times*, 22 January 1956, 224. On the similarities with the Whitney book in particular see Herman, *Douglas MacArthur*, 840.
23. 'In writing this book in his old age', a not altogether unsympathetic Orville Prescott observed, 'the lordly warrior and majestic proconsul found no cause for regret, remembered no occasions of self-doubt.' *New York Times*, 28 September 1964, 27. Even a more pro-MacArthur reviewer, after agreeing

that Inchon was his 'military masterpiece', noted that the 'seriousness of the defeat sustained by the forces under his command in North Korea is somewhat glossed over'. William Henry Chamberlin, *Wall Street Journal*, 15 October 1964, 12.
24. MacArthur, *Reminiscences*, 336, 334.
25. Ibid., 350.
26. Ibid., 353.
27. Ibid., 353–5.
28. Ibid., 348–53, 334–5.
29. See *Chicago Tribune*, 22 November 1964, 20.
30. George Marshall died in 1959; Omar Bradley retired in 1953; Lawton Collins retired in 1956.
31. J. Lawton Collins, *War in Peacetime: The History and Lessons of Korea* (Boston, MA, 1969),129, 125, 126.
32. Ibid., 141–2.
33. See J. Lawton Collins, *Lightning Joe: An Autobiography* (Baton Rouge, LA, 1979), 367.
34. See Matthew B. Ridgway as told to Harold H. Martin, *Soldier: The Memoirs of Matthew B. Ridgway* (New York, 1956), 192–3.
35. Matthew B. Ridgway, *The Korean War* (Garden City, NJ, 1967), 38.
36. Ibid., 42; see also ibid., 42–76, 142.
37. Omar Bradley and Clay Blair, *A General's Life* (New York, 1983), 556, 544, 547.
38. Ibid., 567.
39. Victor H. Krulak, *First to Fight: An Inside View of the U.S. Marine Corps* (Annapolis, MD, 1984). On this storied USMC officer see Robert Coram, *Brute: The Life of Victor Krulak, U.S. Marine* (New York, 2010). It is worth noting that, while MacArthur remained alive, Krulak was careful not to cross him, writing to the general that 'had it not been for your personal genius, vision and resolution, there would have been no Inchon'. MacArthur Memorial Archive, MacArthur Papers, RG-10, Box 6, Folder 59, Krulak to MacArthur, 22 February 1958.
40. Krulak, *First to Fight*, 125–6.
41. See ibid., 120–9.
42. Ibid., 130–1.
43. Ibid., 131–2.
44. Ibid., 133.
45. Ibid., 133–5.
46. Ibid., 137.
47. Ibid.
48. Ibid., 138.
49. See e.g. the published positive recollections of mid-level and junior members of MacArthur's staff: William W. Quinn, *Buffalo Bill Remembers: Truth and Courage* (Fowlerville, MI, 1991), 274–5; Lynn D. Smith, 'A Nickel after a

Dollar', *Army* 20 (September 1970), 24–34. MacArthur had died in 1964; Whitney in 1969; Willoughby in 1972; and Almond in 1979.
50. Arthur W. Radford, *From Pearl Harbor to Vietnam* (Stanford, CA, 1980), 231, 235.
51. Alexander M. Haig, Jr. *Inner Circles: How America Changed the World: A Memoir* (New York, 1992), 25.
52. Ibid., 36.
53. Ibid., 37.
54. Edward L. Rowny, 'Intelligence Failures and the Political Objectives of the War', in Daniel J. Meador (ed.), *The Korean War in Retrospect: Lessons for the Future* (Lanham, MD, 1998), 163.
55. Edward L. Rowny, *An American Soldier's Saga of the Korean War* (Washington, DC, 2013). This book was in essence a substantial excerpt from a longer autobiographical work published later that year under the title *Smokey Joe and the General* (Washington, DC, 2013).
56. Rowny, *American Soldier's Saga*, 9.
57. Ibid., 17.
58. Ibid., 19.
59. See ibid., 21–3.

Chapter 6

1. See e.g. William Manchester, *American Caesar: Douglas MacArthur, 1880–1964* (Boston, MA, 1978); D. Clayton James, *The Years of MacArthur*, Volume 3 (Boston, MA, 1985); Geoffrey Perret, *Old Soldiers Never Die: The Life of Douglas MacArthur* (New York, 1996); Yi Sang-ho, *Maegadŏ Han'guk chŏnjaeng* (Seoul, 2012). Even his most sympathetic recent biographers have conceded that MacArthur occasionally made errors, something that the general himself would never admit: see Richard B. Frank, *MacArthur* (New York, 2007); Arthur Herman, *Douglas MacArthur: American Warrior* (New York, 2016).
2. D. Clayton James with Anne Sharp Wells, *Refighting the Last War: Command and Crisis in Korea, 1950–1953* (New York, 1993), 49; for 'courage' see also T. R. Fehrenbach, *This Kind of War: A Study in Unpreparedness* (New York, 1963), 244; for 'outstanding' see John Toland, *In Mortal Combat: Korea, 1950–1953* (New York, 1991), 7 and Edward L. Daily, *MacArthur's X Corps in Korea: Inchon to the Yalu, 1950* (Paducah, KY, 1999), 15; for 'masterstroke' see Max Hastings, *The Korean War* (London, 1987), 116; for 'without parallel' see Brian Catchpole, *The Korean War, 1950–53* (New York, 2000), 51; for 'twentieth-century Cannae' see David Rees, *Korea: The Limited War* (London, 1964), 96; see also e.g. Bevin Alexander, *Korea: The First War We Lost* (New York, 1986), 149; Joseph C. Goulden, *Korea: The Untold Story of the War* (New York, 1982), 232; Michael Hickey, *The Korean War: The West Confronts Communism, 1950–1953* (Woodstock,

NY, 2000), 16; Burton I. Kaufman, *The Korean War: Challenges in Crisis, Credibility, and Command* (Philadelphia, PA, 1986), 81–2; Gavin Long, *MacArthur as Military Commander* (London, 1969), 209; Callum A. MacDonald, *Korea: The War before Vietnam* (New York, 1986), 208–9; Robert L. O'Connell, *Team America: Patton, MacArthur, Marshall, Eisenhower, and the World They Forged* (New York, 2022), 397–8; Yi Sŏnho, 'Inch'ŏn sangnyuk chakchŏn simch'ŭng punsŏk p'yŏngga', *Anbo nontan* 2, 6 (2007), 142.

3. David Halberstam, *The Coldest Winter: America and the Korean War* (New York, 2007), 293. Or as an otherwise fairly sceptical biographer put it, 'on one day of his long life—September 15, 1950, at Inchon—he proved himself to be a military genius'. Perret, *Old Soldiers*, 587. See also e.g. Edwin Simmons interview, 3 February 1997, George Washington University, https://nsarchive2.gwu.edu/coldwar/interviews/episode-5/simmons2.html (accessed 10 May 2022). For a rare recent dissent on Inchon as the general's finest hour see James Ellman, *MacArthur Reconsidered: General Douglas MacArthur as a Wartime Commander* (Essex, CT, 2023), 177–89.
4. Walt Sheldon, *Hell or High Water: MacArthur's Landing at Inchon* (New York, 1968), 38; for 'brave' see Michael Langley, *Inchon: MacArthur's Last Triumph* (London, 1979), 21; see also e.g. Bill Sloan, *The Darkest Summer: Pusan and Inchon 1950: The Battles That Saved South Korea—and the Marines—from Extinction* (New York, 2009), 167, 251; Earle Rice, Jr., *Korea 1950: Pusan to Chosin* (Philadelphia, PA, 2004), 67, 79; Gerry Van Tonder, *Inchon Landing: MacArthur's Korean War Masterstroke September 1950* (Barnsley, 2019).
5. H. Pat Tomlinson, 'Inchon: The General's Decision', *Military Review* 47, 4 (1967), 34. This piece was reproduced in William M. Leary (ed.), *MacArthur and the American Century: A Reader* (Lincoln, NB, 2001), 345–51.
6. Robert Debs Heinl, Jr., *Victory at High Tide: The Inchon-Seoul Campaign* (Philadelphia, PA, 1968), 267.
7. James F. Totten, 'Operation Chromite: A Study in Generalship', *Armor* 85 (November/December 1976), 38.
8. Clark G. Reynolds, 'MacArthur as Maritime Strategist', *Naval War College Review* 33, 2 (1980), 86.
9. Bruce R. Pirnie, 'The Inchon Landing: How Great Was the Risk?', *Joint Perspectives* 3, 1 (1982), 95.
10. Wilson A. Heefner, 'The Inch'on Landing', *Military Review*, 75, 2 (1995), 76.
11. John R. Ballard, 'Operation Chromite: Counterattack at Inchon', *JFQ: Joint Force Quarterly* 28 (2001), 36.
12. Jeffrey A. Bradford, 'MacArthur, Inchon and the Art of Battle Command', *Military Review* 81, 2 (2001), 86.
13. Russel H. S. Stolfi, 'A Critique of Pure Success: Inchon Revisited, Revised, and Contrasted', *Journal of Military History* 68, 2 (2004), 505–6.
14. Jim Dorschner, 'Douglas MacArthur's Last Triumph', *Military Historian* 22, 6 (2005), 36.

15. See e.g. Bevin Alexander, *MacArthur's War: The Flawed Genius Who Challenged the American Political System* (New York, 2013), 99; John D. Caldwell, *Anatomy of Victory: Why the United States Triumphed in World War II, Fought to a Stalemate in Korea, Lost in Vietnam, and Failed in Iraq* (Lanham, MD, 2019), 191–9; Tony R. Mullis, 'MacArthur', in James H. Willbanks, *Generals of the Army: Marshall, MacArthur, Eisenhower, Arnold, Bradley* (Lexington, KY, 2013), 99–100; Curtis A. Utz, 'Assault from the Sea: The Amphibious Landing at Inchon', in Edward J. Marolda (ed.), *The U.S. Navy in the Korean War* (Annapolis, MD, 2007), 52–109; see also Pascal Vennesson and Amanda Huan, 'The General's Intuition', *Armed Forces and Society* 44 (2018), 498–520; Kim Sŏngu and Kim Yonghyŏn, *Han'guk chŏnjaengsa* (Seoul, 2008), 127–49; Yi Sŏnho, 'Inch'ŏn sangnyuk chakchŏn simch'ŭng punsŏk p'yŏngga', *Anbo nontan* 2, 6 (2007), 119–47; Yu Mijŏng, 'T'ŭkchip kihoek: 6.25 chŏnjaeng 62 chunyŏn: Inch'ŏn sangnyuk chakchŏn 1-Maekadŏ ŭi sinnyŏm i iruŏnaen sŏnggŏng', *Voice of America*, 25 June 2012.
16. To cite what may have been the earliest published example, Commander Malcolm M. Cagle, USN, though he lauded the Inchon landing in other contexts, in an article for a professional journal published within six months of the armistice cautioned that the huge risks involved meant that Operation Chromite ought *not* be considered an exemplary case study of how to properly mount an amphibious attack. See 'Inchon: The Analysis of a Gamble', *U.S. Naval Institute Proceedings* 80, 1 (1954), 47–51.
17. Don McB. Curtis, 'Inchon Insight', *Army* 35, 7 (July 1985), 6.
18. Stanley L. Falk, 'Comments on Reynolds: "MacArthur as Maritime Strategist"', *Naval War College Review* 33, 2 (1980), 96–7.
19. Karl G. Larew, 'Inchon Invasion: Not a Stroke of Genius or Even Necessary', *Army* 38 (December 1988), 15.
20. Ibid. This piece was reproduced in Leary, *MacArthur in the American Century*, 152–6.
21. On his career see D. Clayton James, Goodreads, https://www.goodreads.com/author/show/222143.D_Clayton_James (accessed 22 April 2022).
22. James with Wells, *Refighting the Last War*, 178.
23. On positive responses see Indiana University Press, Truman and MacArthur, https://iupress.org/9780253350664/truman-and-macarthur/ (accessed 22 April 2022).
24. Michael D. Pearlman, *Truman and MacArthur* (Bloomington, IN, 2008), 102.
25. Ibid., 106.
26. Allan R. Millett, *The War For Korea, 1950–1951: They Came from the North* (Lawrence, KS, 2010), 240.
27. See Herman, *Douglas MacArthur*, 845, 847.
28. Inchon Landing, Encyclopaedia Britannica, https://www.britannica.com/event/Inchon-landing (accessed 24 April 2022); see also e.g. Battle of Inchon, Wikipedia, https://en.wikipedia.org/wiki/Battle_of_Inchon (accessed 24 April 2022).

29. There were in fact a variety of such contingency plans for a landing at Inchon dating back to the Second World War (see Sheldon, *Hell or High Water*, 102–3 n. 7; Stanley Weintraub, *MacArthur's War: Korea and the Undoing of an American Hero* [New York, 2000], 106–7), and the initial planning in Tokyo for a landing at Inchon—the abortive Operation Bluehearts—began as early as 2 July (see Donald W. Boose, Jr., *Over the Beach: US Army Amphibious Operations in the Korean War* [Fort Leavenworth, KS, 2008], 119). As a leading revisionist historian of Korea in this period has noted, the idea that the Pentagon 'specialized in clairvoyance' to the extent of producing a prewar contingency plan that exactly met MacArthur's requirements in light of how the first months of the war unfolded strains credulity. See Bruce Cumings, *The Origins of the Korean War*, Volume 2 (Princeton, NJ, 1990), 615.
30. As one otherwise hostile biographer conceded, the results 'did show his brilliance'. Robert Smith, *MacArthur in Korea: The Naked Emperor* (New York, 1982), 70.
31. On the mine danger and stored mines at Inchon see Arthur D. Struble, *The Reminiscences of Admiral Arthur D. Struble U.S. Navy (Retired)* (Annapolis, MD, 2011), 382–3.
32. On MacArthur's personal lack of security discipline concerning Chromite see Vernon A. Walters, *Silent Missions* (Garden City, NY, 1978), 197. On the prevalence of enemy spies in Tokyo see e.g. William J. Sebald with Russell Brines, *With MacArthur in Japan* (New York, 1965), 196. On Chinese awareness of landing preparations see Institute of Military History Research, Academy of Military Science (comp.), *The War to Resist US Aggression and Aid Korea*, Volume 1 (Beijing, 2020), 207 n. 1. On the Chinese warning and Kim Il Sung's contrary assessment see ibid., 208; Chen Jian, *China's Road to the Korean War: The Making of the Sino-American Confrontation* (New York, 1994), 147–9; Shen Zhihua, *Mao, Stalin and the Korean War: Trilateral Communist Relations in the 1950s* (London, 2012), 137, 143; Lim Ŭn, *The Founding of a Dynasty in North Korea: An Authentic Biography of Kim Il-sŏng* (Tokyo, 1982), 188; Cho Sanggŭn. 'Han'guk chŏnjaeng esŏ Chunggong chidobu ŭi Inch'ŏn sangnyuk chakchŏn yech'ŭk kwajŏng', *Kunsa* 71 (2009), 55–80. On the other hand Kim had indicated at least some awareness of the dangers of an American amphibious landing in conversation with the Soviet ambassador as far back as early July: see Shtykov to Stalin, 4 July 1950, quoted in Kathryn Weathersby, 'New Russian Documents on the Korean War', *Cold War International History Project Bulletin* 6/7 (Winter 1995/6), 43. At least some local KPA commanders, moreover, were on the alert for a landing at Inchon in the days preceding Chromite: see Robert M. Collins, 'Korean People's Army', in James I. Matray and Donald W. Boose, Jr. (eds), *The Ashgate Research Companion to the Korean War* (Farnham, 2014), 262; Cumings, *Origins*, Volume 2, 663. The KPA units present at Inchon when Operation Chromite

began were, nonetheless, understrength and woefully unprepared: see Chang Ka-pong testimony in Fyodor Tertitskiy, *The Forgotten Political Elites of North Korea: Woe to the Vanquished* (London, 2024), 77.

33. Signals intelligence suggested a North Korean force around Pusan on the brink of collapse. See Matthew M. Aid, *The Secret Sentry: The Untold History of the National Security Agency* (New York, 2009), 28.
34. While there can be no doubt that the apparent reversal of fortune engendered by the Inchon–Seoul campaign made everyone in Washington just as eager to cross the 38th parallel as MacArthur himself, there is evidence to suggest that while Mao was keen to enter the fray weeks before Chromite, the Inchon–Seoul campaign may have actually caused him temporarily to pause sending Chinese forces across the Yalu for fear that they would be defeated: see Michael Sheng, 'Chinese Intervention', in Matray and Boose, *Ashgate Companion*, 361, 363–7. It certainly shocked him and changed the calculus regarding sending in help: see Chen Jian, *China's Road*, 158ff. Moreover, it is worth noting that there is strong evidence that the Truman administration had decided on the strategic goal of unifying Korea before the Inchon landing had taken place: see James I. Matray, 'Truman's Plan for Victory: National Self-Determination and the Thirty-Eighth Parallel Decision in Korea', *Journal of American History* 66 (1979), 325–9.
35. Arthur Herman, for example, opened his MacArthur biography with a rendering of the dramatic meeting of 23 August: see Herman, *Douglas MacArthur*, prologue. It is noteworthy that a US Special Operations Command historian who took the critiques of MacArthur and Inchon seriously published his interpretative history of the war with an academic rather than a trade press. See Stanley Sandler, *The Korean War: No Victors, No Vanquished* (Lexington, KY, 1999), 92–3.
36. Even the general's most recent sympathetic major biographer agreed that Wonsan had been a 'classic SNAFU' (albeit in his view one 'very unusual for MacArthur') and wrote in respect to the Chinese response to the general's final offensive that 'MacArthur's strategy lay in ruins, almost overnight.' Herman, *Douglas MacArthur*, 777, 756.
37. For actual use of the term in reference to MacArthur see e.g. Dean Acheson, *Present at the Creation: My Years in the State Department* (New York, 1969), 448; Alistair Horne, *Hubris: The Tragedy of War in the Twentieth Century* (New York, 2015), 281–311; Rees, *Korea*, 175.
38. See e.g. Alexander, *Korea*, 149, 154; Halberstam, *Coldest Winter*, 293; Matthew B. Ridgway, *The Korean War* (Garden City, NY, 1967), 61, 76–7; Han'guk yŏksa yŏn'guhoe, *Yŏksahak sisŏn ŭro ingnŭn Han'guk chŏnjaeng* (Seoul, 2010), 231–2.
39. Stephen R. Taaffe, *MacArthur's Korean War Generals* (Lawrence, KS, 2016), 92; see also e.g. Clay Blair, *The Forgotten War: America in Korea 1950–1953* (New York, 1987), 464; Perret, *Old Soldiers*, 566.
40. Edwin H. Simmons, quoted in Halberstam, *Coldest Winter*, 307.

41. Compare the two biographies of Smith (Clifton La Bree, *The Gentle Warrior: General Oliver Prince Smith, USMC* [Kent, OH, 2001] and Gail B. Shisler, *For Country and Corps: The Life of General Oliver P. Smith* [Annapolis, MD, 2009]) with that of Almond (Michael E. Lynch, *Edward M. Almond and the US Army: From the 92nd Infantry Division to the X Corps* [Lexington, KY, 2019]).
42. Almond, as well as being interviewed and contributing notes, was invited to comment on the book draft and did so (see Sheldon, *Hell or High Water*, 58 n. 1, 122 n. 12; see also MacArthur Memorial Archive [hereafter MMA], RG-38, Almond Papers, Box 4, Folder 5, Almond to Sheldon, 10 April 1967). Smith, though not interviewed, was also invited to comment on the book draft and did so (see Sheldon, *Hell or High Water*, 103 n. 17): but only a single comment therefrom was quoted in the book as against multiple citations—quotes and paraphrasing—referencing the Almond interview (see ibid., 21, 39, 85, 102–3, 183, 251, 276, 313, 329).
43. Ibid., 101–2.
44. See ibid., 137–8, 152–3.
45. Ibid., 24; see also e.g. ibid. 263.
46. Ibid., 302.
47. Ibid., 304.
48. Ibid., 314 n. 19; see ibid., 310–11.
49. Ibid., 101–2.
50. On his sources see Heinl, *Victory*, ix–xiv. Heinl did, it should be noted, correspond extensively with Almond. See ibid., xiv; MMA, RG-38, Almond Papers, Box 4, Folder 5, Almond to Hilldrup, 18 March 1968.
51. Heinl, *Victory*, 44, 273 n. 46.
52. Ibid., 45, 274 n. 48.
53. Ibid., 61; see also 72–3.
54. Ibid., 62–3.
55. Ibid., 211.
56. Ibid. In a letter to Heinl, Almond denied that he gave Smith any ultimatum (despite having given an official historian and Sheldon that same impression) and Smith too did not record or recall anything he would describe as such. Yet interviews with both Roy Appleman and subsequently Walt Sheldon made it clear to them that this is what Almond's stated intentions amounted to. See ibid., 286 n. 22; Sheldon, *Hell or High Water*, 302.
57. Heinl, *Victory*, 213. In what was perhaps an illustration of an interviewee giving the answer the interviewee thinks the interviewer wants to hear, Dave Barr, the 7th Division commander, who was present at the conference on the 24th, told Sheldon that 'he did not notice any particular sparks flying between the two commanders' (Sheldon, *Hell or High Water*, 303) but informed Heinl that 'Smith just hit the ceiling' (Heinl, *Victory*, 213, 286 n. 26).
58. See ibid., 261.
59. See ibid., 231–9.

60. Ibid., xiv, 54. See also MMA, RG-38, Box 4, Folder 5, Almond to Childs, 25 March 1968. Heinl was blunt in a private letter to Smith: in his view Almond had shown himself to be 'vain, arbitrary, cavalier, and injudicious'. Heinl to Smith, 28 December 1966, quoted in Shisler, *For Country and Corps*, 156.
61. See Heinl, *Victory at High Tide*, 36.
62. See e.g. Boose, *Over the Beach*, 161; Donald Chisolm, 'Negotiated Joint Command Relationships: Korean War Amphibious Operations, 1950', *Naval War College Review* 53, 2 (2000), 84–5; Taaffe, *MacArthur's Generals*, 70. Some observers have argued that the two generals shared blame for not making a greater effort to get along: see e.g. Shelby L. Stanton, *America's Tenth Legion: X Corps in Korea, 1950* (Novato, CA, 1989), 113.
63. See e.g. Halberstam, *Coldest Winter*, 160–3, 167, 207, 297, 302, 303, 308–11, 546–7. Almond tended to blame his men's race rather than assuming any personal responsibility for setbacks while and after leading the ill-starred 93rd Infantry Division (Colored) during the Second World War. For a careful scholarly portrait that places Almond in the context of his times see Lynch, *Edward M. Almond and the U.S. Army*.

Chapter 7

1. In the West early works included US Army film documentaries such as *Operation Inchon* (National Archives and Records Administration, College Park, MD [hereafter NARA], NAID 4523057, RG 330, US Army Misc. 7883, 1951)—on which see also MacArthur Memorial Archive, RG 10, Box 1, Folder 8, Almond to MacArthur, 15 July 1952—and episodes in the US Army television documentary series *The Big Picture* (see NARA, NAID 2569440-2569441, RG 111, Series 1 Episode 2, 'Turning of the Tide' and Series 1 Episode 3, 'The United Nations Offensive'). On *The Big Picture* see Jeffrey Crean, 'Something to Compete with "Gunsmoke"', *War & Society* 35, 3 (2016), 204–16; John W. Lemza, *The Big Picture: The Cold War on the Small Screen* (Lawrence, KS, 2021). Later television documentaries often either more or less echoed the established line on the war—e.g. *Korea: The Forgotten War* (prod. Lou Reda, 1987); *Battle for Korea* (prod. Dave Flitton *et al.*, 2001), on which see Suhi Choi, 'The New History and the Old Present: Archival Images in PBS Documentary *Battle for Korea*', *Media, Culture & Society* 31, 1 (2009), 67—or took a more sceptical approach—e.g. *Korea: The Unknown War* (dir. Mike Dormer *et al.*, 1988), on which see Bruce Cumings, *War and Television* (London, 1992); *Korea: The Unfinished War* (dir. Brian McKenna, 1993), on which see e.g. *Montreal Gazette*, 8 November 2003, D1; *Korea: The Never-Ending War* (prod. John Maggio, 2019), on which see PBS, Korea: The Never-Ending War, https://www.pbs.org/weta/korea-never-ending-war/ (accessed 20 August 2022). In the communist world documentary records

of the war took the standard communist line on unprovoked imperialist aggression on the Korean peninsula. See e.g. the various versions of *Choguk haebang chŏjaeng: Chŏson kirok yŏnghua* in https://www.worldcat.org (accessed 17 January 2022); on which see also KRT: The Fatherland Liberation War, AP Archive, www.aparchive.com (accessed 17 January 2022). Documentaries produced in the People's Republic of China on the Korean War followed a roughly similar line, especially in the 1950s. See Hauzhi Qin, 'A Floating History: The Korean War and China's Political Use of War Memory' (MA thesis, Georgetown University, 2020), 24.
2. See Lawrence H. Suid, 'Hollywood, the Marines, and the Korean War', *Marine Corps Gazette* 86, 3 (2002), 41–4.
3. The title came from an alleged remark made by the commander of the 1st Marine Division, Oliver P. Smith, who was reported to have said in response to a question concerning the withdrawal: 'Retreat, Hell! We're just advancing in another direction.' *TIME*, 18 December 1950, 26. Smith, characteristically, denied having used a swear word. Gail B. Shisler, *For Country and Corps: The Life of General Oliver P. Smith* (Annapolis, MD, 2009), 266. This campaign would become the single most storied event in the history of the corps in Korea, as multiple popular history titles over the decades attest: see e.g. Eric Hammel, *Chosin: Heroic Ordeal of the Korean War* (New York, 1981); William B. Hopkins, *One Bugle, No Drums: The Marines at Chosin Reservoir* (Chapel Hill, NC, 1986).
4. *Retreat, Hell!* earned $2 million in domestic rentals in the course of 1952: *Variety*, 7 January 1953, 61. On criticism of the film as formulaic see e.g. *Austin Statesman*, 16 February 1952, 8; *Boston Globe*, 7 March 1952, 26; *Christian Science Monitor*, 7 March 1952, 5; *New York Times*, 20 February 1952, 26; *Washington Post*, 22 February 1952, F18.
5. See Paul M. Edwards, *A Guide to Films on the Korean War* (Westport, CT, 1997); Robert J. Lentz, *Korean War Filmography* (Jefferson, NC, 2003): see also Cortland Rankin, 'Forgettable Tales of a Forgotten War: Narrative, Memory, and the Erasure of the Korean War in American Cinema', *Journal of Popular Film and Television* 50, 4 (2022), 178–95.
6. Hence the television play *Collision Course*, broadcast on the American Broadcasting Company network at the start of January 1976, about the conflict between Truman (played by E. G. Marshall) and MacArthur (played by Henry Fonda): see *Variety*, 22 September 1976, 46. For reviews see e.g. *Boston Globe*, 2 January 1976, 27; *Christian Science Monitor*, 2 January 1976, 22; *Los Angeles Times*, 3 January 1976, B5.
7. See Gary Fishgall, *Gregory Peck: A Biography* (New York, 2002), 293; *Los Angeles Times*, 20 February 1976, E11.
8. Inchon was one of the few things about MacArthur that scriptwriter Hal Barwood knew about before he and Matthew Robbins began researching their subject. AP story, *Austin American Statesman*, 28 August 1974, 41.

9. In reality, Truman did not ask Marshall about Chromite when inviting him to be Secretary of Defense: see Forrest C. Pogue, *George C. Marshall: Statesman, 1945–1959* (New York, 1987), 422.
10. This scene involving MacArthur's dark night of the soul was clearly based on Whitney's account of a conversation with the general aboard the *Mount McKinley*; though according to Whitney this took place in MacArthur's cabin rather than on the bridge.
11. AP story, *Austin American Statesman*, 28 August 1974, 41.
12. The resulting compromises left nobody happy: see Fishgall, *Gregory Peck*, 293–6; Lynn Hanley, *Gregory Peck: A Charmed Life* (New York, 2004), 370; Lawrence H. Suid, *Guts and Glory: The Making of the American Military Image in Film* (Lexington, KY, 2002), 306–10. One thing most everyone agreed on was that Universal detrimentally pared the budget, so that planned location shooting could not take place and left *MacArthur* with a distinctly back-lot look.
13. *Washington Post*, 1 July 1977, B1.
14. See e.g. *Austin American Statesman*, 10 August 1977, C10; *Hartford Courant*, 21 August 1977, 2G; *Los Angeles Times*, 24 July 1977, O9; *New York Times*, 1 July 1977, 47; *Newsweek*, 4 July 1977, 77; *Variety*, 29 June 1977, 26; see also *Boxoffice*, 17 October 1977, 11. For more mixed or negative assessments of the film see e.g. *Boston Globe*, 4 August 1977, 37; *Philadelphia Inquirer*, 7 August 1977, L1; *TIME*, 4 July 1977, 54.
15. Fishgall, *Gregory Peck*, 298; *Austin American Statesman*, 10 August 1977, C10.
16. For exposés of questionable Unification Church activity in the United States see Robert Boettcher, *Gifts of Deceit: Sun Myung Moon, Tongsun Park, and the Korean Scandal* (New York, 1980); John Gorenfeld, *Bad Moon Rising: How Reverend Moon Created The Washington Times, Seduced the Religious Right, and Built an American Kingdom* (Sausalito, CA, 2008).
17. See e.g. *Washington Post*, 13 April 1997, G7; Michael Sauter, *The Worst Movies of All Time, or What Were They Thinking?* (New York, 1999), 197.
18. On the motives of Sun Myung Moon see his speech on *Inchon* as reported in *Korea Times*, 9 October 1982, 1.
19. *Korea Times*, 1 March 1978, 5; *Boxoffice*, 6 March 1978, 13; *Variety*, 29 March 1978, 6; *Screen International*, 8 April 1978, 10.
20. *Korea Times*, Tuesday, 8 May 1979, 5; *Los Angeles Times*, 16 May 1982, 1; Stephen B. Armstrong, *Andrew V. McLaglen: The Life and Hollywood Career* (Jefferson, NC, 2011), 23.
21. Meanwhile, Ben Gazzara was paid $750,000 and Richard Roundtree $200,000. *Los Angeles Times*, 16 May 1982, 1; see also Terry Coleman, *Olivier* (New York, 2005), 423. Terence Young apparently also billed the production for lavish entertainment expenses: see Ben Gazzara, *In the Moment: My Life as an Actor* (New York, 2004), 195. On location shoot extravagance see also e.g. *Chosŏn ilbo* 14 September 1979.

22. See *New York Times*, 13 August 1979, C13; *Variety*, 26 September 1979, 43; Gazzara, *In the Moment*, 201–2. Omar Sharif was advertised as a cast member, but—perhaps because his asking price was too high given money already spent—did not in fact take part. See *Hollywood Reporter*, 28 June 1978, 7; *Variety*, 25 July 1979, 46. Italian actor Gabriele Ferzetti played the commander of the Turkish brigade instead. Korean actress Yun Mi-ra, meanwhile, had to be replaced by Karen Kahn due to an adultery case she became embroiled in and problems with her English. See *Korea Times*, 22 June 1979, 8, 13 July 1979, 5, 10 February 1980, 5; *Variety*, 26 September 1979, 43. The original story by Hall Moore was script-doctored by Laird Koenig and Barry Backerman. See *Variety*, 26 September 1979, 43.
23. Coleman, *Olivier*, 423; *Korea Times*, 29 May 1980, 5. For cost estimates see e.g. *Korea Times*, 19 May 1982, 5, 23 September 1982, 5; *Los Angeles Times*, 16 May 1982, 26–7. On infighting see e.g. *Kyŏnghyang sinmun*, 22 February 1981.
24. For comments by Robin Moore on writing for *Inchon* see *Boston Globe*, 17 September 1982, 23.
25. Compare the scenes covering the 23 August 1950 planning meeting in *Inchon* with e.g. Douglas MacArthur, *Reminiscences* (New York, 1964), 347–50.
26. It is strongly implied that the power of prayer on the part of MacArthur prevented disaster at Inchon, and the penultimate scene of the film shows the general—as played by Olivier—reciting the Lord's Prayer in thanks. On Unification Church ideology and the film see Kim Namhyŏk, 'Han'guk chŏnjaeng yŏnghwa *Inch'ŏn* e t'uyŏngdoen pangong chuŭi wa T'ongilgyo ŭi inyŏm', *Hyŏndae yŏnghwa yŏn'gu* 30 (2018), 113–42.
27. Coleman, *Olivier*, 423; *Observer*, 5 July 1981, 2.
28. See e.g. *Washington Post*, 22 April 1981, B1, 5 May 1981, B1. On the political bribery scandal see Boettcher with Freedman, *Gifts of Deceit*.
29. See *Washington Post*, 5 May 1981, B1; Brigham Young University, *Inchon: Love, Destiny, Heroes* motion picture brochure, 42; David L. Robb, *Operation Hollywood: How the Pentagon Shapes and Censors the Movies* (Amherst, NY, 2004), 267–70.
30. *Washington Post*, 5 May 1981, B1.
31. *Variety*, 6 May 1981, 20.
32. *Washington Post*, 5 May 1981, B1; *Variety*, 6 May 1981, 20; *Boxoffice*, 1 June 1981, 28.
33. *Variety*, 12 May 1982, 35, 15 September 1982, 12; *Korea Times*, 19 May 1982, 5; *Los Angeles Times*, 16 May 1982, 26.
34. *Pittsburgh Post-Gazette*, 20 September 1982, 14; *Philadelphia Inquirer*, 20 September 1982, 6D; *Minneapolis Star and Tribune*, 24 September 1982, 16C; *Hartford Courant*, 22 September 1982, C3; *Chicago Tribune*, 20 September 1982, B7; *Boston Globe*, 18 September 1982, 8; *Baltimore Sun*, 20 September 1982, B1; *Atlanta Constitution*, 17 September 1982, 6B.
35. See e.g. *Atlanta Constitution*, 17 September 1982, 6B; *Boxoffice*, 1 December 1982, 116–18; *Globe and Mail* [Toronto], 21 September 1982, 13; *Nation*, 16

October 1982, 380; *New York Times*, 17 September 1982, C9; *Philadelphia Inquirer*, 20 September 1982, 1D, 6D; *Washington Post*, 17 September 1982, Style Section D1, Weekend supplement, 13. Some critics, it must be noted, actually thought Olivier did a good job: see *Boston Globe*, 18 September 1982, 8; *Chicago Tribune*, 20 September 1982, B7; *Hartford Courant*, 22 September 1982, C3; *Women's Wear Daily*, 16 September 1982, 20. Olivier seems to have taken literally the opinion of a former MacArthur aide that the general sounded like W. C. Fields: see Harry Medved and Michael Medved, *The Hollywood Hall of Shame: The Most Expensive Flops in Movie History* (London, 1984), 192.
36. See e.g. *Detroit Free Press*, 17 September 1982, 3C. There were, it should be noted, also one or two more or less positive reviews: see e.g. *Los Angeles Times*, 16 May 1982, 1; *Korea Times*, 3 October 1982, 5. See e.g. Jack Kroll review of *Inchon* in *Newsweek*, 27 September 1982, 76; see also e.g. Alun Evans, *Brassey's Guide to War Films* (Washington, DC, 2000), 103.
37. *Washington Post* weekend section, 17 September 1982, 13.
38. *Atlanta Constitution*, 2 October 1982, D16; *Variety*, 22 September 1982, 3, 29 September 1982, 1, 16; IMDB, Inchon, https://www.boxofficemojo.com/release/rl2942010881/weekend/ (accessed 24 January 2021).
39. See Sun Myung Moon, *As a Peace-Loving Global Citizen* (Seoul, 2010); *The Times*, 12 October 1982, 12. On *Inchon* never being released in South Korea see Kim Chongguk, 'Inch'ŏn (1981) ŭi chejak kwajŏng kwa yŏnghwajŏk yusan', *Han'guk pangsong hakpo* 28, 1 (2014), 167.
40. *New York Times*, 13 August 1978, C13.
41. On Kim Jong Il and film-drama propaganda see Jae-Cheon Lim, 'Kim Jong Il and His Leadership' (PhD thesis, University of Hawai'i at Manoa, 2007), 267–8; Kim Jong Il, *The Art of the Cinema* (Honolulu, HI, 2001); as cineaste see also Paul Fischer, *A Kim Jong-Il Production: The Incredible True Story of North Korea and the Most Audacious Kidnapping in History* (London, 2015). Cinemagoing remained very popular in the DPRK down to and beyond the turn of the century: see Ralph Hassig and Kongdan Oh, *The Hidden People of North Korea: Ordinary Life in the Hermit Kingdom* (Lanham, MD, 2015), 103; Andrei Lankov, *North of the DMZ: Essays on Daily Life in North Korea* (Jefferson, NC, 2007), 62; see also e.g. Hyok Kang, *This Is Paradise! My North Korean Childhood* (London, 2005), 3–4.
42. Korean Film Export & Import Corporation, *Korean Film Art* (Pyongyang, 1985), entry on *Wolmi Island*.
43. 'A North Korean actor in a ragged red wig appears', as an Australian filmmaker commented, 'attempting—and failing—to portray an American soldier [Major James Crawby, USMC]. His exaggerated scowls and bad makeup turn what has until now been a riveting drama into a sketch from the British World War II [TV] comedy *'Allo 'Allo!*' Anna Brionowski, *Aim High in Creation! A One-of-a-Kind Journey inside North Korea's Propaganda Machine* (New York, 2015), 150.

44. Johannes Schönherr, *North Korean Cinema: A History* (Jefferson, NC, 2012), 67, 197; see also in particular Hwang Gon, 'The Island in Flames' (1955) in *North Korean Short Stories* (Pyongyang, 1966), 5–28; Hyangjin Lee, *Contemporary Korean Cinema: Identity, Culture and Politics* (Manchester, 2001), 115–18; Travis Workman, 'The Partisan, the Worker, and the Hidden Hero', in Kyung Hyun Kim and Yougmin Choe (eds), *The Korean Popular Culture Reader* (Durham, NC, 2014), 153; Tatiana Gabroussenko, *Soldiers on the Cultural Front: Developments in the Early History of North Korean Literature and Literary Policy* (Honolulu, 2010), 19. *Wolmi Island* also seems to have inspired the kind of self-sacrifice required by the regime: see e.g. Suk-Young Kim, *Illusive Utopia: Theater, Film and Everyday Performance in North Korea* (Ann Arbor, MI, 2010), 339–40 n. 121.
45. See *Yŏnhap nyusŭ*, 2 September 2013.
46. Korean Film Export & Import Corporation, *Korean Film Art*, entry on *Don't Wait for Us*. See Lee, 'How Are Historical Events Remembered?', 182.
47. See e.g. BBC Monitoring Service Asia Pacific, 26 July 2002, 1—North Korean agency reports on activities during anti-US month. Text of report in English by North Korean news agency KCNA: Pyongyang, 26 July 2002, http://www.infoweb.newsbank.com (23 July 2023); BBC Monitoring Service Asia Pacific, 18 July 2013, 1—A ten-day film show was opened in the DPRK to mark the sixtieth anniversary of the Korean people's victory in the Fatherland Liberation War. Text of report by state-run news agency KCNA: Pyongyang, 18 July, http://www.infoweb.newsbank.com (23 July 2023). See also Paek Yosep, 'Puk Han yŏnghwa "Wŏlmido" wa Nam Han yŏnghwa "nch'ŏn sangnyuk chakchŏn"', *Mirae Han'guk*, 4 August 2016.
48. 'Thousands of North Koreans enjoy 'rhythmic' 4D cinema', The Guardian, 21 May 2014, https://www.theguardian.com/world/2014/may/21/north-korea-4d-cinema-rhythmic (accessed 29 January 2022).
49. A number of these films can be found on YouTube. See also Darcy Paquet, 'South Korean Films about the Korean War (1950–53)', *Korean Quarterly* 12, 4 (Summer 2009), 71–2; Hanna Lee, 'How Are Historic Events Remembered? North Korean War Films on the Inchon Landing Operation', in Andrew David Jackson and Colette Balmain (eds), *Korean Screen Cultures: Interrogating Cinema, TV, Music and Online Games* (Bern, 2016), 179–80; Hyunseon Lee, 'Korean War Films', in Lee, *Korean Film and History*, 138, 140; Lee Young-il and Choe Young-chol, *The History of Korean Cinema* (Seoul, 1998), 100–4, 170, 185; Heonik Kwon, *After the Korean War: An Intimate History* (Cambridge, 2020), 123–4; Dong-Yeon Koe, *The Korean War and Postmemory Generation: Contemporary Korean Arts and Films* (Abingdon, 2022), 105.
50. See e.g. *Legend of the Patriots* television miniseries (dir. Kim Sang-hwi and Song Hyeon-wook, 2010), and the films *The Brotherhood of War* (dir. Kang Je-gyu, 2004) and *The Front Line* (dir. Jang Hoon, 2011). On the shift towards ambiguity see e.g. Young Eun Chae, 'Screening the Past: Historiography of Contemporary South Korean Cinema' (PhD thesis, University of North

Carolina, 2011), 119–52; Suh Ji-moon, 'The Korean War in Korean Films', in Philip West and Suh Ji-moon (eds), *Remembering the "Forgotten War": The Korean War through Literature and Art* (Armonk, NY, 2001), 137–51; Alexandra Urman, 'Perception of Korean Political History through Modern South Korean Films', *Dálný východ/Far East* 5, 1 (2015), 78–9. On the changing environment that made this possible see Seung Hyun Park, 'Korean Cinema after Liberation: Production, Industry and Regulatory Trends', in Francis Gateward (ed.), *Seoul Searching: Culture and Identity in Contemporary Korean Cinema* (Albany, NY, 2007), 15–35.

51. *The Incheon Landing Operation* (2016) was released in the English-speaking world as *Operation Chromite*. The latter title is used here to distinguish it more easily from the 1965 movie. The CJ conglomerate, which acted as distributor, was said to have invested heavily in the film as a means of mending fences with then-president Park Geun-hye, daughter of Park Chung-hee. See Park Jin-hai, 'CJ Made Several Films Pressured by President', Korea Times, 16 January 2017, http://www.infoweb.newsbank.com (accessed 24 September 2024).

52. See e.g. comments by Jeong Tae-won and Lee Jai-han in 'making of' material attached to *Operation Chromite* DVD; see also Chin-hong An, *Inch'ŏn sangnyuk chakcŏn* (Seoul, 2014). The extent to which the main storyline was fictional was elided through the incorporation at the end of the film of the reflections of actual X-Ray survivors. See also Kristen Frances Sun, 'Memorialization and the Limits of Reconciliation: Transnational Memory Circuits of the Korean War' (PhD thesis, University of California, Berkeley, 2019), 45, 55–7. On a budget figure of $12.88 million see *Korea Times*, 8 October 2016, 15.

53. Sŏ Yusŏk, 'K'üllik! T'ongil kyoyuk Uni Movie: Inch'on sangnyuk chakchŏn Maekadŏ wa ich'yŏjin yŏngung ŭl malhada', *T'ongil Han'guk* 394 (2016), 65.

54. *Chungang ilbo*, 22 July 2016; see also e.g. *Chosŏn ilbo*, 22 July 2016; *Tonga ilbo*, 21 July 2016: Chonghyun Choi, 'Between Protector and Oppressor: Representation of the United States as a Geopolitical Entity in Korean Blockbusters', in Lee, *Korean Film and History*, 165–6. See also, for more mixed critical reactions internationally, Levi Fox, 'Not Forgotten: The Korean War in American Public Memory, 1950–2017' (PhD thesis, Temple University, 2018), 207–8.

55. *Korea Times*, 3 August 2016, 16, 8 October 2016, 15. See also The Numbers, 'Operation Chromite', https://www.the-numbers.com/movie/Operation-Chromite-(South-Korea)#tab=summary (accessed 26 January 2021). *The Battle of Jangsari*, a semi-sequel to *Operation Chromite* released in late September 2019 that dealt with one of the small landings meant to divert attention from Inchon, opened well enough (see *Variety*, 30 September 2019) but was ultimately far less successful after the Covid-19 pandemic arrived, earning under $8 million in theatrical release. The Numbers, 'Battle of Jangsari', https://m.the-numbers.com/movie/Jangsa-ri-9-15-(South-Korea) (accessed

26 January 2021). A fictional diversionary operation directed at Wonsan had been depicted four decades earlier in *Abengo Airborne Corps* (dir. Im Kwon-tack, 1982), on which see Lee, 'How Are Historic Events Remembered?', 179–80.

56. As of the time of writing (2024) the most recent example of a feature film being used to propagate perceptions of Inchon comes not from the countries that fought the battle, but from the People's Republic of China, where, in the context of deteriorating contemporary PRC–US relations, the propaganda ministry helped produce the domestically popular 2021 war epic *The Battle at Lake Changjin* (dir. Chen Kaige et al.), in which Chromite is briefly depicted—emphasizing navy firepower and airpower at work against an apparently undefended port—as the start of MacArthur's plan to conquer Korea in its entirety while bombing both sides of the Yalu River.

Chapter 8

1. Ministry of Patriots and Veterans Affairs, *Korean War Memorials in Pictures: Remembering UN Participation 60 Years Later*, 3 vols. (Seoul, 2010).

2. For the story of the itinerant Korean War National Museum see Levi Fox, 'Not Forgotten: The Korean War in American Public Memory, 1950–2017' (PhD thesis, Temple University, 2018), 55–6; Michael J. Devine, *The Korean War Remembered: Contested Memories of an Unended Conflict* (Lincoln, NB, 2023), 106. On the complex history of the exhibits on display at the Memorial Hall of the War to Resist US Aggression and Aid Korea in Dandong, a city on the China–Korea border, see Jung Keun-sik, 'China's Memory and Commemoration of the Korean War in the Memorial Hall of the "War to Resist U.S. Aggression and Aid Korea"', *Cross-Currents* 4 (2015), 17–20; see also, on contents and representation, Tessa Morris-Suzuki, 'Remembering the Unfinished Conflict', in Tessa Morris-Suzuki, Morris Low, Leonid Petrov, and Timothy Y. Tsu (eds), *East Asia beyond the History Wars: Confronting the Ghosts of Violence* (London, 2013), 139–44. Both what is on display and accessibility have varied here and in the relevant section of the Military Museum in Beijing (see Jung, 'China's Memory', 25–6) depending on the state of PRC–DPRK relations. See e.g. Eddie Burdick, *Three Days in the Hermit Kingdom: An American Visits North Korea* (Jefferson, NC, 2010), 266–7; John Everard, *Only Beautiful, Please: A British Diplomat in North Korea* (Stanford, CA, 2012), 88.

3. In Pyongyang the Victorious Fatherland Liberation War Museum and in Seoul the War Memorial of Korea, both discussed with reference to Inchon in this chapter. The former also deals with the guerrilla war against Japanese occupation while the latter covers the entirety of Korean history, albeit with a lot of emphasis on the Six-Two-Five War. Wartime atrocity memorials for massacres of Korean civilians blamed on American troops can be found

NOTES

elsewhere on both sides of the DMZ at, for instance, Sinchon in the DPRK (on which see Han Sunghoon 'The Ongoing Korean War at the Sinch'ŏn Museum in North Korea', *Cross-Currents* 4 [2015], 95–125; see also Travis Jeppesen, *See You Again in Pyongyang: A Journey into Kim Jong Un's North Korea* [New York, 2018], 140–6), and at No Gun Ri in the ROK (on which see e.g. Suhi Choi, *Right to Mourn: Trauma, Empathy, and Korean War Memorials* [New York, 2019], 101–25).

4. Japan remains the exception, since for constitutional and diplomatic reasons it did and does not wish to draw attention to indirect Japanese participation in the Korean War.
5. See Ministry of Patriots and Veterans Affairs, *Korean War Memorials*, Volume 1, 58–61; *New York Times*, 15 September 1957, 31. On the inscription and positive conservative press reaction to the MacArthur statue see Kim Chinung, 'Maekadŏ changgun ŭi che 2 ŭi Inch'ŏn sangnyuk chakchŏn: Tongsang ŭl pullŏssan punjaeng ŭi hamŭi', *Yŏksa kyoyuk nontan* 39, 8 (2007), 416. On the origins, planning, and development of the MacArthur statue and an invitation to MacArthur to attend (eventually declined) see Suhi Choi, *Embattled Memories: Contested Meanings in Korean War Memorials* (Reno and Las Vegas, NV, 2014), 102; *Korea Times*, 23 April 1957, 1; *Korea Times*, 25 April 1957, 4; *Korea Times*, 21 June 1957, 3; *Korea Times*, 2 August 1957, 1; *Korea Times*, 2 September 1957, 2; *Korea Times*, 7 September 1957, 3; *New York Times*, 12 May 1957, 32; *St. Louis Post-Dispatch*, 11 July 1957, 1D.
6. 'For decades, any notion of anti-U.S. feeling was simply unthinkable to [South] Koreans.' Brent (Won-ki) Choi, 'Anti-Americanism or "Antibase-ism": U.S.–South Korean Relations through Changing Generations', in David A. Steinberg (ed.), *Korean Attitudes towards the United States: Changing Dynamics* (London, 2015), 310.
7. Suhi Choi, *Embattled Memories*, 105; Heonik Kwon and Jun Hwan Park, 'American Power in Korean Shaminism', *Journal of Korean Religions* 9, 1 (2018), 54. A decade later little had apparently changed: see Devine, *Korean War Remembered*, xii.
8. *Korea Times*, 15 September 1970, 4.
9. Ministry of Patriots and Veterans Affairs, *Korean War Memorials*, Volume 1, 56; see ibid., 54–7; *Korea Times*, 16 September 1980, 6.
10. On the Inchon Landing Operation Memorial Hall see Ministry of Patriots and Veterans Affairs, *Korean War Memorials*, Volume 1, 48–53; Yŏksaga sumsuinŭn konggan 6, 'Chŏnhang ŭl kŭkjŏk ŭro panjŏnsik'in taejakchŏn Inch'ŏn sangnyuk chakjŏn kinyŏmgwan', *T'ongil Han'guk* 8 (2006), 97–9. See also, with reference to MacArthur's longstanding shamanistic place in Inchon, Kwon and Park, 'American Power in Korean Shamanism', 45, 47, 50, 55–65.
11. The Yangju highway incident of 2002 involved a US Army armoured vehicle which had struck and killed two Korean schoolgirls on a public

road whose crew were court-martialled but found not guilty of negligent homicide, sparking considerable anger in South Korea: see Meredith Woo-Cumings, 'Unilateralism and its Discontents', in Steinberg, *Korean Attitudes*, 67. News of the involvement of US forces in the 1950 killing of Korean civilians at No Gun Ri only became widespread at the end of the century thanks to investigative reporting, the image of the United States in South Korea becoming tarnished by a reluctance to admit murderous intent: see Charles J. Hanley, Sang-Hun Choe, and Martha Mendoza, *The Bridge at No Gun Ri: A Hidden Nightmare from the Korean War* (New York, 2001); Charles J. Hanley, 'No Gun Ri: Official Narrative and Inconvenient Truths', *Critical Asian Studies* 42, 4 (2010), 589–622. Curiously, the initial public response in South Korea was comparatively muted, perhaps because at least some degree of responsibility was accepted by the United States: see Woo-Cumings, 'Unilateralism', 67–8; see also Lara M. Corer, 'Assertive Nationalism in Korean Youth: Anti-American Protest in the 2000s' (MA thesis, Indiana University, 2012), 24–5; Suhi Choi, *Embattled Memories*, 7–29. The No Gun Ri episode nonetheless over time became firmly entrenched in Korean popular culture through books, graphic novels, and a feature film. See 'Nogeun-ri tragedy retold in cartoon book', 27 November 2006, Hankyoreh, https://english.hani.co.kr/arti/english_edition/e_national/174654.html (accessed 17 May 2022); *A Little Pond* (dir. Yi Sang-woo, 2009). On the events at Gwangju see e.g. Henry Scott-Stokes and Lee Jai Eui (eds), *The Kwangju Uprising: Eyewitness Accounts of Korea's Tiananmen* (Armonk, NY, 2000). On the postwar generations linking US support for the Chun Doo-hwan regime with the Gwangju Massacre see Brent (Won-ki) Choi, 'Anti-Americanism'; Bruce Cumings, 'The Korean War: What Is It That We Are Remembering to Forget?', in Sheila Miyoshi Jager and Ranna Mitter (eds), *Ruptured Histories: War, Memory, and the Post-Cold War in Asia* (Cambridge, MA, 2007), 285; John L. Linantud, 'War Memorials and Memories', *International Journal of Heritage Studies* 14, 4 (2008), 356.

12. Hyung Gu Lynn, *Bipolar Orders: The Two Koreas since 1989* (London, 2007), 154.
13. See e.g. AP report on the 1995 anniversary events in Inchon, *Las Vegas Review-Journal*, 16 September 1995, 16A.
14. Gen. McArthur statue spawns Korea protest, China Daily, 18 July 2005, https://www.chinadaily.com.cn/english/ (accessed 19 May 2022); Prompt Removal of Murderer's Statue Demanded, Korea Central News Agency, 14 June 2005, Past News, Korea Central News Agency, http://www.kcna.jp (accessed 19 May 2022); see also e.g. Cho Sŏnghun, 'Inch'ŏn sangnyuk chakchŏn ŭl chŏnhunhan Maekadŏ yŏk'hal ŭi chaep'yŏngga', *Chŏngsin munhwa yŏn'gu* 29, 3 (2006), 135; Devine, *Korea Remembered*, 156, 176.
15. See Kim Jinwung *A History of Korea* (Bloomington, IN, 2012), 595–6; Kim Chinung, 'Maekadŏ changgun ŭi che 2 ŭi Inch'ŏn sangnyuk chakchŏn: Tongsang ŭl pullŏssan punjaeng ŭi hamŭi', *Yŏksa kyoyuk nontan* 39, 8

(2007), 452; Linantud, 'War Memorials', 157–8. On demonstrations and counter-demonstrations in Inchon in the run-up to the September 2005 anniversary and beyond in Inchon see e.g. BBC Monitoring Service Asia Pacific, 11 September 2005, 'Pro- anti-US activists clash in South Korean city', Yonhap, 11 September 2005, http://www.infoweb.newsbank.com (23 July 2023); BBC Monitoring Service Asia Pacific, 28 September 2005, 'Thousands protest on South Korea over fate of Gen MacArthur statue', Icheon, 28 September 2005, http://www.infoweb.newsbank.com (23 July 2023).
16. See e.g. Kan Zhisen, 'Future of Gen. McArthur statue provokes debate', Global Times, 10 September 2009, https://www.globaltimes.cn (accessed 20 May 2022); 'Miguk ŭi kansŏp ch'aekdong ŭl paegyŏkhayŏ', *Rodong sinmun*, 26 October 2018; David Choi, 'Police say anti-US military activist vandalized Douglas MacArthur statue in South Korea', Stars and Stripes, 29 April 2022, https://www.stripes.com (accessed 20 May 2022). For analysis of the MacArthur statue and its endurance see Suhi Choi, *Embattled Memories*, 95–114; ibid., 'Standing between Intransigent History and Transient Memories: The Statue of MacArthur in South Korea', Memory Studies 7 (2014), 191–206.
17. See e.g. 'SKorea re-enacts Incheon Landing despite North's protest', Agence France-Presse, 9 September 2008, https://www.afp.com (accessed 20 May 2022). On North Korean condemnation of the 2008 anniversary events see BBC Monitoring Service Asia Pacific, 6 September 2008, 'North Korea says South's plan to re-enact September 1950 landing "war hysteria"', North Korean News Agency (KCNA), Pyongyang, 6 September 2008, http://www.infoweb.newsbank.com (accessed 23 July 2023); BBC Monitoring Service Asia Pacific, 7 September 2008, 'North Korea reacts to South plan to commemorate Inchon landings', North Korean News Agency (KCNA), dateline Pyongyang 7 September 2008, http://www.infoweb.newsbank.com (accessed 23 July 2023); BBC Monitoring Service Asia Pacific, 15 September 2008, 'North Korean Daily decries South's Inchon landing operation commemoration', from North Korean News Agency (KCNA), Pyongyang, 15 September 2008, http://www.infoweb.newsbank.com (accessed 23 July 2023). See also, e.g., on subsequent reenactments, Kim Minuk, 'Wŏlmido appadasŏ yŏllin 'Inch'ŏn sangnyuk chakchŏn chŏnsŭng 62 chunyŏn kinyŏm mit chaeyŏn haengsa', *Kukpang kwa kisul* 404, 10 (2012), 42; 'Anniversary of Incheon Landing', Korea Times, 14 September 2014, https://infoweb.newsbank-com (accessed 20 May 2022); 'Incheon Landing Operation', Korea Times, 13 September 2015, http://www.infoweb.newsbank.com (accessed 20 May 2022); BBC Monitoring Service Asia Pacific, 'North Korean paper condemns South', US operation, North Korea News Agency (KCNA), 13 September 2016, http://www.infoweb.newsbank.com (accessed 25 September 2024).
18. On the symbolism of the Statue of Brothers and the initial lack of anti-North Korean sentiment on display in the War Memorial of Korea see

Sheila Miyoshi Jager and Jiyul Kim, 'The Korean War after the Cold War', in Jager and Rana Ritter, *Ruptured Histories*, 244, 248–9; though see also Sheila Miyoshi Jager, *Narratives of Nation Building in Korea: A Genealogy of Patriotism* (Armonk, NY, 2003), 117–40. On the development of the memorial see Devine, *Korean War Remembered*, 169–70.

19. Incheon Landing, 4D Cinema Exhibit, War Memorial of Korea. On the politically driven change in tone within the War Memorial of Korea see Daniel Y. Kim, *The Intimacies of Conflict: Cultural Memory and the Korean War* (New York, 2020), 269–70; see also Morris-Suzuki, 'Remembering', 131–5.
20. On the ROK–US Alliance sculpture see Song Sang-ho, 'S. Korea-U.S. Alliance Sculpture Unveiled in U.S. Base in Pyeongtaek', Yonhap News Agency, 10 July 2019, https://en.yna.co.kr/view/AEN20190710006200325 (accessed 25 September 2024). For the North Korean reaction see Ŏm Suryŏn, 'Pŏmchoi ryŏksa rul ch'anmi hanŭn ŏlppajin haengwi', *Rodong sinmun*, 23 July 2019.
21. Anon., *Records of Great Victory* (Pyongyang, 1962), foreword, f. 1.
22. Ibid., foreword, f. 2.
23. Ibid., Operations Hall descriptions, Illustrations 15–16.
24. Korea Pictorial, *The Fatherland Liberation War Memorial* (Pyongyang, 1969), 6.
25. See ibid., 18; Suzy Kim, 'Specters of War in Pyongyang', *Cross-Currents* 4, 1 (2014), 76; see also Anon., *Pyongyang* (Pyongyang, 1975), 20–1.
26. See Philipp Meuser (ed.), *Architectural and Cultural Guide: Pyongyang*, Volume 1 (Berlin, 2012), 122–3; Carolina E. Santiago Alvarez, 'Power Play in Pyongyang: City and Space as Theaters of Power under the Early Kim Regime in North Korea, 1950s–1990s' (MA thesis, University of Puerto Rico, 2020), 48–9; see also National Tourism Administration, *Korea Tour* (Pyongyang, 1998), 17, 30–1.
27. Anon., *Victorious Fatherland Liberation War Museum* (Pyongyang, 1990), 16–17; Anon., *The Victorious Fatherland Liberation War Museum* (Pyongyang, 1979), 18.
28. O Hae-yŏn, *Victorious Fatherland Liberation War Museum* (Pyongyang, 2014), 2, 59–61, 96. On the 2013 renovation see Adam Cathcart, 'Kim Jong-un Syndrome', in Adam Cathcart, Robert Winstanley-Chesters, and Christopher Green (eds), *Change and Continuity in North Korean Politics* (London, 2017), 14–16; Kim, 'Specters of War', 73. For an aerial view see Kim Chun-hyŏk, *Panorama of Pyongyang* (Pyongyang, 2017), 59. English-speaking guides for tour groups further emphasized the Kim Il Sung version of the war, including how the United States had to muster all its strength to carry out the Inchon landing and the wise decision of the Great Leader to order a temporary strategic retreat. See Burdick, *Three Days*, 268; see also Morris-Suzuki, 'Remembering', 135–9. On Westerner scepticism about some of the claims made see e.g. Magnus Bärtås and Fredrik Ekman, *All Monsters Must Die: An Excursion to North Korea* (Toronto, 2015), 16; Everard, *Only Beautiful*, 87–8.

29. BBC Monitoring Service, 'Programme summary of North Korea TV 11:00 GMT 23 July 2021', https://global.factiva.com (accessed 23 July 2023).
30. The phrase (or variations thereof) was used repeatedly in book, thesis, article, and documentary titles: e.g. Clay Blair, *The Forgotten War: America in Korea 1950–1953* (New York, 1987); Mason Edward Horrell, 'Reporting the "Forgotten War": Military-Press Relations in Korea, 1950–1954' (PhD thesis, University of Kentucky, 2002); Bill Shinn, *The Forgotten War Remembered: Korea: 1950–1953: A War Correspondent's Notebook and Today's Danger in Korea* (Elizabeth, NJ, 1996); Yonghee Suh, Makito Yurita, and Scott Alan Metzinger, 'What Do We Want Students to Remember about the "Forgotten War"?', *International Journal of Social Education* 23 (2008), 51–75; Philip West and Suh Ji-moon (eds), *Remembering the "Forgotten War": The Korean War through Literature and Art* (Armonk, NY, 2001); *Korea: The Forgotten War* (dir. Don Horan, 1987).
31. See e.g. Melinda Pash interview by Richard Emsberger, Jr., 'Why Is Korea the "Forgotten War"?', *American History*, 1 June 2014, 24–5; see also Melinda L. Pash, *In the Shadow of the Greatest Generation: The Americans Who Fought the Korean War* (New York, 2012), 1–3.
32. See Steve Rajtar and Frances Elizabeth Franks, *War Monuments, Museums, and Library Collections of 20th Century Conflicts: A Directory of United States Sites* (Jefferson, NC, 2002). The situation improved somewhat around the time of the fiftieth anniversary, so that *circa* 2010 over 450 regional and local Korean War monuments were catalogued on top of the ninety-plus monuments dedicated to American forces or individuals in South Korea. See Ministry of Patriots and Veterans Affairs, *Korean War Memorials*, Volume 1, 80–170, Volume 2, 26–463. The creation and upkeep of regional memorials in the United States could depend very much on local initiative (see e.g. Suhi Choi, *Embattled Memories*, 82) and in one case generated considerable public controversy as to its provenance (see Jon Wiener, *How We Forgot the Cold War: A Historical Journey across America* [Berkeley, CA, 2012], 133–9).
33. Rajtar and Franks, *War Monuments*, 43, 45; see also Judith Dupré, *Monuments: America's History in Art and Memory* (New York, 2007), 148–56, 170–3. On the convoluted backstory to the building of the Korean War Veterans Memorial, dedicated in 1995, see Devine, *Korean War Remembered*, 137–56; Jonathan C. Merritt, 'The Remembered War: The Korean War in American Culture, 1953–1995' (PhD thesis, University of Alabama, 2017), 186–266; Sara Weintraub, 'From Design to Completion: The Transformation of U.S. War Memorials on the National Mall' (PhD thesis, City University of New York, 2017), 96–173.
34. See Rajtar and Franks, *War Monuments*, index. The American monuments situation was quite different in the Republic of Korea. There, every effort was made to thank American veterans through battle, unit, and individual figure monuments as well as books and collaboration in veterans' visits to

commemorate e.g. the Inchon landing. See e.g. *Las Vegas Review-Journal*, 16 Sep. 1995, 16A; Anon., *Korea Reborn: A Grateful Nation Honors War Veterans for More Than Sixty Years* (Salt Lake City, UT, 2018); Ministry of Patriots and Veterans Affairs, *Korean War Memorials*, Volume 1, 80–170.

35. On the 'Iwo Jima Memorial' tag see e.g. 'Visiting the Marine Corps War Memorial, Washington DC', https://washington.org/DC-guide-to/marine-corps-war-memorial (accessed 23 May 2022). On the memorial itself see Rajtar and Franks, *War Monuments*, 269; see also Keith Lowe, *Prisoners of History: What Monuments to World War II Tell Us about Our History and Ourselves* (New York, 2020), 24–33.

36. See 'General MacArthur Statue, Milwaukee', https://city.milwaukee.gov/cityclerk/hpc/War-Memorials-of-Milwaukee/MacArthur-Statue.htm (accessed 23 May 2022); 'MacArthur Statue', MacArthur Memorial, https://www.macarthurmemorial.org/144/The-MacArthur-Statue (accessed 23 May 2022); Rod Miller, *West Point U.S. Military Academy: An Architectural Tour* (New York, 2002), 139; Wiener, *How We Forgot*, 282–4. There was also the statue, the centrepiece of a group of bronzes based on the classic photograph of the general and his entourage wading ashore, built in 1977 to commemorate the landing on Leyte in the Philippines in 1944 (on which see Linantud, 'War Memorials', 353–5).

37. Fox, 'Not Forgotten', 55–6.

38. See ibid., 47; Kim, *Intimacies*, 40–1, 49–52.

39. 'Shifting Battlegrounds, Price of Freedom', Smithsonian National Museum of American History, https://americanhistory.si.edu/price-of-freedom/korean-war/shifting-battlefronts (accessed 24 May 2022); Fox, 'Not Forgotten', 57.

40. 'Why Norfolk?', MacArthur Memorial, https://www.macarthurmemorial.org/225/Why-Norfolk (accessed 24 May 2022); see Geoffrey Perret, *Old Soldiers Never Die: The Life of Douglas MacArthur* (New York, 1996), 586.

41. MacArthur Memorial Museum, Podcast Tour, Gallery 7, https://www.macarthurmemorial.org/193/Podcast-Tour (accessed 9 August 2020); see also ibid., 'The MacArthur Murals', Montage Korea, https://www.macarthurmemorial.org/gallery.aspx?PID=27 (accessed 9 August 2020); Fox, 'Not Forgotten', 78. Even here, however, Korea can seem a mere coda to MacArthur's Second World War career: see Wiener, *How We Forgot*, 282.

42. National Museum of the United States Army, 'Douglas MacArthur', https://www.thenmusa.org/biographies/douglas-macarthur/ (accessed 24 May 2022); ibid., 'Cold War', https://www.usmcmuseum.com/koreanwar.html (accessed 9 August 2020). On the extensive US Army museum system see US Army Center of Military History, 'Find an Army Museum', https://history.army.mil/museums/directory.html (accessed 24 May 2022).

43. See Naval History and Heritage Command, National Museum of the US Navy, 'Korea 1950–53: The Navy in the Forgotten War', https://www.history.navy.mil/content/history/museums/nmusn/explore/exhibits/korea-1950–53–

the-navy-in-the-forgotten-war.html (accessed 9 August 2020); Naval History and Heritage Command, National Museum of the US Navy, 'Korean War', https://www.history.navy.mil/content/history/museums/nmusn/pamphlets/nmusn-pamphlets/korean-war.html (accessed 24 May 2022). It should also be noted that the final *Iwo Jima*-class amphibious assault ship built for the USN was commissioned in 1970 as the USS *Inchon*.
44. National Museum of the Marine Corps, 'Korean War', https://www.usmcmuseum.com/koreanwar.html (accessed 9 August 2020).
45. 'Virtual Tour', USMC Museum, www.virtualusmcmuseum.com/Korea_3.asp (accessed 9 August 2020); see also 'Related Media, Landing at Inchon', USMC Museum, www.virtualusmcmuseum.com/Korea_3.asp# (accessed 9 August 2020).
46. Fox, 'Not Forgotten', 89.

Conclusion

1. Though the People's Republic of China had not yet entered the Korean War at the time of the landing, what flowed from Inchon—the reversal of the North Korean invasion and the American advance deep into North Korea toward the Yalu River border—was, and still is, presented as the *casus belli* in terms of protecting the PRC from outright invasion and heeding the call for help from a socialist neighbour in dire need: compare e.g. Hao Yufan and Zhai Zhihai 'China's Decision to Enter the Korean War', in Kim Chull Baum and James I. Matray (eds), *Korea and the Cold War* (Claremont, CA, 1993), 141–66, with Gary Rawnsley, '"The Great Movement to Resist America and Assist Korea": How Beijing Sold the Korean War', *Media, War & Conflict* 2, 3 (2009), 285–315. There have been, however, significant alterations in emphasis over time for political purposes: see e.g. Zha Ma, 'War Remembered, Revolution Forgotten: Recasting the Sino-North Korean Alliance in China's Post-Socialist Media State', *Cross-Currents* 6, 1 (2017), 205–35; Qin Hauzhi 'A Floating History: The Korean War and China's Political Use of War Memory' (MA thesis, Georgetown University, 2020). Using newly available archival material from the former Soviet Union and China, scholars have debated the factors and timelines involved in Chinese intervention, but often tend to agree that Chromite played a significant—albeit not necessarily decisive—part in Mao's thinking: see e.g. Chen Jian, 'Far Short of a "Glorious Victory": Revisiting China's Changing Strategies to Manage the Korean War', *Chinese Historical Review* 25, 1 (2018), 6–14; Shen Zhihua and Danhui Li, *After Leaning to One Side: China and Its Allies in the Cold War* (Stanford, CA, 2011), 24–60; Michael Sheng, 'Chinese Intervention', in James I. Matray and Donald W. Boose, Jr. (eds), *The Ashgate Research Companion to the Korean War* (Farnham, 2014), 359–70; Son Daekwon, 'Domestic

Instability as a Key Factor in Shaping China's Decision to Enter the Korean War', *China Journal*, 83 (2020), 48–57; Jack Kwoh Tan, 'Korean War June–October 1950: Inchon and Stalin in the "Trigger vs. Justification" Debate' (2006), RIS Working Paper No. 105, Nanyang Technological University, https://hdl.handle.net/10356/09667 (accessed 9 September 2022); Li Xiaobing, *China's War in Korea* (Singapore, 2019), 79–98.

2. See e.g. BBC Monitoring Service Asia Pacific, Korean Central News Agency, Great Feats Recorded in History of Fatherland Liberation War, Korean News, 25 July 2022, https://global.factiva.com (accessed 14 July 2023); BBC Monitoring Asia Pacific, Koreans Work Miracle in World History of War, Pyongyang Times, 30 July 2022, https://global.factiva.com (accessed 14 July 2023).

3. For instance the war drama *Jangsa-ri 9.15* (dir. Kim Tae-hoon and Kwak Kyung-taek, 2019), on which see e.g. *Korea Herald*, 23 September 2019. On ongoing small-scale efforts directed against the MacArthur statue see e.g. *Washington Post*, 21 February 2002, A07.

4. See e.g. Robert L. Durham, 'MacArthur's Last Great Stroke', *Military Heritage* 22, 3 (2020), 35–43; Changing the Game at Incheon, Korean War Legacy Project, https://koreanwarlegacy.org/chapters/changing-the-game-at-incheon/ (accessed 9 September 2022); Michael D. Miller, *General Douglas MacArthur: From Betrayal to Greatness* (Columbia, SC, 2022), 68–9.

5. For recent pro-USMC accounts of Inchon–Seoul see Michael Green, *The United States Marine Corps in the Korean War: Rare Photographs from Wartime Archives* (Barnsley, 2021), 54–66; Paul Westermeyer, *The United States Marine Corps: The Expeditionary Force at War* (Philadelphia, PA, 2019), 81–3. For criticism of Almond, see e.g. Gordon L. Rottman, *Inch'on 1950: The Last Great Amphibious Assault* (Oxford, 2006), 26.

6. See Aaron B. O'Connell, *Underdogs: The Making of the Modern Marine Corps* (Cambridge, MA, 2012), 234–45. Thereafter the profile of amphibious capability would wax and wane, but nonetheless remain important to the USMC: see Joseph H. Alexander and Merrill L. Bartlett, *Sea Soldiers in the Cold War: Amphibious Warfare, 1945–1991* (Annapolis, MD, 1995).

7. Hence the subtitle of Rottman's *Inch'on 1950*; see also e.g. Michael Langley, *Inchon Landing: MacArthur's Last Triumph* (New York, 1979), ix.

8. On the aborted plan to stage a major USMC landing in Kuwait during the Gulf War of 1991 see Michael R. Gordon and Bernard E. Trainor, *The Generals' War: The Inside Story of the Conflict in the Gulf* (Boston, MA, 1995), 292–3. On the abandoned plans to land in North Vietnam in 1967 see Michael F. Morris, 'Invading North Vietnam', *Naval History Magazine* 43, 5 (October 2020), https://www.usni.org/magazines/naval-history-magazine/2020/october/invading-north-vietnam (accessed 24 April 2024).

9. Berger quoted in: (2020) The future of amphibious operations, Strategic Comments, 26:1, iv, DOI: 10.1080/13567888.2020.1727696 (accessed 24 March 2024).

10. See e.g. on the major USMC landings in the Pacific, Chris K. Hemler, *Delivering Destruction: American Firepower and Amphibious Assault from Tarawa to Iwo Jima* (Annapolis, MD, 2023).
11. Jason Q. Bohm, preface to Timothy Heck and B. A. Friedman, *On Contested Shores: The Evolving Role of Amphibious Operations in the History of Warfare* (Quantico, VA, 2020), x. The Chinese armed forces have paid serious attention to both success and failure in examining amphibious operations of the twentieth century, including in relation to Chromite. See Lyle Goldstein, 'The Hard School of Amphibious Warfare', *Asian Security* 19, 1 (2023), 26–42.
12. As the overall naval commander put it in retrospect, if the enemy had been able to fully mine the approaches 'I don't believe we would ever have gotten up to Inchon.' *Reminiscences of Admiral Arthur D. Struble, U.S. Navy (Retired)*, US Naval Institute transcript, 2011, 383. On lack of intelligence about what the North Koreans had been able to accomplish in way of mining in the run-up to Chromite see e.g. ibid., 366; *Reminiscences of Admiral Arleigh Burke, USN Retired*, Volume 1, US Naval Institute transcript, 1979, 26. On the north-to-south deployment of sea mines sent from the Soviet Union in the early months of the war see James A. Field, Jr. *History of United States Naval Operations: Korea* (Washington, DC, 1962), 183. On a store of mines being spotted ashore at Inchon in the first stages of Chromite see Heinl, *Victory*, 82, 83. On the problems caused subsequently by intensive enemy sea mining at Wonsan see Theodore L. Gatchel, *At the Water's Edge: Defending against Modern Amphibious Assault* (Annapolis, MD, 1996), 181–3.
13. On intelligence estimates see Bruce R. Pirnie, 'The Inchon Landing: How Great Was the Risk?', *Joint Perspectives* 3, 1 (1982), 92–3. On the success of American signals intelligence see Matthew Aid, *Secret Sentry: The Untold History of the National Security Agency* (New York, 2009), 28–9.
14. 'Although some awareness of the fall of Seoul affected the KPA's defeat,' as the elder statesman among military historians who have studied the war has put it, 'the Communist army simply fell victim to the bludgeoning of the Eighth Army and the Fifth Air Force.' Allan R. Millett, *War for Korea, 1950–1951: They Came from the North* (Lawrence, KS, 2010), 271.
15. See Gertrud Koch, 'A Law's Tale: *The Man Who Shot Liberty Valance*', *Philosophy and Social Criticism* 36, 6 (2008), 685–92.

BIBLIOGRAPHY

National Archives and Records Administration II, College Park, MD

RG 111 – Records of the Office of the Chief Signal Officer, 1860–1985.
RG 127 – Records of the U.S. Marine Corps, 1775–.
RG 319 – Records of the Army Staff, 1903–2009.
RG 330 – Records of the Office of the Secretary of Defense, 1921–2008.
RG 428 – General Records of the Department of the Navy, 1941–2004.

Other U.S. Government Documents

American Consulate General, Hong Kong, Review of the Hong Kong Chinese Press, 177–178/50.
American Consulate General, Hong Kong, Survey of China Mainland Press, No. 1.
Congressional Record, 1951.
Foreign Relations of the United States 1951: Korea and China, Volume 7, Part I (Washington, DC, 1983).
Foreign Relations of the United States 1950, Volume 7: *Korea* (Washington, DC, 1976).
Inchon Seoul Invasion: Headquarters X Corps: Operations Instructions: Nos 1–10: 15 Sep–4 Oct (U.S. Army Military History Research Collection).
Summary of messages exchanged between CINCFE and JCS concerning the Inchon landing conducted in Korea in September 1950 (Department of the Army, Office of the Chief of Staff, G-3, Operations).

Other Documents

Inchon: Love, Destiny, Heroes motion picture publicity booklet (Brigham Young University).

Transcripts and Papers

Edward M. Almond (MacArthur Memorial Archives; Virginia Military Institute); Roy E. Appleman (United States Army History Education Center); David G. Barr

(United States Army History Education Center); Frank Goldsworthy (Imperial War Museum); Arleigh A. Burke (United States Naval Institute); Victor H. Krulak (United States Marine Corps University); D. Clayton James (MacArthur Memorial Archives); Douglas MacArthur (MacArthur Memorial Archives); Raymond L. Murray (United States Marine Corps University); Lemuel C. Shepherd, Jr. (United States Marine Corps University); Edwin H. Simmons (George Washington University); Arthur D. Struble (United States Naval Institute); Oliver P. Smith (University of California, Berkeley; United States Marine Corps University); Edwin K. Wright (MacArthur Memorial Archives).

Newspapers and Magazines

Atlanta Constitution; Atlanta Daily World; Austin American Statesman; Baltimore Sun; Boston Globe; Boxoffice; Chicago Daily Tribune; China Daily; Chosŏn ilbo; Christian Science Monitor; Chungang ilbo; Daily Express; Daily Herald; Detroit Free Press; Global Times; Globe and Mail; Guardian; Hartford Courant; Korea Times; Kyŏnghyang sinmun; Leatherneck; LIFE; Los Angeles Times; Manchester Guardian; Minneapolis Star Tribune; Minneapolis Sunday Tribune; Morning Call; Nation; National Post; New York Daily Worker; New York Herald Tribune; New York Times; Newsweek; Observer; Philadelphia Inquirer; Pittsburgh Post-Gazette; Pyongyang Times; Rodong sinmun; Saturday Evening Post; Screen International; South China Morning Post; South China Sunday Post; Stars and Stripes; TIME; The Times; Times of India; Tonga ilbo; Variety; Washington Post; Women's Wear Daily; Yŏnhap nyusŭ.

News Agencies

Agence France-Presse; Korea Central News Agency.

News Monitoring Services

BBC Monitoring; KCNA Watch.

Books, Articles, and Theses

Abramson, Rudy, *Spanning the Century: The Life of W. Averell Harriman, 1891–1986* (New York, 1992).

Acheson, Dean, *Present at the Creation: My Years in the State Department* (New York, 1969).

Aguirre, Emilio, *We'll Be Home for Christmas: A True Story of the United States Marine Corps in the Korean War* (New York, 1959).

Aid, Matthew M., *The Secret Sentry: The Untold History of the National Security Agency* (New York, 2009).

BIBLIOGRAPHY

Alexander, Bevin, *MacArthur's War: The Flawed Genius Who Challenged the American Political System* (New York, 2013).

Alexander, Bevin, *Korea: The First War We Lost*, revised edition (New York, 1998).

Alexander, James Edwin, *Inchon to Wonsan: From the Deck of a Destroyer in the Korean War* (Annapolis, MD, 1996).

Alexander, Joseph H., *Fleet Operations in a Mobile War: September 1950–June 1951, The U.S. Navy in the Korean War* (Washington, DC, 2001).

Alexander, Joseph H., *Battle of the Barricades: U.S. Marines in the Recapture of Seoul*, Marines in the Korean War Commemorative Series (Washington, DC, 2000).

Alexander, Joseph H. and Merrill L. Bartlett, *Sea Soldiers in the Cold War: Amphibious Warfare, 1945–1991* (Annapolis, MD, 1995).

An, Chin-hong, *Inch'ŏn sangnyuk chakcŏn* (Seoul, 2014).

Anon., *Korea Reborn: A Grateful Nation Honors War Veterans for More Than Sixty Years* (Salt Lake City, UT, 2018).

Anon., *Victorious Fatherland Liberation War Museum* (Pyongyang, 1990).

Anon., *The Victorious Fatherland Liberation War Museum* (Pyongyang, 1979).

Anon., *Pyongyang* (Pyongyang, 1975).

Anon., *Fatherland Liberation War Memorial* (Pyongyang, 1969).

Anon., *Records of Great Victory* (Pyongyang, 1962).

Anon (ed.), *Eight Years of the Chinese People's Volunteers' Resistance to American Aggression and Aiding Korea* (Beijing, 1958).

Appleman, Roy E., *Escaping the Trap: The U.S. Army's X Corps in Northeast Korea, 1950* (College Station, TX, 1990).

Appleman, Roy E., *Ridgway Duels for Korea* (College Station, TX, 1990).

Appleman, Roy E., *Disaster in Korea: The Chinese Confront MacArthur* (College Station, TX, 1989).

Appleman, Roy E., *East of Chosin: Entrapment and Breakout in Korea, 1950* (College Station, TX, 1987).

Appleman, Roy E., *United States Army in the Korean War: South to the Naktong, North to the Yalu (June–November 1950)* (Washington, DC, 1961).

Armstrong, Charles K., *The North Korean Revolution, 1945–1950* (Ithaca, NY, 2003).

Armstrong, Stephen B., *Andrew V. McLaglen: The Life and Hollywood Career* (Jefferson, NC, 2011).

Axelrod, Alan, *Bradley* (New York, 2008).

Baik, Bong, *Kim Il Sung Biography (II): From Building Democratic Korea to Chullima Fight* (Beirut, 1973).

Ballard, John R., 'Operation Chromite: Counterattack at Inchon', *JFQ: Joint Force Quarterly* 28 (2001), 31–6.

Barlow, Jeffrey G., *Revolt of the Admirals: The Fight for Naval Aviation, 1945–1950* (Washington, DC, 1998).

Barron, Leo, *High Tide in the Korean War: How an Outnumbered American Regiment Defeated the Chinese at the Battle of Chipyong-ni* (Mechanicsburg, PA, 2015).

Bärtås, Magnus and Fredrik Ekman, *All Monsters Must Die: An Excursion to North Korea*, Saskia Vogel, trans. (Toronto, 2015).
Bartlett, Merrill L. (ed.), *Assault from the Sea: Essays on the History of Amphibious Warfare* (Annapolis, MD, 1982).
Beech, Keyes, *Tokyo and Points East* (Garden City, NY, 1954).
Berry, Henry, *Hey, Mac, Where Ya Been? Living Memories of the U.S. Marines in the Korean War* (New York, 1988).
Blair, Clay, *The Forgotten War: America in Korea 1950–1953* (New York, 1987).
Blomstedt, Larry, *Truman, Congress, and Korea: The Politics of America's First Undeclared War* (Lexington, KY, 2016).
Boettcher, Robert with Gordon L. Freedman, *Gifts of Deceit: Sun Myung Moon, Tongsun Park, and the Korean Scandal* (New York, 1980).
Bonner, Nicholas with Simon Cockerell and James Banfill, *Printed in North Korea: The Art of Everyday Life in North Korea* (London, 2019).
Boose, Donald W., Jr., *Over the Beach: US Army Amphibious Operations in the Korean War* (Fort Leavenworth, KS, 2008).
Bowers, Ian (ed.), *Coalition Navies during the Korean War: Understanding Combined Naval Operations* (London, 2024).
Bradford, Jeffrey A., 'MacArthur, Inchon and the Art of Battle Command', *Military Review* 81, 2 (2001), 83–95.
Bradley, Omar and Clay Blair, *A General's Life: An Autobiography* (New York, 1983).
Brainard, Morgan, *Men in Low Cut Shoes: A Marine Rifle Company in Korea, 1950–1951* (Great Neck, NY, 1986).
Brands, H. W., *The General vs. the President: MacArthur and Truman on the Brink of Nuclear War* (New York, 2016).
Brazinsky, Gregg, *Nation Building in South Korea: Koreans, Americans, and the Making of a Democracy* (Chapel Hill, NC, 2007).
Breuer, William B., *Shadow Warriors: The Covert War in Korea* (New York, 1996).
Brionowski, Anna, *Aim High in Creation! A One-of-a-Kind Journey inside North Korea's Propaganda Machine* (New York, 2015).
Buhite, Russell D., *Douglas MacArthur: Statecraft and Stagecraft in America's East Asian Policy* (Lanham, MD, 2008).
Burdick, Eddie, *Three Days in the Hermit Kingdom: An American Visits North Korea* (Jefferson, NC, 2010).
Cagle, Malcolm W., 'Inchon: The Analysis of a Gamble', *U.S. Naval Institute Proceedings* 80, 1 (1954), 47–51.
Cagle, Malcolm W. and Frank A. Manson, *The Sea War in Korea* (Annapolis, MD, 1957).
Caldwell, John D., *Anatomy of Victory: Why the United States Triumphed in World War II, Fought to a Stalemate in Korea, Lost in Vietnam, and Failed in Iraq* (Lanham, MD, 2019).
Cameron, James, *Point of Departure: Experiment in Biography* (London, 1967).
Carmin, Charles L., *My Twenty and Then Some* (Ellinwood, KS, 2011).

Carpenter, Ronald H., 'General Douglas MacArthur's Oratory on Behalf of Inchon: Discourse that Altered the Course of History', *Southern Communications Journal* 58, 1 (1992), 1–12.

Casey, Stephen, *Selling the Korean War: Propaganda, Politics, and Public Opinion in the United States, 1950–1953* (New York, 2008).

Catchpole, Brian, *The Korean War, 1950–53* (New York, 2000).

Cathcart, Adam, 'Kim Jong-un Syndrome: North Korean Commemorative Culture and the Succession Process', in Adam Cathcart, Robert Winstanley-Chesters, and Christopher Green (eds), *Change and Continuity in North Korean Politics* (London, 2017), 6–22.

Cha, Victor, *The Impossible State: North Korea, Past and Future*, updated edition (New York, 2018).

Chae, Young Eun, 'Screening the Past: Historiography of Contemporary South Korean Cinema' (PhD thesis, University of North Carolina, 2011).

Chen, Jian, 'Far Short of a "Glorious Victory": Revisiting China's Changing Strategies to Manage the Korean War', *Chinese Historical Review* 25, 1 (2018), 1–22.

Chen, Jian, *China's Road to the Korean War: The Making of the Sino-American Confrontation* (New York, 1994).

Chisolm, Donald, 'Amphibious Assault as Decisive Maneuver in Korea', in Bruce A. Elleman and S. C. M. Paine (eds), *Naval Power and Expeditionary Wars: Peripheral Campaigns and New Theatres of Naval Warfare* (Abingdon, 2011), 114–28.

Chisolm, Donald, 'Negotiated Joint Command Relationships: Korean War Amphibious Operations, 1950', *Naval War College Review* 53, 2 (2000), 65–124.

Cho, Sanggŭn, 'Han'guk chŏnjaeng esŏ Chunggong chidobu ŭi Inch'ŏn sangnyuk chakchŏn yech'ŭk kwajŏng', *Kunsa* 71 (2009), 55–80.

Cho, Sanghun, 'Memory as Propaganda: The Molding of Official Memory of the Korean War and Its Employment in the DPRK from 1953 to 1958' (MA thesis, University of Toronto, 2007).

Cho, Sŏnghun, 'Inch'ŏn sangnyuk chakchŏn ŭl chŏnhunhan Maekadŏ yŏk'hal ŭi chaep'yŏngga', *Chŏngsin munhwa yŏn'gu* 29, 3 (2006), 133–67.

Choi, Brent (Won-ki), 'Anti-Americanism or "Antibaseism": U.S.–South Korean Relations through Changing Generations', in David A. Steinberg (ed.), *Korean Attitudes towards the United States: Changing Dynamics* (London, 2015), 307–15.

Choi, Chonghyun, 'Between Protector and Oppressor: Representation of the United States as a Geopolitical Entity in Korean Blockbusters', in Hyunseon Lee (ed.), *Korean Film and History* (London, 2024), 161–79.

Choi, Suhi, *Right to Mourn: Trauma, Empathy, and Korean War Memorials* (New York, 2019).

Choi, Suhi, *Embattled Memories: Contested Meanings in Korean War Memorials* (Reno and Las Vegas, NV, 2014).

Choi, Suhi, 'Standing between Intransigent History and Transient Memories: The Statue of MacArthur in South Korea', *Memory Studies* 7 (2014), 191–206.

Choi, Suhi, 'The New History and the Old Present: Archival Images in PBS Documentary *Battle for Korea*', *Media, Culture & Society* 31, 1 (2009), 59–77.
Chŏnjaeng kinyŏm saŏphoe, *Han'guk chŏnjaengsa kwŏn 1–6* (Seoul, 1992).
Chosŏn Rondongang Ch'ulp'ansa, *Cha-ju Toknip eul wihan Chosun In-min ui Chokuk Hae-bang Cheon-Chaeng* (Pyongyang, 1959).
Chung, Henry, *Korea and the United States through War and Peace, 1943–1960* (Seoul, 2000).
Clark, Eugene Franklin, *Secrets of Inchon: The Untold Story of the Most Daring Covert Mission of the Korean War* (New York, 2002).
Cleaver, Thomas McKelvey, *The Frozen Chosen: The 1st Marine Division and the Battle of the Chosin Reservoir* (Oxford, 2016).
Coker, Kathryn Roe and Jason Wetzel, *The U.S. Army Combat Historian and Combat Operations: World War I to the Vietnam War* (Philadelphia, PA, 2023).
Coleman, J. D., *Wonju: The Gettysburg of the Korean War* (Washington, DC, 2000).
Coleman, Terry, *Olivier* (New York, 2005).
Collins, J. Lawton, *Lightning Joe: An Autobiography* (Baton Rouge, LA, 1979).
Collins, J. Lawton, *War in Peacetime: The History and Lessons of Korea* (Boston, MA, 1969).
Collins, Robert M., 'Korean People's Army', in James I. Matray and Donald W. Boose, Jr. (eds), *The Ashgate Research Companion to the Korean War* (Farnham, 2014), 255–67.
Conant, Jennet, *Fierce Ambition: The Life and Legend of War Correspondent Maggie Higgins* (New York, 2023).
Condit, Doris M., *History of the Office of the Secretary of Defense*, Volume 2: *The Test of War, 1950–1953* (Washington, DC, 1988).
Connor, John W., *Let Slip the Dogs of War: A Memoir of the GHQ 1st Raider Company (8245th Army Unit) a.k.a. Special Operations Company. Korea, 1950–51* (Bennington, VT, 2008).
Cooke, John Bryne, *Reporting the War: Freedom of the Press from the American Revolution to the War on Terrorism* (New York, 2007).
Coram, Robert, *Brute: The Life of Victor Krulak, U.S. Marine* (New York, 2010).
Corer, Lara M., 'Assertive Nationalism in Korean Youth: Anti-American Protest in the 2000s' (MA thesis, Indiana University, 2012).
Cornfield, Justin, *Historical Dictionary of Pyongyang* (London, 2013).
Crane, Conrad C., *American Airpower Strategy in the Korean War* (Lawrence, KS, 2000).
Cumings, Bruce, *The Korean War: A History* (New York, 2010).
Cumings, Bruce, 'The Korean War: What Is It That We Are Remembering to Forget?', in Sheila Miyoshi Jager and Rana Ritter (eds), *Ruptured Histories: War, Memory, and the Post-Cold War in Asia* (Cambridge, MA, 2007), 266–90.
Cumings, Bruce, *War and Television* (London, 1992).
Cumings, Bruce, *The Origins of the Korean War*, Volume 2: *The Roaring Cataract, 1947–1950* (Princeton, NJ, 1990).

Cutler, Thomas J., 'Sea Power and Defense of the Pusan Pocket, June-September 1950', in Edward J. Marolda (ed.), *The U.S. Navy in the Korean War* (Annapolis, MD, 2007), 1–51.
Daily, Edward L., *MacArthur's X Corps in Korea: Inchon to the Yalu, 1950* (Paducah, KY, 1999).
Davies, Robert B., *Baldwin of the Times: Hanson W. Baldwin, a Military Journalist's Life, 1903–1991* (Annapolis, MD, 2011).
Davis, Burke, *Marine! The Life of Lt. Gen. Lewis B. (Chesty) Puller, USMC (Ret.)* (Boston, MA, 1962).
Desfor, Max, 'The Korean War through the Camera of an American War Correspondent', in Philip West and Suh Ji-moon (eds), *Remembering the "Forgotten War": The Korean War through Literature and Art* (Armonk, NY, 2001), 77–91.
Devine, Michael J., *The Korean War Remembered: Contested Memories of an Unended Conflict* (Lincoln, NB, 2023).
Dickerson, Bryan J., *Marine General from the Ranks: The Life of Lieutenant General Homer L. Litzenberg, Jr., USMC* (Middleton, DE, 2016).
Dockery, Jared, 'Return to the Pentagon: Marshall and the Korean War', in William A. Taylor (ed.), *George C. Marshall and the Early Cold War* (Norman, OK, 2020), 189–217.
Dorschner, Jim, 'Douglas MacArthur's Last Triumph', *Military History* 22, 6 (2005), 30–6.
Dougherty, Leo J., III, *Train Wreckers and Ghost Killers: Allied Marines in the Korean War* (Washington, DC, 2003).
Drifte, Reinhard, 'Japan's Involvement in the Korean War', in James Cotton and Ian Neary (eds), *The Korean War in History* (Atlantic Highlands, NJ, 1989), 120–34.
Duffy, Bernard K. and Ronald H. Carpenter, *Douglas MacArthur: Warrior as Wordsmith* (Westport, CT, 1997).
Duncan, David Douglas, *This Is War! A Photo-Narrative of the Korean War* (Boston, MA, 1990).
Dupré, Judith, *Monuments: America's History in Art and Memory* (New York, 2007).
Durham, Robert L., 'MacArthur's Last Great Stroke', *Military Heritage* 22, 3 (2020), 35–43.
Editing Committee of the Album of the Korean Revolution Museum, *The Korean Revolution Museum*, Volume 2 (Tokyo, 1975).
Edwards, Paul M., *The Mistaken History of the Korean War: What We Got Wrong, Then and Now* (Jefferson, NC, 2018).
Edwards, Paul M., *To Acknowledge a War: The Korean War in American Memory* (Westport, CT, 2000).
Edwards, Paul M., *A Guide to Films on the Korean War* (Westport, CT, 1997).
Edwards, Paul M., *The Inchon Landing, Korea, 1950: An Annotated Bibliography* (Westport, CT, 1994).

Ehrhart, William D., 'Above All, the Waste: American Soldier-Poets and the Korean War', in Philip West and Suh Ji-moon (eds), *Remembering the "Forgotten War": The Korean War through Literature and Art* (Armonk, NY, 2001), 40–54.

Elliott, Oliver, *The American Press and the Cold War: The Rise of Authoritarianism in South Korea, 1945–1954* (London, 2018).

Ellman, James, *MacArthur Reconsidered: General Douglas MacArthur as a Wartime Commander* (Essex, CT, 2023).

Estes, Kenneth W., *Into the Breach at Pusan: The 1st Provisional Marine Brigade in the Korean War* (Norman, OK, 2012).

Evans, Alun, *Brassey's Guide to War Films* (Washington, DC, 2000).

Everard, John, *Only Beautiful, Please: A British Diplomat in North Korea* (Stanford, CA, 2012).

Falk, Stanley L., 'Comments on Reynolds: "MacArthur as Maritime Strategist"', *Naval War College Review* 33, 2 (1980), 92–9.

Farrar-Hockley, Anthony, *The British Part in the Korean War*, Volume 1: *A Distant Obligation* (London, 1990).

Fehrenbach, T. R., *This Kind of War: A Study in Unpreparedness* (New York, 1963).

Field, James A., Jr., *History of United States Naval Operations: Korea* (Washington, DC, 1962).

Fischer, Paul, *A Kim Jong-Il Production: The Incredible True Story of North Korea and the Most Audacious Kidnapping in History* (London, 2015).

Fishgall, Gary, *Gregory Peck: A Biography* (New York, 2002).

Foreign Languages Publishing House, *They Fought for the Fatherland: Reminiscences of the Korean War* (Pyongyang, 1963).

Fox, Levi, 'Not Forgotten: The Korean War in American Public Memory, 1950–2017' (PhD thesis, Temple University, 2018).

Foy, David A., *Loyalty First: The Life and Times of Charles A. Willoughby, MacArthur's Chief Intelligence Officer* (Philadelphia, PA, 2023).

Frank, Richard B., *MacArthur* (New York, 2007).

Fujiwara, Kazuki, *Han'guk chŏnjaeng esŏ ssaun Ilbonin: ilgŭp pimil konggae ro tŭrŏnan Ilbonin ŭi Han'guk chŏnjaeng ch'amjŏn kirok*, Yong-jun Pak, trans. (Seoul, 2023).

Futrell, Robert Frank, *The United States Air Force in Korea, 1950–1953* (New York, 1961).

Gabroussenko, Tatiana, *Soldiers on the Cultural Front: Developments in the Early History of North Korean Literature and Literary Policy* (Honolulu, 2010).

Gatchel, Theodore L., *At the Water's Edge: Defending against the Modern Amphibious Assault* (Annapolis, MD, 1996).

Gateward, Francis (ed.), *Seoul Searching: Culture and Identity in Contemporary Korean Cinema* (Albany, NY, 2007).

Gazzara, Ben, *In the Moment: My Life as an Actor* (New York, 2004).

Geer, Andrew, *The New Breed: The Story of the U.S. Marines in Korea* (New York, 1952).

Gilbert, Oscar E., *Marine Corps Tank Battles in Korea* (Havertown, PA, 2003).

Gilbert, Oscar E. and Romain C. Cansière, *Amphibious Warfare: Battle on the Beaches* (Oxford, 2018).
Goldstein, Lyle, 'The Hard School of Amphibious Warfare: Examining the Lessons of the 20th Century's Major Amphibious Campaigns for Contemporary Chinese Strategy', *Asian Security* 19, 1 (2023), 26–42.
Goldstein, Stephen M., 'Chinese Perspectives on the Origins of the Korean War: An Assessment at Sixty', *International Journal of Korean Studies* 14, 2 (2010), 45–70.
Goldsworthy, Frank, *Want You Soonest . . . : Memoirs of a War Reporter* (Pittsburgh, PA, 1997).
Gordon, Michael R. and Bernard E. Trainor, *The Generals' War: The Inside Story of the Conflict in the Gulf* (Boston, MA, 1995).
Gorenfeld, John, *Bad Moon Rising: How Reverend Moon Created The Washington Times, Seduced the Religious Right, and Built an American Kingdom* (Sausalito, CA, 2008).
Goulden, Joseph C., *Korea: The Untold Story of the War* (New York, 1982).
Gray, John Edward, *Called to Honor: Memoirs of a Three-War Veteran* (Ashville, NC, 2006).
Green, Michael, *The United States Marine Corps in the Korean War: Rare Photographs from Wartime Archives* (Barnsley, 2021).
Grey, Jeffrey (ed.), *The Last Word? Essays on Official History in the United States and British Commonwealth* (Westport, CT, 1999).
Haebyŏngdae, *Haebyŏngdae chŏnu 70-yŏnsa*, 2 vols. (Seoul, 2019).
Haebyŏndae Saryŏngbu, *Sajin ŭro pon haebyŏndae 50-yŏnsa, 1949–1999* (Seoul, 1999).
Haebyŏngdae Saryŏngbu, *Haebyŏngdae chŏnt'usa* (Seoul, 1962).
Haebyŏngdae Saryŏngbu, *Haebyŏng palchŏnsa: haebyŏng sibinyŏns,a: cha 1949, 04, 15 chi 1960, 12, 31* (Seoul, 1961).
Haig, Alexander M., Jr., with Charles McCary, *Inner Circles: How America Changed the World: A Memoir* (New York, 1992).
Hajima, Masuda, *Cold War Crucible: The Korean Conflict and the Postwar World* (Cambridge, MA, 2015).
Halberstam, David, *The Coldest Winter: America and the Korean War* (New York, 2007).
Hallion, Richard P., *The Naval Air War in Korea* (Tuscaloosa, AL, 2011).
Hammel, Eric, *Chosin: Heroic Ordeal of the Korean War* (New York, 1981).
Hammes, T. X., *Forgotten Warriors: The 1st Provisional Marine Brigade, the Corps Ethos, and the Korean War* (Lawrence, KS, 2010).
Han, Sunghoon, 'The Ongoing Korean War at the Sinch'ŏn Museum in North Korea', *Cross-Currents* 4 (2015), 95–125.
Hand, Jesse A. with Michael Hudson Arnold, *The Change Is Forever: Memories, 1931–2022* (Middletown, DE, 2022).
Han'guk yŏksa yŏn'guhoe, *Yŏksahak sisŏn ŭro ingnŭn Han'guk chŏnjaeng* (Seoul, 2010).

Hanson, Thomas E., *Combat Ready? The Eighth U.S. Army on the Eve of the Korean War* (College Station, TX, 2010).

Hanley, Charles J., *Ghost Flames: Life and Death in a Hidden War* (New York, 2020).

Hanley, Charles J., 'No Gun Ri: Official Narrative and Inconvenient Truths', *Critical Asian Studies* 42, 4 (2010), 589–622.

Hanley, Charles J., Sang-Hun Choe, and Martha Mendoza, *The Bridge at No Gun Ri: A Hidden Nightmare from the Korean War* (New York, 2001).

Hanley, Lynn, *Gregory Peck: A Charmed Life* (New York, 2004).

Hao, Yufan and Zhai Zhihai, 'China's Decision to Enter the Korean War: History Revisited', in Kim Chull Baum and James I. Matray (eds), *Korea and the Cold War: Division, Destruction, and Disarmament* (Claremont, CA, 1993), 141–66.

Harden, Blaine, *King of Spies: The Dark Reign of America's Spymaster in Korea* (New York, 2017).

Hass, Kristin, 'Remembering the "Forgotten War" and Containing the "Remembered War": Insistent Nationalism and the Transnational Memory of the Korean War', in Udo J. Hebel (ed.), *Transnational American Memories* (Berlin, 2009), 267–84.

Hassig, Ralph and Kongdan Oh, *The Hidden People of North Korea: Ordinary Life in the Hermit Kingdom*, 2nd edition (Lanham, MD, 2015).

Hastings, Max, *The Korean War* (London, 1987).

Heck, Timothy and B. A. Friedman (eds), *On Contested Shores: The Evolving Role of Amphibious Operations in the History of Warfare* (Quantico, VA, 2020).

Heefner, Wilson A., *Patton's Bulldog: The Life and Service of General Walton H. Walker* (Shippensburg, PA, 2001).

Heefner, Wilson A., 'The Inch'on Landing', *Military Review* 75, 2 (1995), 65–77.

Heinl, Robert Debs, Jr., *Victory at High Tide: The Inchon-Seoul Campaign* (Philadelphia, PA, 1968).

Heinl, Robert Debs, Jr., *Soldiers of the Sea: The United States Marine Corps, 1775–1962* (Annapolis, MD, 1962).

Hellier, Francis H. (ed.), *The Korean War: A 25-Year Retrospective* (Lawrence, KS, 1977).

Hemler, Chris K., *Delivering Destruction: American Firepower and Amphibious Assault from Tarawa to Iwo Jima* (Annapolis, MD, 2023).

Herman, Arthur, *Douglas MacArthur: American Warrior* (New York, 2016).

Hermes, Walter G., *United States Army in the Korean War: Truce Tent and Fighting Front* (Washington, DC, 1966).

Hickey, Michael, *The Korean War: The West Confronts Communism, 1950–1953* (Woodstock, NY, 1999).

Higgins, Marguerite, *War in Korea: The Report of a Woman Combat Correspondent* (Garden City, NY, 1951).

Higham, Robin (ed.), *The Writing of Official Military History* (Westport, CT, 1999).

Higham, Robin (ed.), *Official Histories: Essays and Bibliographies from around the World* (Manhattan, KS, 1970).

Ho, Jong Ho, Kang Sok Hui, and Pak Thae Ho, *The U.S. Imperialists Started the Korean War* (Pyongyang, 1977/1993).
Hoffman, Jon T., *Chesty: The Story of Lieutenant General Lewis B. Puller, USMC* (New York, 2001).
Hong, Seunghei Clara, 'Silenced in Memoriam: Consuming Memory at the Nogŭnri Peace Park', *Cross-Currents*, 4 (2015), 126–50.
Hong, Yong-Pyo, *State Security and Regime Security: President Syngman Rhee and the Insecurity Dilemma in South Korea, 1953–60* (Basingstoke, 2000).
Hopkins, William B., *One Bugle, No Drums: The Marines at Chosin Reservoir* (Chapel Hill, NC, 1986).
Horrell, Mason Edward, 'Reporting the "Forgotten War": Military-Press Relations in Korea, 1950–1954' (PhD thesis, University of Kentucky, 2002).
Horne, Alastair, *Hubris: The Tragedy of War in the Twentieth Century* (New York, 2015).
Howard, Keith, *Songs for "Great Leaders": Ideology and Creativity in North Korean Music and Dance* (New York, 2020).
Hwang, Gon, *The Island in Flames* (Pyongyang, 1966).
Hwang, Yun Sik, 'Nationalism in Crisis: The Reconstruction of South Korean Nationalism in Korean History Textbooks' (MA thesis, University of Toronto, 2016).
Isserman, Maurice, *Korean War* (New York, 2003).
Jackson, Andrew David, 'South Korean Films about the Korean War', *Acta Koreana* 16 (2013), 281–301.
Jager, Sheila Miyoshi, *Brothers at War: The Unending Conflict in Korea* (New York, 2013).
Jager, Sheila Miyoshi and Jiyul Kim, 'The Korean War after the Cold War: Commemorating the Armistice Agreement in South Korea', in Sheila Miyoshi Jager and Rana Ritter (eds), *Ruptured Histories: War, Memory, and the Post-Cold War in Asia* (Cambridge, MA, 2007), 233–65.
Jager, Sheila Miyoshi, *Narratives of Nation Building in Korea: A Genealogy of Patriotism* (Armonk, NY, 2003).
James, D. Clayton, *The Years of MacArthur, Volume 3: Triumph and Disaster, 1945–1964* (Boston, MA, 1985).
James, D. Clayton with Anne Sharp Wells, *Refighting the Last War: Command and Crisis in Korea, 1950–1953* (New York, 1993).
Jang, Jin-sun, *Dear Leader: North Korea's Senior Propagandist Exposes Shocking Truths behind the Regime* (London, 2014).
Jeppesen, Travis, *See You Again in Pyongyang: A Journey into Kim Jong Un's North Korea* (New York, 2018).
Jones, Charles and Eugene Jones, *The Face of War* (New York, 1951).
Jung, Keun-sik, 'China's Memory and Commemoration of the Korean War in the Memorial Hall of the "War to Resist U.S. Aggression and Aid Korea"', *Cross-Currents* 4 (2015), 14–29.

Kang, Hyok with Philippe Grangeau, *This Is Paradise! My North Korean Childhood*, trans. Shaun Whiteside (London, 2005).
Kang, Sŏkhŭi, *Chosŏn inmin ŭi chŏngŭi ŭi choguk haebang chŏnjaengsa 2* (Pyŏngyang, 1983).
Karig, Walter, Malcolm W. Cagle, and Frank A. Manson, *Battle Report: The War in Korea* (New York, 1952).
Kaufman, Burton I., *The Korean War: Challenges in Crisis, Credibility, and Command* (Philadelphia, PA, 1986).
Keiser, Gordon W., *The US Marine Corps and Defense Unification, 1944–47: Politics of Survival* (Washington, DC, 1982).
Kim, Chae-yŏp, *Taehan Min'guk Haebyŏngdae: segye esŏ kajang kanginham kundae ŭi chopko* (Seoul, 2009).
Kim, Chinung, 'Maekadŏ changgun ŭi che 2 ŭi Inch'ŏn sangnyuk chakchŏn: Tongsang ŭl pullŏssan punjaeng ŭi hamŭi', *Yŏksa kyoyuk nontan* 39, 8 (2007), 415–54.
Kim, Chongguk, 'Inch'ŏn (1981) ŭi chejak kwajŏng kwa yŏnghwajŏk yusan', *Han'guk pangsong hakpo* 28, 1 (2014), 167–205.
Kim, Chum-kon, *The Korean War* (Seoul, 1973).
Kim, Chun-hyŏk, *Panorama of Pyongyang* (Pyongyang, 2017).
Kim, Daniel Y., *The Intimacies of Conflict: Cultural Memory and the Korean War* (New York, 2020).
Kim, Daniel Y., 'Nationalist Technologies of Cultural Memory and the Korean War: Militarism and Neo-Liberalism in *The Price of Freedom* and the War Memorial of Korea', *Cross-Currents* 4 (2015), 40–70.
Kim, Do Young, 'Heroes of Wolmi Island', in *They Fought for the Fatherland: Reminiscences of the Korean War* (Pyongyang, 1963), 151–8.
Kim, Hakjoon, 'A Review of Korean War Studies since 1992–1994', in James I. Matray (ed.), *Northeast Asia and the Legacy of Harry S. Truman: Japan, China, and the Two Koreas* (Kirksville, MO, 2012), 315–46.
Kim, Il Sung, *Reminiscences: With the Century*, 8 vols. (Pyongyang, 1994–8).
Kim, Il Sung, *Works, Volume 6: June 1950–December 1951* (Pyongyang, 1981).
Kim, Il Sung, *The Just Fatherland Liberation War of the Korean People for Freedom and Independence* (Pyongyang, 1955).
Kim, Jinwung, *A History of Korea: From Land of the Morning Calm to States in Conflict* (Bloomington, IN, 2012).
Kim, Jong Il, *On the Art of the Cinema: April 11, 1973*, reprint edition (Honolulu, 2001).
Kim, Minu, 'Wŏlmido appadasŏ yŏllin 'Inch'ŏn sangnyuk chakchŏn chŏnsŭng 62 chunyŏn kinyŏm mit chaeyŏn haengsa', *Kukpang kwa kisul* 404, 10 (2012), 42.
Kim, Sŏngu and Kim Yonghyŏn, *Han'guk chŏnjaengsa* (Seoul, 2008).
Kim, Suk-young, *Illusive Utopia: Theater, Film and Everyday Performance in North Korea* (Ann Arbor, MI, 2010).
Kim, Sun-A, 'Life and War in Korea: Photographic Portrayals of the Korean War in LIFE Magazine, July 1950–August 1953' (PhD thesis, University of Missouri, 2008).

Kim, Suzy, 'Specters of War in Pyongyang: The Victorious Fatherland Liberation War Museum in North Korea', *Cross-Currents* 4 (2015), 71–98.

Kim, Suzy, *Everyday Life in the North Korean Revolution, 1945–1950* (Ithaca, NY, 2013).

Kim, Won-chung, 'The Korean War, Memory and Nostalgia', *Comparative Literature and Culture* 17, 3 (2015), https://doi.org/10.7771/1481-4374.2786 (accessed 12 December 2020).

Kim, Youngjun, *Origins of the North Korean Garrison State: The People's Army and the Korean War* (London, 2018).

King, O. H. P., *Tail of the Paper Tiger* (Caldwell, ID, 1961).

Kiper, Richard L., *Spare Not the Brave: The Special Activities Group in Korea* (Kent, OH, 2014).

Knight, Peter G., '"MacArthur's Eyes": Reassessing Military Intelligence Operations in the Forgotten War, June 1950–April 1951' (PhD thesis, Ohio State University, 2006).

Knightley, Philip, *The First Casualty: The War Correspondent as Hero and Myth-Maker from the Crimea to Iraq* (Baltimore, MD, 2004).

Knox, Donald, *The Korean War: Pusan to Chosin: An Oral History* (San Diego, CA, 1985).

Koe, Dong-Yeon, *The Korean War and Postmemory Generation: Contemporary Korean Arts and Films* (Abingdon, 2022).

Korea Institute of Military History, *The Korean War*, Volumes 1–3 (Lincoln, NB, 2000).

Korean Film Export and Import Corporation, *Korean Film Art* (Pyongyang, 1985).

Korean People's Army, *The Heroic KPA, the Invincible Revolutionary Armed Forces* (Pyongyang, 1990).

Kosh, Gertrude, 'A Law's Tale: *The Man Who Shot Liberty Valance*', *Philosophy and Social Criticism* 36, 6 (2008), 685–92.

Kotowski, Matthew, 'The Battle at Lake Changjin: The Influence of Korean War Memory on Contemporary Chinese War Films', *Journal of Chinese Military History* 13, 1 (2024), 53–92.

Krulak, Victor H., *First to Fight: An Inside View of the U.S. Marine Corps* (Annapolis, MD, 1984).

Kukpangbu p'yŏnch'an wiwŏnhoe, *Han'guk chŏnjaengsa* 1–11 (Seoul, 1970–80).

Kwon, Heonik, *After the Korean War: An Intimate History* (Cambridge, 2020).

Kwon, Hoenik and Jun Hwan Park, 'American Power in Korean Shamanism', *Journal of Korean Religions* 9, 1 (2018), 43–68.

La Bree, Clifton, *The Gentle Warrior: General Oliver Prince Smith, USMC* (Kent, OH, 2001).

Lange, Dorian, 'The Republic of Korea's Public Libraries: A Critical Examination of Censorship Practices' (PhD thesis, University of Missouri, 2013).

Langley, Michael, *Inchon: MacArthur's Last Triumph* (London, 1979).

Lankov, Andrei, *North of the DMZ: Essays on Daily Life in North Korea* (Jefferson, NC, 2007).

Lankov, Andrei, *From Stalin to Kim Il Sung: The Formation of North Korea, 1945–1960* (New Brunswick, NJ, 2002).

Larew, Karl G., 'Inchon Invasion: Not a Stroke of Genius or Even Necessary', *Army* 38 (December 1988), 15–20.

Leary, William M. (ed.), *MacArthur and the American Century: A Reader* (Lincoln, NB, 2001).

Leckie, Robert, *Conflict: The History of the Korean War, 1950–53* (New York, 1962).

Lee, Hanna, 'How Are Historic Events Remembered? North Korean War Films on the Inchon Landing Operation', in Andrew David Jackson and Colette Bailman (eds), *Korean Screen Cultures: Interrogating Cinema, TV, Music and Online Games* (Bern, 2016), 177–92.

Lee, Hyangjin, 'The "Division Blockbuster" in South Korea: The Evolution of Cinematic Representations of War and Division', in Michael Berry and Chiho Sawada (eds), *Divided Lenses: Screen Memories of War in East Asia* (Honolulu, 2018), 62–73.

Lee, Hyangjin, *Contemporary Korean Cinema: Identity, Culture and Politics* (Manchester, 2001).

Lee, Hyunseon, 'Korean War Films: Generational Memory of North Korean Soldiers, Partisans, Brothers, and Women', in Hyunseon Lee (ed.), *Korean Films and History* (London, 2024), 133–60.

Lee, Jongsoo, *The Partition of Korea after World War II: A Global History* (New York, 2006).

Lee, Young-il and Choe Young-chol, *The History of Korean Cinema*, trans. Richard Lynn Greever (Seoul, 1998).

Lemza, John W., *The Big Picture: The Cold War on the Small Screen* (Lawrence, KS, 2021).

Lenz, Robert J., *Korean War Filmography* (Jefferson, NC, 2003).

Leonzini, Alexandra and Peter Moody, 'From MacArthur's Landing to Trump's Fire and Fury: Sonic Depictions of Struggle and Sacrifice in a North Korean Short Story, Film and Opera', *Korean Studies* 44 (2022), 73–107.

Levine, Alan J., *Stalin's Last War: Korea and the Approach to World War III* (Jefferson, NC, 2005).

Li, Xiaobing, *Attack at Chosin: The Chinese Second Offensive in Korea* (Norman, OK, 2020).

Li, Xiaobing, *China's War in Korea: Strategic Culture and Geopolitics* (Singapore, 2019).

Li, Xiaobing, *China's Battle for Korea: The 1951 Spring Offensive* (Bloomington, IN, 2014).

Li, Xiaobing, Allan R. Millett, and Bin Yu (trans. and eds), *Mao's Generals Remember the Korean War* (Lawrence, KS, 2001).

Lim, Jae-cheon, *Leader Symbols and Personality Cult in North Korea: The Leader State* (London, 2015).

Lim, Jae-cheon, 'Kim Jong Il and His Leadership' (PhD thesis, University of Hawai'i at Manoa, 2007).

Lim, Ŭn, *The Founding of a Dynasty in North Korea: An Authentic Biography of Kim Il-sŏng* (Tokyo, 1982).

Linantud, John L., 'War Memorials and Memories: Comparing the Philippines and South Korea', *International Journal of Heritage Studies* 14, 4 (2008), 347–61.

Lindsay, Robert, *This High Name: Public Relations and the U.S. Marine Corps* (Madison, WI, 1956).
Long, Gavin, *MacArthur as Military Commander* (London, 1969).
Lott, Arnold S., *Most Dangerous Sea: A History of Mine Warfare, and an Account of U.S. Navy Mine Warfare Operations in World War II and Korea* (Annapolis, MD, 1959).
Lowe, Keith, *Prisoners of History: What Monuments to World War II Tell Us about Our History and Ourselves* (New York, 2020).
Lynch, Michael E., *Edward M. Almond and the US Army: From the 92nd Infantry Division to the X Corps* (Lexington, KY, 2019).
Lynn, Hyung Gu, *Bipolar Orders: The Two Koreas since 1989* (London, 2007).
MacArthur, Douglas, *Reminiscences* (New York, 1964).
MacDonald, Callum A., *Korea: The War before Vietnam* (New York, 1987).
Mahony, Kevin, *Formidable Enemies: The North Korean and Chinese Soldier in the Korean War* (Novato, CA, 2001).
Manchester, William, *American Caesar: Douglas MacArthur, 1880–1964* (Boston, MA, 1978).
Marshall, S. L. A., *Pork Chop Hill: The American Fighting Man in Action, Korea, Spring, 1953* (New York, 1956).
Marshall, S. L. A., *The River and the Gauntlet: Defeat of the Eighth Army by the Chinese Communist Forces, November 1950, in the Battle of the Chongchon River, Korea* (New York, 1953).
Martin, Bradley K., *Under the Loving Care of the Fatherly Leader: North Korea and the Kim Dynasty* (New York, 2004).
Masuda, Hiroshi, *MacArthur in Asia: The General and His Staff in the Philippines, Japan, and Korea*, trans. Reiko Yamamoto (Ithaca, NY, 2012).
Matray, James I., 'Koreans Invade Korea', in James I. Matray and Donald W. Boose, Jr. (eds), *The Ashgate Research Companion to the Korean War* (Farnham, 2014), 309–20.
Matray, James I., 'Korea's War at 60: A Survey of the Literature', *Cold War History* 11, 1 (2011), 99–129.
Matray, James I., 'Truman's Plan for Victory: National Self-Determination and the Thirty-Eighth Parallel Decision in Korea', *Journal of American History* 66, 2 (1979), 314–33.
McFarland, Keith D., *Louis Johnson and the Arming of America: The Roosevelt and Truman Years* (Bloomington, IN, 2005).
McGibbon, Ian, *New Zealand and the Korean War, Volume 2: Combat Operations* (Auckland, 1996).
McWilliams, Bill, *On Hallowed Ground: The Last Battle for Pork Chop Hill* (Annapolis, MD, 2003).
Medved, Harry and Michael Medved, *The Hollywood Hall of Shame: The Most Expensive Flops in Movie History* (London, 1984).
Merritt, Jonathan C., 'The Remembered War: The Korean War in American Culture, 1953–1995' (PhD thesis, University of Alabama, 2017).

Meuser, Philipp (ed.), *Architectural and Cultural Guide: Pyongyang*, 2 vols. (Berlin, 2012).
Miller, Michael D., *General Douglas MacArthur: From Betrayal to Greatness* (Columbia, SC, 2022).
Miller, Rod, *West Point U.S. Military Academy: An Architectural Tour* (New York, 2002).
Millett, Allan R., *The War for Korea, 1950–1951: They Came from the North* (Lawrence, KS, 2010).
Millett, Allan R., *The War for Korea, 1945–1950: A House Burning* (Lawrence, KS, 2005).
Millett, Allan R., 'The Korean War: A 50-Year Critical Historiography', *Journal of Strategic Studies* 24, 1 (2001), 188–224.
Millett, Allan R., *Semper Fidelis: The History of the United States Marine Corps*, revised and expanded edition (New York, 1991).
Ministry of Patriots and Veterans Affairs, *Korean War Memorials in Pictures: Remembering UN Participation 60 Years Later*, 3 vols. (Seoul, 2010).
Mitchell, Thomas M., *Winds, Waves and Warriors: Battling the Surf at Normandy, Tarawa, Inchon* (Baton Rouge, LA, 2019).
Montross, Lynn, *The United States Marine Corps: A Pictorial History* (New York, 1959).
Montross, Lynn, 'The Inchon Landing: Victory over Time and Tide', *Marine Corps Gazette* 35, 7 (1951), 26–35.
Montross, Lynn and Nicholas A. Canzona, *U.S. Marine Corps Operations in Korea, 1950–1953*, Volume 3: *The Chosin Reservoir Campaign* (Washington, DC, 1957).
Montross, Lynn and Nicholas A. Canzona, *U.S. Marine Corps Operations in Korea, 1950–1953*, Volume 2: *The Inchon-Seoul Operation* (Washington, DC, 1955).
Moon, Sun Myung, *As a Peace-Loving Global Citizen* (Seoul, 2010).
Morin, Relman, *A Reporter Reports* (New York, 1960).
Morris, Michael F., 'Invading North Vietnam', *Naval History Magazine* 43, 5 (October 2020), https://www.usni.org/magazines/naval-history-magazine/2020/october/invading-north-vietnam (accessed 24 April 2024).
Morris-Suzuki, Tessa, 'A Fire on the Other Shore?: Japan and the Korean War Order', in Tessa Morris-Suzuki (ed.), *The Korean War in Asia: A Hidden History* (Lanham, MD, 2018), 7–38.
Morris-Suzuki, Tessa, 'Remembering the Unfinished Conflict: Museums and the Contested Memory of the Korean War', in Tessa Morris-Suzuki, Morris Low, Leonid Petrov, and Timothy Y. Tsu (eds), *East Asia beyond the History Wars: Confronting the Ghosts of Violence* (London, 2013), 128–52.
Morris-Suzuki, Tessa, 'Post-War Warriors: Japanese Combatants in the Korean War', *Asia-Pacific Journal: Japan Focus* 10, 31 (2012), 1–19.
Mossman, Billy C., *United States Army in the Korean War: Ebb and Flow, November 1950–July 1951* (Washington, DC, 1990).
Moten, Matthew, *Presidents and Their Generals: An American History of Command in War* (Cambridge, MA, 2014).

Mullis, Tony R., 'Douglas MacArthur', in James H. Willbanks (ed.), *Generals of the Army: Marshall, MacArthur, Eisenhower, Arnold, Bradley* (Lawrence, KS, 2013), 63–111.

Mun, Hui Sok, 'War History in Korea: War History Compilation Committee, the Ministry of National Defense', in Robin Higham (ed.), *Official Histories: Essays and Bibliographies from around the World* (Manhattan, KS, 1970), 294–5.

Myers, Brian, *Han Sŏrya and North Korean Literature: The Failure of Socialist Realism in the DPRK* (Ithaca, NY, 1994).

Nasca, David S., *The Emergence of American Amphibious Warfare, 1898–1945* (Annapolis, MD, 2020).

National Tourism Administration, *Korea Tour* (Pyongyang, 1998).

Noble, Harold Joyce, *Embassy at War*, ed. Frank Baldwin (Seattle, 1975).

O, Hae-yŏn, *The Victorious Fatherland Liberation War Museum* (Pyongyang, 2014).

Oberdorfer, Gon and Robert Carlin, *The Two Koreas: A Contemporary History*, 3rd edition (New York, 2014).

O'Connell, Aaron B., *Underdogs: The Making of the Modern Marine Corps* (Cambridge, MA, 2012).

O'Connell, Robert L., *Team America: Patton, MacArthur, Marshall, Eisenhower, and the World They Forged* (New York, 2022).

O'Donnell, Patrick K., *Give Me Tomorrow: The Korean War's Greatest Untold Story—The Epic Stand of the Marines of George Company* (Cambridge, MA, 2010).

O'Neill, Robert, *Australia in the Korean War, 1959–53*, Volume 2: *Combat Operations* (Canberra, 1985).

Office of Information, *Republic of Korea Army*, Volume 1 (Seoul, 1954).

Owen, Joseph R., *Colder than Hell* (Annapolis, MD, 1996).

Paik, Sun Yup, *From Pusan to Panmunjom* (Washington, DC, 1992).

Park, Il-Song, 'Republic of Korea Army', in James I. Matray and Donald W. Boose, Jr. (eds), *The Ashgate Companion to the Korean War* (Farnham, 2014), 241–53.

Park, Seung Hyun, 'Korean Cinema after Liberation: Production, Industry and Regulatory Trends', in Francis Gateward (ed.), *Seoul Searching: Culture and Identity in Contemporary Korean Cinema* (Albany, NY, 2007), 15–35.

Party History Research Institute, *History of the Revolutionary Activities of the Great Leader Kim Il Sung* (Pyongyang, 1983).

Pash, Melinda L., *In the Shadow of the Greatest Generation: The Americans Who Fought the Korean War* (New York, 2012).

Pearlman, Michael, 'The Inch'ŏn Landing', in James I. Matray and Donald W. Boose, Jr. (eds), *The Ashgate Research Companion to the Korean War* (Farnham, 2014), 333–44.

Pearlman, Michael D., *Truman and MacArthur: Policy, Politics, and the Hunger for Honor and Renown* (Bloomington, IN, 2008).

Peng, Dehuai, *Memoirs of a Chinese Marshal: The Autobiographical Notes of Peng Dehuai (1898–1974)* (Honolulu, 1984).

Perret, Geoffrey, *Old Soldiers Never Die: The Life of Douglas MacArthur* (New York, 1996).

Peters, Richard and Xiaobing Li, *Voices from the Korean War: Personal Stories of American, Korean, and Chinese Soldiers* (Lexington, KY, 2004).

Petrov, Leonid, 'Turning Historians into Party Scholar-Bureaucrats: North Korean Historiography from 1955–1958', *East Asian History* 31 (June 2007), 101–19.

Piehler, G. Kurt, *Remembering War the American Way* (Washington, DC, 1995).

Pirnie, Bruce R., 'The Inchon Landing: How Great Was the Risk?', *Joint Perspectives* 3, 1 (1982), 86–97.

Poats, Rutherford M., *Decision in Korea: An Authentic History of the Korean War* (New York, 1954).

Pogue, Forrest C., *George C. Marshall: Statesman, 1945–1959* (New York, 1987).

Qin, Hauzhi, 'A Floating History: The Korean War and China's Political Use of War Memory' (MA thesis, Georgetown University, 2020).

Qing, Semei, 'The US-China Confrontation in Korea: Assessment of Intentions', in James I. Matray (ed.), *Northeast Asia and the Legacy of Harry S. Truman: Japan, China, and the Two Koreas* (Kirksville, MO, 2012), 93–118.

Quigley, Bill, *Passage through a Hell of Fire and Ice: Korea ... the First Five Months: A Marine Epic* (New York, 2015).

Quinn, William W., *Buffalo Bill Remembers: Truth and Courage* (Fowlerville, MI, 1991).

Radford, Arthur W., *From Pearl Harbor to Vietnam: The Memoirs of Admiral Arthur W. Radford*, ed. Stephen Jurika, Jr. (Stanford, CA, 1980).

Rankin, Cortland, 'Forgettable Tales of a Forgotten War: Narrative, Memory, and the Erasure of the Korean War in American Cinema', *Journal of Popular Film and Television* 50, 4 (2022), 178–95.

Ratjar, Steve and Frances Elizabeth Franks, *War Monuments, Museums, and Library Collections of 20th Century Conflicts: A Directory of United States Sites* (Jefferson, NC, 2002).

Rawnsley, Gary, '"The Great Movement to Resist America and Assist Korea": How Beijing Sold the Korean War', *Media, War & Conflict* 2, 3 (2009), 285–315.

Rees, David, *Korea: The Limited War* (London, 1964).

Research Institute of History, Academy of Sciences of the Democratic People's Republic of Korea, *History of the Just Fatherland Liberation War of the Korean People* (Pyongyang, 1961).

Reynolds, Clark G., 'MacArthur as Maritime Strategist', *Naval War College Review* 33, 2 (1980), 79–91.

Rice, Earle Jr., *Korea 1950: Pusan to Chosin* (Philadelphia, PA, 2004).

Ridgway, Matthew B., *The Korean War* (Garden City, NY, 1967).

Ridgway, Matthew B. as told to Harold H. Martin, *Soldier: The Memoirs of Matthew B. Ridgway* (New York, 1956).

Robb, David L., *Operation Hollywood: How the Pentagon Shapes and Censors the Movies* (Amherst, NY, 2004).

ROK Marine Corps, *Marine Album for 10th Foundation Anniversary* (Seoul, 1959).

Ron, Yok Min, *Outstanding Leadership and Brilliant Victory* (Pyongyang, 1993).
Rottman, Gordon L., *Inch'on: The Last Great Amphibious Assault* (Oxford, 2006).
Rowny, Edward L., *An American Soldier's Saga of the Korean War*, ed. Anne Kazel-Wilcox (Washington, DC, 2013).
Rowny, Edward L., *Smokey Joe and the General*, ed. Anne Kazel-Wilcox (Washington, DC, 2013).
Rowny, Edward L., 'Intelligence Failures and the Political Objectives of the War', in Daniel J. Meador (ed.), *The Korean War in Retrospect: Lessons for the Future* (Lanham, MD, 1998), 161–4.
Ruetten, Richard T., 'General Douglas MacArthur's "Reconnaissance in Force": The Rationalization of a Defeat in Korea', *Pacific Historical Review* 36 (1967), 79–83.
Ryang, Sonia, *Reading North Korea: An Ethnological Enquiry* (Cambridge, MA, 2012).
Ryu, Youngju, *Writers of the Winter Republic: Literature and Resistance in Park Chung Hee's Korea* (Honolulu, 2015).
Salmon, Andrew, *To the Last Round: The Epic British Stand on the Imjin River, Korea 1951* (London, 2009).
Saluzzi, Joseph A., *Red Blood... Purple Hearts: The Marines in the Korean War*, revised edition (Brooklyn, NY, 1993).
Sandler, Stanley, *The Korean War: No Victors, No Vanquished* (Lexington, KY, 1999).
Santiago Alvarez, Carolina E., 'Power Play in Pyongyang: City and Spaces as Theaters of Power under the Early Kim Regime in North Korea, 1950s–1990s' (MA thesis, University of Puerto Rico, 2020).
Sauter, Michael, *The Worst Movies of All Time, or What Were They Thinking?* (New York, 1999).
Schaller, Michael, *Douglas MacArthur: The Far Eastern General* (New York, 1989).
Schnabel, James F., *United States Army in the Korean War: Policy and Direction: The First Year* (Washington, DC, 1972).
Schnabel, James F. and Robert J. Watson, *The History of the Joint Chiefs of Staff: The Joint Chiefs of Staff and National Policy*, Volume 3: *The Korean War, Part I* (Washington, DC, 1998).
Schönherr, Johannes, *North Korean Cinema: A History* (Jefferson, NC, 2012).
Schuon, Karl (ed.), *The Leathernecks: An Informal History of the U.S. Marine Corps* (New York, 1963).
Scott-Stokes, Henry and Lee Jai Eui (eds), *The Kwangju Uprising: Eyewitness Accounts of Korea's Tiananmen* (Armonk, NY, 2000).
Sebald, William J. with Russell Brines, *With MacArthur in Japan* (New York, 1965).
Seiler, Sydney A., *Kim Il-sŏng, 1941–1948: The Creation of a Legend, the Building of a Regime* (Lanham, MD, 1994).
Seth, Michael J., *Korea at War* (Rutland, VT, 2023).
Seth, Michael J., *North Korea: A History* (London, 2018).
Setzekorn, Eric, 'The Battle for Seoul, September 1950', in Gregory Fremon-Barnes (ed.), *Urban Battlefields: Lessons Learned from World War II to the Modern Era* (Annapolis, MD, 2024), 172–96.

Sheldon, Walt, *Hell or High Water: MacArthur's Landing at Inchon* (New York, 1968).
Shen, Zhihua, *A Misunderstood Friendship: Mao Zedong, Kim Il-sung, and Sino-North Korean Relations, 1949–1976* (New York, 2018).
Shen, Zhihua, *Mao, Stalin and the Korean War: Trilateral Communist Relations in the 1950s*, trans. Neil Silver (London, 2012).
Shen, Zhihua and Danhui Li, *After Leaning to One Side: China and Its Allies in the Cold War* (Stanford, CA, 2011).
Sheng, Michael, 'Chinese Intervention', in James I. Matray and Donald W. Boose, Jr. (eds), *The Ashgate Research Companion to the Korean War* (Farnham, 2014), 359–70.
Shinn, Bill, *The Forgotten War Remembered: Korea: 1950–1953: A War Correspondent's Notebook and Today's Danger in Korea* (Elizabeth, NJ, 1996).
Shisler, Gail B., *For Country and Corps: The Life of General Oliver P. Smith* (Annapolis, MD, 2009).
Shrader, Charles R., *Communist Logistics in the Korean War* (Westport, CT, 1995).
Sides, Hampton, *On Desperate Ground: The Marines, the Reservoir, and the Korean War's Greatest Battle* (New York, 2018).
Simmons, Edwin H., *Over the Seawall: U.S. Marines at Inchon*, Marines in the Korean War Commemorative Series (Washington, DC, 2000).
Simmons, Edwin Howard, *Dog Company Six* (Annapolis, MD, 2000).
Simmons, Edwin Howard, *The United States Marines: A History*, 3rd edition (Annapolis, MD, 1998).
Sin, Nayŏng, 'Inch'ŏn sangnyuk chakchŏn VR keim ŭro t'ansaeng', *Inch'ŏn ilbo*, 13 September 2017.
Sloan, Bill, *The Darkest Summer: Pusan and Inchon 1950: The Battles that Saved South Korea—and the Marines—from Extinction* (New York, 2009).
Smith, Lynn D., 'A Nickel after a Dollar', *Army* 20 (September 1970), 24–34.
Smith, Robert, *MacArthur in Korea: The Naked Emperor* (New York, 1982).
Sŏ, Yusŏk, 'K'ŭllik! T'ongil kyoyuk Uni Movie: Inch'on sangnyuk chakchŏn Maekadŏ wa ich'yŏjin yŏngung ŭl malhada', *T'ongil Han'guk* 394 (2016), 64–5.
Sŏk, Chŏng-nae, *Pobyŏngdŭl: K'at;usa 6.25 ch'amjŏn hoegorok* (Taegu Kwangyŏski, 2014).
Son, Daekwon, 'Domestic Instability as a Key Factor in Shaping China's Decision to Enter the Korean War', *China Journal* 83 (2020), 34–57.
Stallard, Katie, *Dancing on Bones: History and Power in China, Russia, and North Korea* (New York, 2022).
Stanton, Shelby L., *America's Tenth Legion: X Corps in Korea, 1950* (Novato, CA, 1989).
Stolfi, Russel H. S., 'A Critique of Pure Success: Inchon Revisited, Revised, and Contrasted', *Journal of Military History* 68 (2004), 505–25.
Stuek, Willam and Boram Yi, '"An Alliance Forged in Blood": The American Occupation of Korea, the Korean War, and the US-South Korean Alliance', *Journal of Strategic Studies* 33, 2 (2010), 177–209.

Suh, Dae-Sook, *Kim Il Sung: The North Korean Leader* (New York, 1988).
Suh, Ji-moon, 'The Korean War in Korean Films', in Philip West and Suh Ji-moon (eds), *Remembering the "Forgotten War": The Korean War through Literature and Art* (Armonk, NY, 2001), 137–51.
Suh, Yonghee, Makito Yurita, and Scott Alan Metzinger, 'What Do We Want Students to Remember about the "Forgotten War"? A Comparative Study of the Korean War as Depicted in Korean, Japanese, and U.S. Secondary School History Textbooks', *International Journal of Social Education* 23 (2008), 51–75.
Suid, Lawrence H., *Guts and Glory: The Making of the American Military Image in Film*, revised and expanded edition (Lexington, KY, 2002).
Suid, Lawrence H., 'Hollywood, the Marines, and the Korean War', *Marine Corps Gazette* 86, 3 (March 2002), 41–4.
Sun, Kenzhi and Dan Xu, 'Chinese Documentaries and the Korean War', *International Journal of Korean History* 19, 2 (2014), 137–68.
Sun, Kristen Frances, 'Memorialization and the Limits of Reconciliation: Transnational Memory Circuits of the Korean War' (PhD thesis, University of California Berkeley, 2019).
Sweeney, Michael S., *The Military and the Press: An Uneasy Truce* (Evanston, IL, 2006).
Taaffe, Stephen R., *MacArthur's Korean War Generals* (Lawrence, KS, 2016).
Takeo, Takagi, *Kim Il Sung: Master of Leadership* (Pyongyang, 1976).
Tallent, Robert W., 'Inchon to Seoul', *Leatherneck* 34, 1 (1951), 12–17.
Tan, Jack Kwoh, 'Korean War June–October 1950: Inchon and Stalin in the "Trigger vs. Justification" Debate' (2006), RIS Working Paper 105, Nanyang Technological University, https://hdl.handle.net/10356/09667 (accessed 9 September 2022).
Taplett, Robert D., *Darkhorse Six: A Memoir of the Korean War, 1950–1951* (Williamstown, NJ, 2002).
Tertitskiy, Fyodor, *The Forgotten Political Elites of North Korea: Woe to the Vanquished* (London, 2024).
Thompson, Reginald, *Cry Korea* (London, 1951).
Thorgrimsson, Thor, *Canadian Naval Operations in Korean Waters, 1950–1955* (Ottawa, 1965).
Thornton, Richard C., *Odd Man Out: Truman, Stalin, Mao, and the Origins of the Korean War* (Washington, DC, 2000).
Toland, John, *In Mortal Combat: Korea, 1950–1953* (New York, 1991).
Tomlinson, H. Pat, 'Inchon: The General's Decision', *Military Review* 47, 4 (1967), 28–34.
Tonder, Gerry Van, *Inchon Landing: MacArthur's Korean War Masterstroke, September 1950* (Barnsley, 2019).
Torkunov, Anatoly, *The War in Korea, 1950–1953: Its Origin, Bloodshed and Conclusion* (Tokyo, 2000).
Totten, James F., 'Operation Chromite: A Study in Generalship', *Armor* 85 (November/December 1976), 33–8.

Truman, Harry, *Memoirs*, Volume 2: *Years of Trial and Hope* (Garden City, NY, 1956).
Tudor, Daniel, *Ask a North Korean* (Tokyo, 2017).
Urman, Alexandra, 'Perception of Korean Political History through Modern South Korean Cinema', *Far East/Dálný východ* 5, 1 (2015), 72–85.
Utz, Curtis A., 'Assault from the Sea: The Amphibious Landing at Inchon', in Edward J. Marolda (ed.), *The U.S. Navy in the Korean War* (Annapolis, MD, 2007), 52–109.
Vennesson, Pascal and Amanda Huan, 'The General's Intuition: Overconfidence, Pattern Matching, and the Inchon Landing Decision', *Armed Forces & Society* 44, 3 (2018), 498–520.
Wada, Haruki, *The Korean War: An International History*, updated edition, trans. Frank Baldwin (Lanham, MD, 2018).
Wade, Betsy, *Forward Positions: The War Correspondence of Homer Bigart* (Fayetteville, AK, 1991).
Wahlman, Alec, *Storming the City: U.S. Military Performance in Urban Warfare from World War II to Vietnam* (Denton, TX, 2015).
Walters, Vernon A., *Silent Missions* (Garden City, NY, 1978).
Wang, Ban, *China in the World: Culture, Politics, and World Vision* (Durham, NC, 2022).
War History Compilation Committee, *The History of the United Nations Forces in the Korean War*, 6 vols. (Seoul, 1972–7).
Weathersby, Katherine, 'New Russian Documents on the Korean War', *Cold War International History Project Bulletin* 6, 7 (Winter 1995/6), 30–119.
Weintraub, Sara, 'From Design to Completion: The Transformation of U.S. War Memorials on the National Mall' (PhD thesis, City University of New York, 2017).
Weintraub, Stanley, *MacArthur's War: Korea and the Undoing of an American Hero* (New York, 2000).
Wells, Samuel F., *Fearing the Worst: How the Korean War Transformed the Cold War* (New York, 2020).
Westermeyer, Paul, *The United States Marine Corps: The Expeditionary Force at War* (Philadelphia, PA, 2019).
Whelan, Richard, *Drawing the Line: The Korean War, 1950–1953* (Boston, MA, 1990).
Whitney, Courtney, *MacArthur: His Rendezvous with History* (New York, 1955).
Wiener, Jon, *How We Forgot the Cold War: A Historical Journey across America* (Berkeley, CA, 2012).
Willoughby, Charles A. and John Chamberlain, *MacArthur, 1941–1951* (New York, 1954).
Woo-Cumings, Meredith, 'Unilateralism and its Discontents', in David A. Steinberg (ed.), *Korean Attitudes towards the United States: Changing Dynamics* (London, 2015), 56–79.
Workman, Travis, 'The Partisan, the Worker, and the Hidden Hero: Popular Icons in North Korean Film', in Kyung Hyun Kim and Youngmin Choe (eds), *The Korean Popular Culture Reader* (Durham, NC, 2014), 145–67.

Youm, Kyo Ho, 'Freedom of the Press in South Korea, 1945–1983: A Sociopolitical and Legal Perspective' (PhD thesis, University of Southern Illinois, 1985).

Yi, Sang-ho, *Maegadŏ Han'guk chŏnjaeng* (Seoul, 2012).

Yi, Sŏnho, 'Inch'ŏn sangnyuk chakchŏn simch'ŭng punsŏk p'yŏngga', *Anbo nontan* 2, 6 (2007), 119–47.

Yŏksaga sumsuinŭn konggan 6., 'Chŏnhang ŭl kŭkjŏk ŭro panjŏnsik'in taejakchŏn Inch'ŏn sangnyuk chakjŏn kinyŏmgwan', *T'ongil Han'guk* 8 (2006), 97–9.

Yu, Bin, 'Chinese People's Volunteers Force', in James I. Matray and Donald W. Boose, Jr. (eds), *The Ashgate Research Companion to the Korean War* (Farnham, 2014), 269–82.

Yu, Mijŏng, 'T'ŭkchip kihoek: 6.25 chŏnjaeng 62 chunyŏn: Inch'ŏn sangnyuk chakchŏn 1-Maekadŏ ŭi sinnyŏm i iruŏnaen sŏnggŏng', *Voice of America*, 25 June 2012.

Yukkun sagwan hakkyo, *Han'guk chŏnjaengsa* (Seoul, 1959).

Yukkun pangmulgwang, *Yukkun pangmulgwang: Collection of Korea Army Museum* (Seoul, 2011).

Zha, Ma, 'War Remembered, Revolution Forgotten: Recasting the Sino-North Korean Alliance in China's Post-Socialist Media State', *Cross-Currents* 6, 1 (2017), 205–35.

Zur, Dafna, 'Textual and Visual Representations of the Korean War in North and South Korean Children's Literature', in Rüdiger Frank, Jim Hoare, Patrick Köllner, and Susan Pares (eds), *Korea 2010: Politics, Economy and Society*: Volume 4: *Korea Yearbook* (Leiden, 2010), 271–303.

PICTURE ACKNOWLEDGEMENTS

3.1 – courtesy Alamy
3.2 – courtesy Alamy
3.3 – courtesy Alamy
4.1 – courtesy Eastern National
4.2 – courtesy Alamy
4.3 – courtesy Alamy
5.3 – courtesy U.S. Naval Institute Press
6.1 – courtesy Alamy
7.1 – courtesy Alamy
7.3 – courtesy Getty Images
8.1 – courtesy Alamy
8.2 – courtesy Alamy
8.3 – courtesy Alamy

INDEX

Alexander, Joseph H. 44
Almond, Edward M. 'Ned' 10, 13, 17, 19, 29, 42, 64–5, 66, 67, 75–83, 102, 115, 123 n. 25 n. 24
American Battle Monuments Commission 109
An American Soldier's Saga of the Korean War (book) 66–7
Appleman, Roy E. 41–3

Baldwin, Hanson 55
Ballard, John 69–70
Barr, David G. 13, 77, 149 n. 57
Battle at Lake Changjin (film) 119 n. 2, 156 n. 57
Battle of the Barricades (book) 44
Battle of Jangsari (film) 156 n. 56
Bentley, Elbie 4
Berger, David 116
Bigart, Homer 33
Bissett, Jacqueline 88, 89
Blair, Bill 31, 32
Blair, Clay 61
Bluehearts operation 146 n. 29
Bohm, Jason Q. 116
Bradford, Jeffrey 70
Bradley, Omar 58, 61–2, 73, 116
Brines, Russell 27
British Pathé 36
Burke, Arleigh 123 n. 25

Cagle, Malcolm M. 145 n. 16
Cameron, James 29, 34
Canzona, Nicholas A. 39
Carlson, Richard 85
Chamberlain, John 53–4
Chang, Hak-pong 139 n. 1
Chao, Son Ju 108
China, Peoples Republic of 20, 116, 125 n. 43, 132 n. 1, 140 n. 5, 163–4 n. 1

Chinese People's Volunteers 21–2, 74, 140 n. 5
Cho, Gung-ha 96
Cho, Gyong Sun 94
Choe, Sang Su 75
Chosin Reservoir 17, 84, 119 n. 2, 150 n. 3
Chromite operation, *see* Inchon landing: Chromite
Chung, Il-kwan 27
Cold War 115
Coletta, Paolo E. 40
Collins, J. Lawton 10–11, 54, 58, 59–61, 73, 121 n. 6
Costello, Ward 86
Crane, Lionel 129 n. 36
Cumings, Bruce 146 n. 29
Curtis, Don 70

Davidson, Michael 37
Davies, John 129 n. 36
Democratic People's Republic of Korea, *see* North Korea
documentaries 149–50 n. 1
Donovan, Warde 86
Don't Wait for Us (film) 95–6
Dorschner, Jim 70
Doyle, James H. 10, 12, 13, 64, 65, 69

Eighth Army 6, 16, 21, 22, 28, 4, 72, 112, 117, 166 n. 14
Eller, E. M. 40

Falk, Stanely 70–1
Falklands War 116
Fatherland Liberation War Museum 106–9, 157 n. 3
Field, James A. 40
First to Fight (book) 62–5
Five Marines (film) 96
Flanders, Ed 86
Fleet Operations in a Mobile War (book) 44

INDEX

Fleming, Art 86
Freedom Park (Inchon) 100–1, 104–5, 112, 114

Gazzara, Ben 88, 89
A General's Life (book) 61
Gibney, Frank 30
A Glorious Operation (film) 96
Goldsmith, Jerry 89
Gulf War 115
Gwangju Uprising 103

Haig, Alexander 66
Han River 16, 17, 28, 32, 77, 112
Handleman, Howard 56
Heefner, Wilson 69
Heinl, Robert D., Jr. 69, 78, 80–3
Hell or High Water (book) 75–9
Herman, Arthur 73, 147 n. 35–6
Heroes of Wolmido statue 107–8
Higgins, Marguerite 30, 32, 33, 34, 35–6, 129 n. 36
History of the Just Fatherland Liberation War (book) 46
History of the Korean War (book) 48
Hoberecht, Ernest 36
Howard, Michael 43
Hungnam 17, 84
Hwang, Gon 95

Im, Kwon-taek 96
Inchon landing:
　blue beach 12, 14, 15
　Chromite 10–13, 40, 53–5, 59, 61–2, 64–7, 68–73, 116–17
　games 2
　green beach 12, 13, 15, 30
　Japanese role 37, 47, 157 n. 4
　music 2
　red beach 12, 14, 15, 30–1
　toys 2
Inchon (film) 87–93
Inchon Landing Memorial Hall 101–2
Inchon Landing Operation (film) 96
Inchon-Seoul Operation (book) 39
Inchon, USS 163 n. 43
Inner Circles (book) 66
Ishii, Mitsuharu 88

James, D. Clayton 71–2
James, Michael 33
Janssen, David 88, 89, 91

Japan 8, 37, 157 n. 4
Jaskilka, Samuel 91
Jeong, Tae-won 97
Joint Chiefs of Staff 10–11, 13, 19, 20, 23, 43, 58, 59, 61–2, 71, 72–3, 86
Joint Task Force 7, 12, 80
Jones, F. C. 41
Jones, Gene 32
Joy, C. Turner 65

Kahn, Karen 89, 152 n. 23
Keiley, Larry 30
Kim, Il Sung 3, 5, 20, 21, 25, 45–7, 49, 52–3, 74, 93, 94, 106–9, 113–4, 146–7 n. 32
Kim, Jae-jung 105
Kim, Jong Il 93–4, 96
Kim, Jong Un 96
Kim, Ki-duk 96
Kim, Kyuk-sing 100
Kim, Yu Sam 95
Kimpo airfield 16, 31, 76, 80
Keonig, Laird 89
Koh, Yŏng-nam 96
Korean civilians 34–6
Korean People's Army 5–7, 9, 16–17, 19, 25–6, 30–3, 42, 45, 71, 106–7, 113, 147 n. 32
　8th Coastal Artillery Regiment 15
　18th Rifle Division 16
　25th Rifle Brigade 17
　47th Tank Regiment 16
　78th Independent Brigade 17
　87th Infantry Regiment 16
Korean War National Museum 99, 110–11, 112
Korean War Veterans Memorial 109
Krulak, Victor 'Brute' 62–5, 142 n. 39
Kunsan 10, 71, 122 n. 18

Lambert, Tom 36
Larew, Karl 71
Lee, Beom-su 97
Lee, Jung-jae 97
Lee, Kyu-chnag 97
Lee, Man-hee 96, 97
Lee, Myung-bak 105
Lee, Yong-woon 27
Levine, Harold 30
Lei, Lydia 89
Lewis, Joseph H. 85
Li, Dai Hoon 46, 95, 106, 108

INDEX

Li, Jin U 94, 95
Li ,Tai Un *see* Li Dai Hoon
Lightning Joe (book) 61
Lovejoy, Frank 85

M26 Pershing tank 15, 112
MacArthur, Douglas 1–2, 6, 8–15, 16, 19–23, 26–9, 36, 40, 41, 42, 43, 45, 47, 49, 50, 52–9, 60–3, 65–7, 68–75, 80, 83, 85, 87–90, 95, 98, 100, 102, 111, 112, 113–14, 117, 120 n. 4, 121 n. 6, 123 n. 21, 141 n. 20
MacArthur Memorial 111
MacArthur statue (Inchon) 99–101, 104–5, 112, 114
MacArthur statues (United States) 110
MacArthur (film) 86–7
MacArthur: 1941–1951 (book) 53–4
MacArthur: His Rendezvous with History (book) 44–5
Mao, Zedong 20–1, 125 n. 43, 128 n. 13, 147 n. 34
Marine Corps War Memorial 110
The Marines Who Never Returned (film) 96
Marshall, George C. 19, 58, 86
Marshall, S. L. A. 42–3
McCarthy, Frank 86
McLaglen, Andrew V. 88
Memorial Hall of the War to Resist US Aggression and Aid Korea 99
Mifune, Toshiro 88, 89
Millett, Alan 73
Montross, Lynn 39
Monument to the Inchon Region Battle 101–2
Moon, Sun Myung 87–8, 90, 93
Moore, Robin 88
Morin, Relman 34
Morton, Louis 40–1
Mount McKinley USS 13, 26, 27, 29, 55, 58, 65, 86, 102
Murray, Raymond L. 27, 28

Naktong River 6, 72
Nam, Goon Won 89
National Broadcasting Company 32
National Infantry Museum 111
National Museum of the Marine Corps 112
National Museum of the United States Army 111
National Museum of the US Navy 111
Neeson, Liam 97

No Gun Ri 104, 158 n. 11
North Korea 1–3, 5–6, 19–22, 42, 44–7, 52, 72, 93–5, 106–9, 154 n. 42

Olivier, Laurence 88–93
O'Neill, Dick 86
Operation Chromite, *see* Inchon landing: Chromite
Operation Chromite (film) 97–8, 155 n. 52
Osan 17
Over the Seawall (book) 44

Park, Chung-hee 48–9, 96, 97
Park, Geun-hye 105, 155 n. 52
Pearlman, Michael 72
Peck, Gregory 86–7
Peng, Duhai 21
Pernie, Bruce 69
Pieper, Daniel 3–4
Policy and Direction: The First Year (book) 43
Posung-myon 10, 64, 71, 76, 80
Pusan 3, 16, 27
Pusan perimeter 6–9, 13, 16, 41, 48, 62, 71, 72, 80, 86, 112
Pyeongtaek sculpture 105–6
Pyongyang 20, 22, 98, 105–8, 113–14
Pyongyang radio 24–5

Radford, Arthur W. 65–6
Reminiscences (book) 56–8, 59
Reminiscences: With the Century (book) 52–3
Republic of Korea, *see* South Korea
Republic of Korea Army 6, 8, 19, 20, 21, 88
  17th Regiment 17, 122 n. 17
Republic of Korea Marine Corps 12–13, 96, 101, 122 n. 17, 138 n. 47, 139 n. 58
Retreat, Hell! (film) 84–5
Reynolds, Clark 69
Rhee, Syngman 5, 19, 28, 36, 48, 100, 140 n. 6
Ridgway, Matthew 22, 61
Roh, Moon-hyun 105
Ropp, Theodore 43
Roskill, Stephen 40
Roundtree, Richard 88, 89
Rowny, Edward 66–7

Savage, Paul 88
Schnable, James F. 43
Second World War 5, 8, 39, 40, 52, 109, 115, 116

INDEX

Seoul 2, 6, 9, 13, 17, 18, 19, 22, 24, 28, 33, 36, 40, 41, 46, 52, 62, 76–8, 81, 83, 98, 103, 105, 106, 112
Sharif, Omar 152 n. 23
Shaw, E. Clay 91
Sheldon, Walt 75–8
Shepherd, Lemuel C. 11, 62, 64, 86, 121 n. 6
Sherman, Forrest 11, 55, 64
Shinn, Bill 26–7
Simmons, Edwin H. 44
Simmons, Robert R. 43
Simmons, Walter 55
Smith, Oliver P. 12, 15, 17, 59, 65, 69, 75–83, 150 n. 3
Smithsonian National Museum of American History 110–11
South Korea 2–3, 5–6, 47–50, 52, 96–8, 99–106, 114
South to the Naktong, North to the Yalu (book) 41–3, 44
Spaatz, Carl 37
Sperling, Milton 85
Statue of Brothers 105
Stolfi, Russel 70
Struble, Arthur D. 12, 165 n. 12
Suez Crisis 116
Sunderland, Riley 43
Suwon 16, 78

T-34 tank 5
Taegu 6
Taejon 6
Taiwan 116
Tamblyn, Russ 85
Task Force 90 12, 15
Testimony (film) 96
Thompson, Regnald 34
Toho Studios 88
Tokyo 8, 10–11, 15, 26–7, 28, 36, 43, 58, 59, 64, 66, 73, 78
Tomlinson, Pat 69
Totten, James 69
Tremaine, Frank 28
Trudy Jackson operation 122 n. 15
Truman, Harry S. 19, 20, 23, 54, 58, 62, 86, 87, 141 n. 19

Um, Sun Il 50
Unification Church 87–91
United Nations 6, 19, 21, 37, 71, 74
United States Air Force 39, 41, 166 n. 14

United States Army, *see also* Eighth Army
   1st Cavalry Division 9, 16, 17
   2nd Infantry Division 9
   7th Infantry Division 13, 16, 17, 41, 77, 81, 122 n. 17
   32nd Regiment 17, 77, 81
United States Army in the Korean War (book series) 41
United States Marine Corps 2–3, 30–3, 39, 52, 64, 67, 84, 90–1, 112, 115–16, 133 n. 5, 150 n. 3
   Fleet Marine Force Pacific 11, 64, 86, 121 n. 6
   1st Marine Division 9, 12, 16, 17, 21, 59, 64, 75, 78, 80, 81, 83, 84, 112, 115
   1st Marine Regiment 13, 15, 16, 17, 77
      1st Battalion 14
      2nd Battalion 14
   5th Marine Regiment 13, 15, 16, 17, 27, 76, 77, 80, 122 n. 16
      3rd Battalion 14
   7th Marine Regiment 16, 17
   1st Tank Battalion 15
U.S. Marine Corps Operations in the Korean War (book series) 39, 44
United States Military Academy (West Point) 86, 87, 110
United States Naval Operations: Korea (book) 40–1, 44
United States Navy 9–15, 24–5, 39, 133 n. 5
United States of America 114, 115

Vandenberg, Hoyt 10
Victory at High Tide (book) 78, 80–3
Vietnam War 109, 115

Wake Island 20
Walberg, Gary 86
Walker, Walton H. 6, 16, 19, 22, 40–1, 86
War in Peacetime (book) 59–61
War Memorial of Korea 105, 157 n. 3
Whitehead, Don 32
Whitney, Courtney 29, 54–5, 56, 63, 86, 102
Williams, John 89
Willoughby, Charles 53–4, 56, 62
Wolmi-do 10, 12, 24, 45–7, 98, 106, 108–9
Wolmi Island (film) 94–6

INDEX

Wonsan 74
Wood, Percy 27
Wright, Edwin K. 'Pinky' 9, 65

X Corps 13, 16, 17, 21, 22, 28, 41, 67, 71, 72, 75, 80, 117

Yalu River 20, 21, 71
Yangju highway incident 104, 158 n. 11
Yi, Sŭng-yŏp 46
Yongdungpo 16, 33, 77
Young, Terence 88–90
Yun, Mi-ra 152 n. 23